THE MANAGEMENT OF HUMAN RESOURCES IN CHINESE INDUSTRY

STUDIES ON THE CHINESE ECONOMY

General Editors: Peter Nolan, Lecturer in Economics and Politics, University of Cambridge, and Fellow and Director of Studies in Economics, Jesus College, Cambridge, England; and Dong Fureng, Professor, Chinese Academy of Social Sciences, Beijing, China

This series analyses issues in China's current economic development, and sheds light upon that process by examining China's economic history. It contains a wide range of books on the Chinese economy past and present, and includes not only studies written by leading Western authorities, but also translations of the most important works on the Chinese economy produced within China. It intends to make a major contribution towards understanding this immensely important part of the world economy.

Published titles include:

Derong Chen
CHINESE FIRMS BETWEEN HIERARCHY AND MARKET

Dong Fureng
INDUSTRIALIZATION AND CHINA'S RURAL MODERNIZATION

Du Runsheng (*edited by Thomas R. Gottschang*)
REFORM AND DEVELOPMENT IN RURAL CHINA

Qimiao Fan and Peter Nolan (*editors*)
CHINA'S ECONOMIC REFORMS

Christopher Findlay, Andrew Watson and Harry X. Wu (*editors*)
RURAL ENTERPRISES IN CHINA

Jiann-Jong Guo
PRICE REFORM IN CHINA, 1979–86

Michael Korzec
LABOUR AND THE FAILURE OF REFORM IN CHINA

Nicholas K. Menzies
FOREST AND LAND MANAGEMENT IN IMPERIAL CHINA

Ryoshin Minami
THE ECONOMIC DEVELOPMENT OF CHINA

The Management of Human Resources in Chinese Industry

Malcolm Warner
Fellow of Wolfson College
Judge Institute of Management Studies
University of Cambridge

St. Martin's Press

First published in Great Britain 1995 by
MACMILLAN PRESS LTD
Houndmills, Basingstoke, Hampshire RG21 6XS
and London
Companies and representatives
throughout the world

A catalogue record for this book is available from the British Library.

ISBN 0-333-60524-1

10   9   8   7   6   5   4   3   2   1
04   03   02   01   00   99   98   97   96   95

Printed and bound in Great Britain by
Ipswich Book Co Ltd, Ipswich, Suffolk

First published in the United States of America 1995 by
Scholarly and Reference Division,
ST. MARTIN'S PRESS, INC.,
175 Fifth Avenue,
New York, N.Y. 10010

ISBN 0-312-12524-0

Library of Congress Cataloging-in-Publication Data
Warner, Malcolm.
The management of human resources in Chinese industry / Malcolm
Warner.
p.   cm.
Studies on the Chinese economy
Includes bibliographical references and index.
ISBN 0-312-12524-0
1. Government business enterprises—China—Management.
2. Government business enterprises—China—Management—Case studies.
3. Industrial relations—China.   4. China—Economic policy—1976–
I. Title.
HD4318.W37   1995
658.3'00951—dc20   95–5131
                                                     CIP

To the memory of
my father, Simon Warner

Contents

List of Tables

List of Figures

Preface

This book attempts to deal with the management of human resources in the emergent economic superpower of the coming decade, namely the People's Republic of China, from 1949 to the present. It particularly focuses on the institutionalization of the 'iron rice-bowl' employment-system covering over one hundred million workers – the core of the Chinese 'proletariat' in the state-owned industries – 'from the cradle to the grave'. It goes on to examine how under the economic reforms in the 1980s and early 1990s these arrangements are now being undermined by the emergence of a nascent labour-market. The research is based on empirical data collected in the North-East (*Dongbei*), China's industrial heartland in Manchuria.

The main field-work involved visits to state-owned enterprises covering a wide range of industries from iron and steel to pharmaceuticals. A case-study methodology was employed and semi-structured interviews were conducted with employees at all levels, via an interpreter, in mid-1993. Documentary evidence was also collected and translated from the Chinese into English by my research colleagues in the respective institutes involved. The project was written up by myself over the winter of 1993/94, and the responsibility for both factual content and evaluation in the manuscript is entirely my own.

The sources, cited in the text, and set out at length in the bibliography, include both Chinese and English language materials, although the majority are in the latter category as these will be most accessible to a wider readership and to those more interested in the comparative industrial relations and human resource management implications.

The study was officially supported by the Joint Exchange Programme of the British Academy, the Chinese Academy of Social Sciences, and the Economic and Social Research Council, to whom I am deeply grateful for their funding arrangements, and was carried out with the practical help of several universities and research institutes in the PRC. I should also like to thank the innumerable Chinese academics and managers in Beijing, Dalian, Harbin and Shenyang, who gave generously of their time in order to assist my field-investigation. Special note should be made of the role of CASS Institute of Industrial Economics in Beijing, and the Provincial Academies of Liaoning and Heilongjiang. I should like to thank the following individuals for their kind encouragement and/or help: Bu Nailin, Jan Borgonjon, Max Boisot, William Brown, John Child, Chen Derong,

Ding Yi, Dong Ferong, Steve Frenkel, Colin Gill, Frank Heller, Chris Hope, Adrian Johnson, Trini Leung, Martin Lockett, Lu Yuan, Peter Nolan, Rosalie Tung, Sasha Ward, Wang Wei, Martyn Wright and Yang Weibin.

I should also like to express my appreciation of the support of Stephen Watson and colleagues at the Judge Institute of Management Studies at the University of Cambridge (and especially Jo Grantham for secretarial and administrative back-up) as well as the President, Vice-President and Fellows of Wolfson College, past and present.

Next, I must mention the important role of the editorial staff at Macmillan, namely Giovanna Davitti, Tim Farmiloe and colleagues, without whom this book would not have appeared.

Last but not least, I thank my family for their forbearance and patience during my long absences in East Asia, respectively my wife Jacqueline and children, Raphael and Natasha: their unstinting support has proved invaluable.

Acknowledgements

I should like to thank the editors and publishers of the following for generously giving permission to quote from earlier versions of my own work: the *International Journal of Human Resource Management* and (for citation from material which I contributed to a chapter) *Organized Labour in the Asia-Pacific: A Comparative Study of Trade Unions*, ed. S. Frenkel, *ILR Press*, School of Industrial and Labor Relations, Cornell University, Ithaca, NY. In addition, I am obliged to the *Journal of Management Studies* for use of a diagram, Figure 3.2 in this monograph.

List of Abbreviations

ACFIC	All-China Federation of Industry and Commerce
ACFTU	All-China Federation of Trade Unions
CASS	Chinese Academy of Social Sciences
CCP	Chinese Communist Party
CPG	Chinese People's Government
CEDEFOP	Centre Européen pour le Développement de la Formation Professionelle
CEMA	Chinese Enterprise Management Association
CMEA	Council for Mutual Economic Assistance
DEDZ	Dalian Economic Development Zone
DLRS	Dalian Locomotive and Rolling-Stock
DPA	Dalian Port Authority
FEC	Foreign Exchange Certificate
FYP	Five Year Plan
GDP	Gross Domestic Product
GNP	Gross National Product
HRM	Human Resource Management
INSEAD	Institut Européen d'Administration
IR	Industrial Relations
JV	Joint Venture
KDK	Knocked-Down Kits
KMT	Kuomintang Nationalist Party
MoLP	Ministry of Labour and Personnel
OB	Organizational Behaviour
OC	Organizational Commitment
PRC	People's Republic of China
QC	Quality Circle
RMB	Renminbi
SCRES	State Commission for Restructuring the Economic System
SEC	State Economic Commission
SEZ	Special Economic Zone
SOE	State Owned Enterprise
SPC	State Planning Commission
SSB	State Statistical Bureau
SWB	*Short Wave Broadcasts (BBC Bulletin of)*
TQM	Total Quality Management
TVE	Township and Village Enterprises

Part One:
Inside the Iron Rice-Bowl

The Chinese proletariat has many outstanding qualities which permit it to be the leading force in the Chinese revolution ... In spite of certain unavoidable weaknesses – for example, its small size (as compared with the peasantry), its youth (as compared with the proletariat in capitalist countries) and its low cultural level (compared with the bourgeosie), the Chinese proletariat has nonetheless become the basic motive force of the Chinese revolution. The Chinese revolution certainly will not succeed without the participation and leadership of the proletariat ...

(Mao Zedong, 1940, cited in Schram, 1963, p.192)

1 Setting the Scene

1.1 INTRODUCTION

The goal of this book is to enhance the understanding of the management of human resources in Chinese industry. It will largely cover the evolution (and eventual erosion) of the so-called 'iron rice-bowl' (*tie fan wan*) employment system, which for many years has been closely associated with the pivotal state-owned industrial sector in the formerly 'top-down' planned economy of the PRC and which since the mid-1980s has seen many reforms.[1]

Since the death of Mao Zedong and Zhou En-Lai in 1976, China has undergone an enormous transformation. The pragmatic policies of Deng Xiaoping have, for example, seen a sea-change in the country's economy and the introduction of the 'Four Modernizations' (of Agriculture, Industry, Science and Technology, and Defence) and the 'Open Door' policies in the latter half of the 1970s, extending to the present day (see Figure 1.1 for a chronology of background events). Deng has encouraged a 'commodity economy' in China not only to achieve his own brand of 'socialism' but also to feed the burgeoning population. The backdrop to the many economic dilemmas of successive Chinese governments in the past, as now, has been the rapid growth of population. Currently, the total number of mainland Chinese exceeds 1.2 billion people, or around one in five persons in the world; it is nine times the number in Japan and five times that in the US. China has a low population density overall, but most people live in the crowded river-valleys and coastal areas. There are 25 cities with over a million inhabitants, together congregating over 65 million citizens, in a growing urban population. The perennial problem of China's rulers has been to feed, clothe, house and employ this expanding total of town and city-dwellers (see Minami, 1994, pp.191–2).

Faced with this challenge at the end of the 1980s, the economy was at a crossroads. Industry was unquestionably the largest economic sector, producing around two-fifths of GNP, with state-owned enterprises contributing just over half of this total. Education and health were largely provided by the State, but in building, commerce, personal services and transport, state firms accounted for less than half of economic activity. Agriculture, which brought forth a quarter of GNP, was predominantly in

3

the hands of peasant families (see Wood, 1994, p.23). Rapid economic growth, averaging nine per cent per annum over the last decade or so, set the scene (see Tables 1.1 and 1.2).

Once a 'command economy', the PRC has slowly moved to what may be called 'marketization' (if not 'privatization' Eastern European-style). This study hypothesizes that as such a market-economy 'with Chinese characteristics' emerges, the state sector will attenuate and many of the institutionalized practices associated with it will accordingly change. One of such arrangements which developed during the 1950s was the life-time tenure employment system offering 'cradle-to-grave' welfare benefits to the industrial 'proletariat', namely to state-sector employees as 'staff and workers'.

The 'iron rice-bowl' was for many decades readily on offer from the work-unit to which employees were assigned after finishing their formal schooling. As Leung (1988, pp.55–6) sums up:

> The work unit then took charge of their wages, housing, living subsidies, medical benefits, political activities, marriage and other family affairs, family planning, the family's medical benefits, education, labour insurance and pensions. All these benefits were based on the worker's grade according to the Employee Grading Ladder. Wherever anyone went, whatever they did, all was done through their work unit. People's citizenship registration was either with their own work unit or that of their parents or spouses, and their livelihood was based on that. Those urban dwellers who did not belong to a work unit lived as 'non-citizens'.

It was a 'wall' between insiders and outsiders, as in the traditional Chinese home, official building or fortification (see Waldron, 1992, p.13).

I hope to show how it became a standard feature of the employment system affecting the lives of the 'industrial elite' in Chinese cities and towns, working in state-owned enterprises (SOEs) in those key sectors of industry such as iron and steel, machine-building, heavy engineering and so on, which constituted the commanding heights of the economy. However, its benefits were not restricted to the industrial 'vanguard' of the working-class but also set the standard for other largely urban employees of state-owned enterprises who constituted less than 20 per cent of the total labour force including agriculture. Thus, job-security became the hallmark of a wide spectrum of occupations but restricted to the urban sector of the Chinese economy from the early 1950s onwards, as we shall see in Chapter 2.

Figure 1.1   Chronology of selected background events in China 1911–93

1911	Outbreak of the Nationalist Revolution
1921	Chinese Communist Party founding Congress in Shanghai
1924	First National Congress of the Kuomintang (Nationalist Party)
1925	Foundation of the All-China Federation of Trade Unions
1927	Abortive Shanghai Workers' Uprising
1931	Japanese invasion
1934–35	The 'Long March'
1945	End of the Second World War: Japanese surrender
1949	The 'Liberation': Communists take power
1950	Eight-grade wage system initiated
1951	Outbreak of the Korean War
1953	First Five-Year Plan announced
1955–56	Nationalization of industry and commerce
1958	The 'Great Leap Forward' begins
1960	Sino-Soviet split: Moscow recalls technicians
1966	The Cultural Revolution: years of strife follow
1976	Death of Premier Zhou En-Lai and later of Chairman Mao Zedong
1967–77	Launch of the 'Four Modernizations'
1978–80	'Open Door' policy initiated by Deng Xiaoping
1978	Start of the new economic reforms in Sichuan Province
1979	Enterprise reforms extended to other areas
1980	Trial of the 'Gang of Four'
1981	Sixth Five-Year Plan (1981–85)
1982	Workers' Congresses set up in 95 per cent of large firms
1983	Substitution of taxation for profit remittance
1984	New Law on enterprise management in urban factories
1985	Enterprise Responsibility Contract System approved
1986	Seventh Five-Year Plan (1986–90)
1986–87	Labour contract and wage reforms set out
1988	Zhao Ziyang approved as Party General Secretary: Li Peng as Premier
1989	Tiananmen Square student demonstrations. Imposition of Martial Law and fall of Zhao Ziyang
1990	Eighth Five-Year Plan (1990–94)
1990–91	Policy of economic retrenchment
1992	Deng Xiaoping's speech on renewal of Economic Reforms
1993	Comprehensive 'three systems' reforms
1994	Approval of new Labour Law

Source: Adapted from Warner, 1992, p.3; Takahara, 1994, p.viiff.

Job-security is, however, a two-faced Janus. On the one hand, it satisfies one of the pre-conditions for motivation put forward by Western work-psychologists (such as Maslow or Herzberg) but at the same time it is anathema to many American and British neo-classical economists who see it associated with factor-immobility (such as Friedman or Minford).[2] Since China embarked on a strategy of planned growth in the 1950s, labour-direction was part and parcel of the mobilization of resources, disregarding the need for labour-markets. The lack of such markets coincided with the presence of a labour-surplus, principally of rural origin. If workers with scarce skills were tied down in enterprises which were much of the time expanding, marginal employees could be brought in by ancillary recruitment and trained in-house. Already-educated graduates could be directed to key firms and jobs, but selection worked only imperfectly. The educational infrastructure itself was relatively undeveloped, and only limited numbers of school-leavers reached higher education, where the total output of qualified engineers and technologists for example was insufficient to meet requirements of rapid industrial growth. Similarly, the mismatch between the outputs of educational institutions and the needs of enterprises, increasing qualitatively as well as quantitatively, became a growing concern after the economic reforms were introduced in the late 1970s.

Labour immobility was also associated with overmanning; hence the labour surplus inside the state enterprises mirrored that outside. Since dismissals were 'out of court' and virtually impossible to carry out, the possibility of raising productivity by getting rid of inefficient and/or lazy workers, or simply reducing over-all numbers, was not available to Chinese managers until recently. There was also a gender implication as the *danwei* protected women's jobs and provided supporter services, such as nurseries, for their employment (see Stockman, 1994).

1.2   ENTERPRISE REFORMS

The push towards economic reforms after 1979 and the rapid growth rates associated with it (see Table 1.1) raised fundamental questions regarding the allocation of resources in the Chinese economy (see Warner, 1987a). It was clear however that change could not be implemented overnight and whether by accident or design a pragmatic approach towards dealing with factor-immobilities and rigidities was incrementally adopted. Enterprise reform was introduced in fits and starts and there was no very obviously linear progression towards a 'socialist market economy'.

Enterprise renewal began in December 1978 when the Third Plenum of the CCP Central Committee launched the initial wave of economic reform. Urban enterprise reform did not however get fully underway until October 1984 when the Central Committee took a major policy decision on reform of the economic structure. The introduction of director responsibility and enterprise autonomy followed from this in a number of steps between 1984 and 1989 to introduce greater efficiency and production. The drive towards such improvements in enterprise performance was not based on any elaborate theoretical justification in terms of Western-style economics and did not lead to any rapid development of factor-markets. In this setting, many economists take the view that the absence of factor-markets holds back the full potential of an economy. The 'allocation of factors, the incentives for using them efficiently, and technological change' are seen to be as frequently important as the growth of factor inputs (see Byrd and Tidrick, 1987, p.60). In China, a policy of intensive growth since 1978 has stressed 'the growth of factor productivity rather than the accumulation of capital as the main source of output growth' (ibid.).

While I have reservations about the feasibility of over-rapidly introducing such markets in the Chinese institutional context (see also Boisot and Child, 1988; 1994), it is clear that reforms have been implemented with varying degrees of official enthusiasm since the early 1980s. The focus of this study will however be mainly restricted to one dimension of the enterprise reforms, namely the introduction of the management of human resources and what are generally referred to as 'labour reforms'.

1.3 LOSSES AND SUBSIDIES

Structural enterprise and labour reform in the Chinese economy must thus be seen in the context of the piecemeal emergence of the 'socialist market economy' since 1978 (see Fan, 1994). The high rate of growth has probably resulted as much from those parts of the economy outside the state-owned enterprise sector as those inside, namely the township and village enterprises (TVEs) and the privately-owned and foreign-funded ones, for example. The state-owned *danwei* (work-units) are however a mixed group, with some allegedly in surplus, some making a moderate

Table 1.1   China: Economic growth, 1978–92

	1992 vs 1978 Annual growth per cent	1979–92 Average annual growth per cent
National income	224.9	8.8
Gross domestic product	223	9
Total industrial output	470.2	13.2
Urban cost of living index	153.8	6.9

Source: SSB, 1993.

loss and some heavily 'in the red' (see Nolan, 1994a and 1994b). Great caution should normally be exercised when invoking Chinese official statistics. Nonetheless, the State Statistical Bureau reported nearly half were loss-making in the first quarter of 1994 (*Financial Times*, 24 May 1994, p.4). Given the strategic importance of many of the large *danwei*, it can be argued that they should be 'turned round'.

In any event, the subsidies on their losses were arguably a drag on the efficient allocation of funds which the state could direct to or invest in more productive firms. If losses revealed convincing inefficiencies or waste of resources, then it could be asserted that 'root and branch solutions' might be needed. Enterprise reforms were put forward as the answer to such market distortions. To date, however, Chinese state-owned enterprises have only recently begun to put their houses in order. Whether the estimate of the percentage of loss-making state-owned enterprises is overestimated or underestimated, however, is hard to judge. In the course of interviewing managers in such enterprises, it emerged that losses could be adjusted to show a worse situation than existed, to bargain more strongly with the municipal, provincial or state authorities for larger subsidies (see Brislin, 1994) and to receive a higher allocation of special funds, for example to counter potential unemployment locally.[3]

It is clear that the losses of many state-owned *danwei* may in part at least be due to their resembling 'company-towns' (in Western terms) and having to carry the high overhead costs of the welfare infrastructure they provided to their employees.[4] Elsewhere, this would not be included in the company's books and paid for by local or central government, in the case of schools, hospitals and so on, out of citizens' taxes or social insurance contributions. It is, of course, true however that in some Western economies, like France, over 20 per cent of welfare costs are paid by employers.

As the pilot-sites for labour reform were initiated in state-owned enterprises already in credit, their experience may not necessarily be influential for enterprises allegedly heavily 'in the red', as the latter's problems may be due to obsolete technology, product inadequacies, declining markets and so on. Such considerations may supersede managerial and human resources shortcomings or reflect built-in strategic and/or structural problems which may not be easily rectified.

A strength and a weakness of the pilot reforms introduced has been their experimental nature:

A salient feature of China's economic reform, and indeed of China's economic reform as a whole, is that it proceeded on an *ad hoc*, trial and error basis, without a coherent or predetermined blueprint. Piecemeal reform measures were introduced on an experimental basis in a single region or sector and, if successful, were then extended to enterprises in other regions or sectors of the country. This *ad hoc*, piecemeal approach has profoundly affected the implementation and success of China's enterprise reform. The absence of a coherent blueprint not only precluded a clear understanding and careful consideration of the interdependence among various components of reform but also made it difficult to determine the necessary conditions for further reform and the means of achieving them. (Fan, 1994, p.138)

It is therefore hard to know whether the policy-makers had carried out a sufficiently robust economic analysis of the problem in hand.

Whilst the absolute level of losses rose in the late 1980s and early 1990s, these were concentrated in a limited number of sectors. Around half of the shortfalls came from coalmining, and oil and natural gas extraction. Industrial firms in credit generated almost five times the sum lost by enterprises in deficit (150bn yuan against 35bn yuan in 1990). Large and medium size state firms produced nearly three-quarters of all profits and tax at the end of the 1980s (see Nolan 1994b). Even so, conventional wisdom – whether World Bank or Chinese government-inspired – held that the subsidies to the SOEs were a drag on growth and had to be reduced. Official economic policy was, and is still therefore geared largely towards this goal (see *Beijing Review*, 17 October 1994, pp. 5–6). Thus, a number of reforms were implemented over the course of 1993 (continuing in 1994) to achieve a higher level of enterprise reform and to extend 'marketization', which will be described in detail in Chapters 4, 5 and 6.

The profitability of the state firms (SOEs) was however consistently lower than in the township and village enterprises (TVEs). In 1986 retained profits were 24 per cent in TVEs but only 11.8 per cent in SOEs; by 1991 TVEs earned 21.5 percent but SOEs only 7.8 per cent. Bolton (1993, p. 10) believes this may explain why TVEs have grown faster than GDP over the period, although it should be noted that the tax burden on SOEs was heavier. Reported pre-tax profits were lower in the TVEs but this may reflect an element of tax evasion.

It is of dubious value to extrapolate such statistical trends but there is a valid argument that emphasizes concentrating resources in enterprises which are less state-controlled (or even 'privatized') on the grounds that they are more efficient. The Chinese experience according to some economists tends to support policies emphasizing small and medium-sized enterprises (SMEs) of all kinds because they can avoid the institutionalized sclerosis of the industrial giants of past years, more rapidly reap greater economies of scale, and so on.[5] The contribution, and hence the importance of large Chinese state enterprises grew nonetheless over the last decade as the output of small state enterprises was shrinking, having been 36 per cent in 1980 and down to just 9 per cent in 1991. As Nolan points out:

By the late 1980s the state sector had relinquished control of the 'foothills' of Chinese industry. However, it still occupied the 'commanding heights' ... The state sector of industry was increasingly concentrated on upstream heavy industry ... (Nolan, 1994b, p.8)

1.4 LABOUR SURPLUSES

The improvement in the Chinese economy has resulted in part from using the labour surplus released from agriculture. However, it may not be an inter-sectoral shift, because even in the Chinese state-owned enterprises labour productivity has risen, according to World Bank evidence. (This has to a degree been true also in Eastern Europe.) In both cases, a market environment has helped increase efficiency. In addition a 'no bail-out' condition may possibly prevail in the Chinese case to accentuate the process according to this view (see Portes, 1993). The 'no bail-out' injunction refers to removing state subsidies to loss-making enterprises and forcing them to sink or swim *vis-à-vis* market forces.

One reason why 'hard-budget constraints' are necessary is to allow the economy to grow fast enough to provide jobs for the labour surplus in the rural sector without 'overheating' (Minami, 1994, p.231). Even if macro-economic and monetary policy tightens, it has been known for the state to bail out SOEs in difficulty. As the same source puts it: 'Banks cannot refuse loans to enterprises with strong political connections' (ibid.). As a result the money supply grows and inflation ensues. One answer is a more robust macro-economic set of controls; the other is to introduce 'hard budget constraints' for SOEs, with possible bankruptcies in view, or even to privatize them. Stronger incentives for both enterprises and individuals are needed to make the above policies effective. Reorganization of SOEs and the encouragement of the collective and private sectors must go in tandem *pari passu* with such tighter policies.

If there are severe underlying inflationary pressures, 'shock treatment' may be counselled; this has been the case in Eastern Europe, but less so in

China. Gradual reform in the latter case has prevailed and been accompanied by rapid growth. However, even in Eastern Europe there were relatively gradual reforms in the 1980s (see Meaney, 1988). The contrast between China and Eastern Europe was probably over-drawn. It is likely too that certain preconditions are necessary for economic transformation, and the incremental Chinese economic reforms from the late 1970s onwards are likely to have helped in this respect, although the costs in terms of environmental pollution have been high. Another important caveat is that some of the economic growth has been of the 'non-sustainable' kind, with the depletion of national assets (see Wall, 1993).[6]

The Chinese experience rests on a balanced judgement as to what must be done first: economics is always about ascertaining alternatives and choosing priorities. The Chinese case was based on initiating micro-economic reforms as well as macro- ones. Micro-economic stabilization was essential, and pragmatically implemented in the state-owned sector, with labour factor-productivity rising considerably. Significant progress was therefore possible without privatization, although exposure to market-forces was essential (see Portes, 1993).

1.5 CONCLUDING REMARKS

Although enterprise reforms were more or less successively introduced throughout the 1980s, the 'iron rice-bowl' proved to be rather resilient and still characterized the SOEs by the early 1990s. If a 'socialist market economy' was slowly emerging, there was limited progress towards what is now called a 'labour-force market' (Gao, 1994, pp.14–16), as we shall see in Chapters 4 and 7. By the mid-1980s for example, jobs for life were still *de rigueur* in the typical large state firm, and seniority-based promotion systems very common. In other words, it was only after 1985/6 that labour contracts and efficiency wages were seriously placed on the economic agenda.

Even after state regulations were implemented to achieve employment and wage reforms in the latter part of the 1980s (see Korzec, 1992, pp.26–50) such reforms could still be described by leading Western writers on Chinese economics as 'ineffectual' (see for example Howe, foreword to Korzec, 1992, p.ix). Indeed, describing the reforms of the decade:

No significant dismissals have taken place, and in any case, the new regulations only allow worker dismissal in terms of infringement of regulations or imminent bankruptcy. Dismissal to cut costs remains illegal. Moreover, from the worker's point of view, the reform has not given him the right to quit work or take a better job elsewhere. Thus neither employer nor employee is in a position to strike a market-style wage/employment bargain. (1992, p.ix)

In order to understand how this state of affairs arose, we have to go back to the origins of the 'iron rice-bowl' system in the late 1940s and early 1950s. The next chapter will deal with the earliest historical roots of the employment system and both its exogenous origins and its endogenous implementation.

2 The Iron Rice-Bowl: The Early Days

2.1 INTRODUCTION

Early industrial enterprises which grew up in China were mostly located in the military sphere and tried to keep to the traditional division of labour, with 'official supervision and merchant management' (Lockett, 1980, p.454). By the turn of the century, foreign- and comprador-owned enterprises were set up in the coastal regions, particularly textile factories and flour mills. These were few in number and by 1912 there were only just over 350 factories using mechanical power and around 750 works employing over 100 operatives each (Feuerwerker, 1958, p.5). In the inter-war years, the textile industry developed extensively, especially in large cities like Shanghai. Many of these factories were Japanese-owned and managed, and it was through their influence that many ideas of the US management theorist F.W. Taylor, as adapted to Japanese practice, were introduced (Warner, 1994). Many British and American businesses were also expanding in the inter-war years and it was largely through their production methods that exogenous management ideas entered China. It was not until the early 1950s that Taylorism in another foreign guise, namely Soviet management practice (see Beissinger, 1988), again became an important influence in Chinese industry.[1]

One authority (Lockett, 1980, p.463) argues that the Scientific Management practices of the Soviet Union were attractive 'because they were modern rather than because of the type of socialist content in them' (ibid.). The popular slogan of the day was 'Let's be modern and Soviet' (Schurmann, 1966, pp.244–5). The supply of Soviet technology and investment aid promoted the spread of Stalinist practices in management and work-organization (see for example Brugger, 1976; Lee, 1987; Kaple, 1994). Chinese industrial organization was thus influenced by Taylorism in varying degrees. Like its application elsewhere, its influence was predominantly indirect. It was in many respects Taylorism without Taylor, in effect 'Hamlet without the Prince'.

The Soviet Union had agreed to set up over 300 new industrial plants from 1953 onwards, as well as to train the Chinese to run them. Soviet technical experts poured into China, considerable numbers of Chinese students were sent to study in Soviet enterprises and universities, and cadre-training was promoted on Soviet lines (see Warner, 1992, pp.127–8). Russian became the main foreign language spoken in the PRC and remains so among the generation who studied and trained in the immediate post-Liberation period, many of whom are still in positions of responsibility in Chinese enterprises.[2]

Another Stalinist policy which was imported at the time was 'one-man management' which had become common in heavy industry (see Andors, 1977). It was one policy among many which were introduced in Chinese enterprises between 1949 and the present day, having its moment of influence in the middle 1950s. It was eventually replaced by variants of the multiple-control mechanisms involving managers, party officials and trade union representatives which were the norm both before and after 'one-man management' (see Schurmann, 1966).

Great attention was paid to the imposition of labour discipline, managerial monitoring of performance and the delineation of individual responsibility for specific tasks at worker-level. It was also at that time that payment by results, another Soviet importation, was introduced. These innovations sat uneasily on top of existing work practices and in many cases were difficult to implement as they were imposed 'top–down' and then only in the most industrialized areas like the north-eastern cities. Party officials were resentful of their role being bypassed or undermined. As a result, 'one-man management' went by the board in 1956.

As Lee points out:

> The origin of China's industrial management system can be examined in two time-periods. Between 1948 and 1952 a command economy and a system of rationalized industrial management developed in North-East China. In the years 1953 to 1955, the First Five-Year Plan was introduced, the State Council with its powerful economic ministries was built and the pattern of the planned economy and industrial management spread throughout China as most of industry became nationalized. (1987, p.21)

The evolution of the command economy in the North-East was characterized by a shift from a lower form of 'state capitalism' (contract-geared planning model) to a higher form (a target-geared planning model). This Administrative Region was highly developed industrially and ready for such a transition. If Shanghai was modern enough, it did not move to the command economy until 1956 because of its large private sector (see Lee, 1987, p.22).

The North-East set the pace for the rest of China, not only in respect of changes in industrial enterprise but also in the growth of the management of human resources and its employment and labour model which will be the focus of this study. However, none of this proceeded evenly and the diffusion of the various practices involved took some years before it became a national pattern. Even then, the Soviet-derived organizational innovations were neither taken up entirely unchanged nor without subsequent modifications.

2.2 JAPANESE OCCUPATION

A further residual influence on Chinese industrial organization was the legacy of Japanese occupation.[3] Manchuria had been colonized in the early thirties and the industrial heartland of contemporary China had been set up and run by the occupiers (see Choucri et al., 1992). The Japanese took an active role in Chinese economic development as part of what has been called its 'informal empire' (Duus, 1989). Furthermore:

> Japanese economic interests in China were as important, in absolute terms, as the economic interests of the Westerners, and more important in relative terms. As the Japanese manufacturing sector grew, and particularly as more and more of its productions depended on export markets in the 1920s, China loomed larger and larger in economic significance. In an uncertain world economy, the market and resources of China came to be linked inextricably in many minds with Japan's well-being. (Duus, 1989, p.xxvi)

Japan particularly invested in the North-East where its 'informal empire' was located on the Liaotung Peninsula, and where the South Manchuria Railway was its economic fiefdom.

By the mid-1930s, Manchuria had become more industrialized than the rest of China (Nakagone, 1989). By late 1936, the Japanese government had set up three basic economic props to their puppet-state of Manchukuo – namely government agencies, banks and manufacturing enterprises, under military guidance. A five-year economic plan was set up to promote rapid industrialization. It was to be a strategy of state-planned 'forced' industrial growth, with funds mostly from Japan and a net capital inflow.

Three-quarters of investment funds were to go to heavy industry. By 1942, a Second Five-Year Plan had been launched. The war however spoilt whatever chances Japan had of profiting in the long-term. Even so, there was a legacy of Japanese economic and industrial planning which had characterized the wartime period. In industrial management the Japanese model, it is said, prevailed until 1953 and synthesized with the Soviet model from 1950 onwards (see Lee, 1987, p.45). Japanese managers and technicians also remained in the North-East in a number of cases after the Liberation and until the early fifties.

The 'Manchurian' management and employment model started with the Russians in the late nineteenth century. Russian enterprises had a privileged employment status for their own nationals working as managers, administrators and engineers but, given the times, not for Chinese workers. The Russians also built and controlled the railways in the North-East, but after 1904 they were replaced by the Japanese (see Beasley, 1963; Nish, 1985). After Manchukuo was set up in 1931, the Japanese control became total and after 1936 all the railways were formally sold to them. The Russians then returned in 1946 and occupied most of Manchuria until 1946, although they stayed in Dalian until 1952, as specified in the Yalta Treaty (see Swearingen, 1978, p.16). The Chinese and Russians jointly ran the railways until 1952. The new People's Republic of China clearly learnt a great deal from the Soviet model in the 1950s. Yet Japanese influence should not be underestimated as they had a strong tradition of 'unified operations' which persisted (Interviews, Heilongjiang Provincial Academy of Social Sciences, August 1993).

The Japanese had created an organizational structure to encompass all firms in a given industry, for example, flour-milling, brewing, rolling-stock and so on. In addition, all the small subcontracting firms in its sphere were linked to it. Prices were controlled by the dominant enterprise group. This 'planned', and possibly 'inflexible', model therefore has a long history. When most of the Japanese left, their influence persisted, and some Japanese managers and technical personnel were still kept on to run the railways and other key installations, as noted earlier. The Japanese employment model, although previously only for Japanese personnel and senior Chinese 'collaborators' in the railways, rolling-stock works and the post-office, was referred to as the 'golden rice-bowl' (*jin fan wan*) and said to be the precursor of the 'iron' version eventually later extended to all Chinese state employees.[3] Even the Chinese, who worked for the Japanese in these enterprises, were described as relatively better off than their fellow-workers elsewhere, in those hard times (Interviews, Heilongjiang Provincial Academy of Social Sciences, August 1993).

2.3 SOVIET INFLUENCES

The 'iron rice-bowl', as the state employment system became known, emerged after 1955 in most areas, but the railways and the post-office were to be state owned straight after the Liberation in 1949. As the Soviet Union was the 'older brother', it was an object of admiration and emulation, but these new Chinese-run state enterprises themselves became exemplars after this date. 'Authority-centred' is the term Lee (1987, p. 32) uses for this 'web' of rights and mutual obligations in the work-units (*danwei*), backed up by state institutions and laws. The life-tenure system was part and parcel of making the trade unions (as representatives of the working-class) 'masters of the country' now the revolution had actually succeeded (to be described in further detail in Chapter 3). Two key policies are cited as institutionalizing the system. One was the decision of the Chinese People's Government (CPG) Administrative Council in 1952 to make each enterprise responsible for its labour, in effect banning dismissals; and second, the 1954 'Outline of Labour Regulations within State-owned Enterprises', making for dismissals to be possible only on higher authority (see Lee, 1987, p.33).

The wage-grading system was also taken over from the Soviets, first applied in the North-East, spreading fairly slowly to the rest of the country. Before mid-1950, wage-systems varied according to local needs, but after that a standard system began to be introduced, though with some cognizance of local conditions. The principle of 'each according to his labour; more pay for more work' was to be recognized. The central government soon introduced national wages and salaries, first in 1952 with homogenization of the work-points system, and later, in 1956, with the eight-grade arrangement, backed up with a subsidy system, and a standard salary system, for economic cadres (see Lee, 1987, p.35). Differentiation of jobs was built into this Taylorist system, with recognition awarded to skills and technical expertise. Piece-rates were extensively used in the North-East, spreading nationally soon after in 1952. By the mid-1950s, just under half of industrial workers were covered by such arrangements (1987, p.36).

Takahara (1992) has clearly outlined this unfolding of Chinese wages policy over time from the Liberation onwards. As noted earlier, the Chinese system was copied from the Soviet one, but 'with Chinese characteristics'. The Soviet-style wage system was only established on a nationwide basis with 1956 reforms. This step launched what he calls 'the long rein of the so-called "rational low-wage system"' (1992, p.8). Urban wages were generally held down and the lowest-paid workers, as they were the 'link' in the chain with the peasantry, were particularly restricted.

2.4 LOCAL ADAPTATIONS

Three factors shaped the CCP's policy on wages, according to Takahara (1992, pp.9–10). First, the theoretical legacy of Marx's views in the *Critique of the Gotha Programme* with distribution according to the worker's labour, but without yet going to the ideal of to each according to his or her needs. Second, the experience of the Chinese Communists in their revolutionary mountain-bases where a rigidly egalitarian reward-system was kept out of industrial sites in order to avoid dampening-down workers' morale. The third factor was the Soviet experience and it was in the Sino-Soviet early joint ventures in the newly liberated Manchurian North-East that the original implementation of the wage system took root. As early as 1947, two years before the Liberation proper, a seven-grade wage system, which expanded across the country in the next decade into eight grades, had been installed in the joint ventures in the Lüda industrial area situated on the Liaotong Peninsula, not too far from Dalian.

The policy was first administered on a pragmatic basis with a Soviet-style productivity drive. The reforms spread first to the whole of the North-East and ultimately to the whole country, in the following sequence:

- North-East, 1950/51
- North, 1951
- East, 1951/52
- Central/South, 1952

However, it was not until the final wave of nationalization of industry and commerce was completed in 1956 that the definitive wage reforms followed.

By the mid-1950s, the average worker earned about 65 yuan per month, with middle managers and key technical staff getting two or three times as much. A chief engineer, for example, could earn around 280 yuan (see Richman, 1969, p.231). Often top managers might earn less than this, but not a great deal less, sometimes as much as 263 yuan monthly (ibid.). There were many difficulties in implementing such incentive schemes, the lack of a proper accounting system notwithstanding. It was difficult to get adequate data to calculate production norms and to judge the performance levels of workers. The Soviet system depended also on economies of scale often not present in the Chinese situation. The lack of managerial and technical expertise in China was additionally a barrier.[4] And finally not to be played down was the 'clash of cultures' between the Chinese and the Soviets.

Wage areas in 1955 numbered 285 and there were 78 price-supplement schemes; the 1956 reforms reduced this to only 12 wage-areas. Higher rewards were offered as an incentive for people to go to less economically attractive areas but the wages in Shanghai remained higher, none the less. In 1963, 1979 and 1985 the first five wage-areas were merged together and subsequently only areas 5 to 11 were retained. Even after the last of these reforms, the largest and medium-sized state enterprises operated with 11 wage-areas (see Korzec, 1992, p.95, note 158).

The mid-1950s wage-system however remained the template for the industrial sector of the Chinese economy, albeit with amendment and reform proceeding in parallel over the 1980s. Wage levels varied from higher pay in heavy industry to lower pay in the light industrial sectors, as in the Soviet example. As Korzec (ibid., pp.56–7) points out, this was not overly complex given that China is a huge country with many industrial and regional variations, nor was it excessively egalitarian given the multiple elements of remuneration built into the system over and above the 'basic wage'.

Similarly, workers' insurance schemes were first introduced in the fifties, in the North-East state industries, with the 1951 Labour Insurance Regulations. These covered accidents, sickness, medical care and so on, as well as pensions. Workers could also claim collective fringe-benefits when production targets were exceeded and such funds could be used to develop schools, canteens, clinics and so on in the enterprise for the use of workers and their families.[5]

The 'responsibility system' had been directly introduced in Manchuria, initially in the joint Sino-Soviet companies, as a way of enforcing labour discipline. The principle of individual responsibility for tasks did not however sit well with the Chinese collectivist tradition. It was first established in the railway system, which in turn would provide a model for the whole economy. Rational management was to be promoted, not only in large enterprises but also in smaller ones (see Schurmann, 1966, p.245–50). While Sino-Soviet plants had introduced Soviet methods, many Chinese plants, such as Anshan Iron and Steel, had not; the latter only did so fully in 1953. Most firms in light industries nationally did not conform here. The degree of implementation (ibid., p.253) depended on the degree of Soviet influence present, especially if such foreign experts were on site. The system enabled Soviet technical staff to run operations effectively, as the Chinese lacked the appropriate 'know-how'.[6]

As Schurmann concludes:

Manchuria had been 'liberated' earlier than the remainder of China and production was resumed even before the civil war had ended. Therefore, methods of management became an issue for the Chinese Communists in Manchuria in the late 1940s. The introduction of Soviet methods of industrial organization was not just a matter of emulation. The Soviets controlled the Central Manchurian Railroad and ran plants and shops connected with it. They also operated enterprises in the Dairen and Port Arthur areas. Moreover, the Manchurian government was under the control of Kao Kang, who presumably was already closely linked to the Soviets. (1966, p. 242)

It was important to follow Soviet methods, it was argued, as capitalist ones were not suitable for a socialist country. In the long run, the new ways of working would save manpower. By taking advantage of the Soviet Union's twenty years of experience, 'costly mistakes could be avoided. By adopting this system, the railroads could provide a model for industry as a whole' (ibid., p.244).

2.5   CONCLUDING REMARKS

We have in this chapter traced the development of the 'iron rice-bowl' system from its earliest days and attempted to show how Chinese, Japanese and Soviet (and previously Imperial Russian) influences blended into a distinctive employment system. The diffusion of the model from the North-East has also been noted (See Yahuda, 1994). The emergence of a differentiated wage-system, based on Soviet practices, was also sketched out. At the same time, it is clear that the management forms adopted after 1949 were institutionalized in an almost cyclical fashion ranging from a 'collective' model at one extreme to 'one-man management' at the other and then a counter-reaction (see Leung, 1988, p.21ff). The 'iron rice-bowl' seemed quite capable of coexisting with these authority structures and what was to come later, as the Cultural Revolution and subsequently the Dengist economic reforms respectively changed the environment in which the *danwei* operated (see Dittmer, 1994), as we shall see next in Chapters 3 and 4.

3 Labour–Management Relations

3.1 INTRODUCTION

In examining how the Chinese employment model evolved, we now focus on the changes in labour–management relations in recent decades. The way in which organized labour in the People's Republic of China fits into existing typologies in both Western and communist societies must first be set out, as well as their effectiveness in representing workers' interests. The Chinese 'proletariat' were, after all, 'masters of the country' (*guojia zhuren*) and the 'leading class' (*lingdao jieji*).

The Leninist conception of trade unions in communist societies, stressing their role as 'transmission-belts', has long been an intrinsic element of 'democratic centralism' (see Poole, 1986, p.92). Accordingly, the Soviet model, with high levels of formal unionization, industrial unions and an apex-governing structure dutifully implementing Party policy, in 'ideal-typical' terms, greatly influenced the emergence of Chinese labour after 1949 (Wilson, 1987, p.221). The trade unions soon became part and parcel of the Soviet-influenced model introduced by Mao and colleagues during the First Five-Year Plan (1953–7), although somewhat modified because of China's position as a 'labour-surplus' economy (Littler and Palmer, 1987, p.268). Trade union structure is, more often than not, a product of its history. Chinese unions are no exception to this axiom; thus we must take note of their beginnings, especially as the formative years prior to the 'Liberation' in 1949 played a major role in shaping the present state of Chinese labour–management relations.[1] As Leung points out:

> The current function and importance of Chinese trade unions can only be understood in the context of the development of the Chinese labour movement. Trade unions evolved in the midst of the immense social upheavals which shaped modern China. The unions' present status, self-image and power reflects their role in these revolutions, regressions and reversals. Their historical development will continue to influence their future role in the changes still sweeping China. (Leung, 1988, p.7)

The organized labour movement had come into being prior to the establishment of the Chinese Communist Party in 1921 and unions had been active even before the turn of the century (see Wales, 1945; Chesneaux, 1969; Chan, 1981; Chen, 1985 for further details). As industrialization had been confined to the coastal areas and especially the large cities such as Canton (now Guangzhou), Hong Kong, Shanghai, and Tientsin (now Tianjin), it is not surprising that labour disputes flared up in those locations. Indeed, the early workers' organizations had started their life there.

In China, the formal national union structure goes back to the early 1920s (see Littler and Lockett, 1983) with the setting-up of the All-China Federation of Trade Unions (ACFTU) in 1925 in Canton. The dominance of the Communist Party was established from the outset, with rule from above rather than below, although collaborating with the 'yellow' unions of the Kuomintang (KMT) and 'grey' unions of the politically unaligned workers (Leung, 1988, p.10). The right within the KMT came to power in 1927, when Chiang Kai-shek organized a coup against the Communists. As many as 13 000 activists were executed in the struggle for political ascendency and over 25 000 died in combat (Guillermaz, 1972, p.226); labour unions were savagely treated, particularly where they could not be taken over by the KMT (Wilson, 1987, p.221). The struggle for power resulted in the disappearance of leftist unions (see Brandt, 1958). As a result of this, the KMT prevented the ACFTU establishing unions all over China, as the CCP could not organize all the industries on a national level (Lee, 1986, p. 14). Some occupational groups could be recruited, however, and seamen, mechanics, railway-workers, print-workers, and miscellaneous unskilled operatives began to play in important role in the leadership of the unions (Chesneaux, 1968, p.400–2). By and large, however, between 1927 and 1949 the ACFTU mostly worked in the agrarian areas. Unions were set up hurriedly and often existed only on paper. The 'industrial' logic was never fully pursued and the number of experienced union cadres was very thinly distributed across the country (Wilson, 1987, p.219).

As a consequence, the unions had a skimpy industrial spread and a limited 'proletarian' base before 1949. This 'weakened their ability to make demands on the party' (Lee, 1986, p.30). A new organizational basis was established by the Constitution of the Sixth Labour Congress in 1948 and the Trade Union Law of 1950. From these, the principle of 'democratic centralism' was consolidated, and the industrial sector basis became pre-eminent in harness with geographically established trade union councils to form a 'dual system' of authority (Littler and Lockett, 1983).

The historical legacy of the pre-1949 period and the difficulties of organizing nationally thus led the CCP to use the ACFTU as essentially a 'transmission-belt', between Party and 'masses', above all other considerations. The problems faced by the regime in terms of grass-roots support in the cities (see Perry, 1993; 1994) were not always clear-cut. From 1949 onwards, however, the ACFTU undertook a national role, until 1966 when it went into abeyance during the Cultural Revolution. By 1979, a speedy restoration of its structure and function had taken place (Littler and Lockett, 1983). The evolution of organized labour over the subsequent decade must now be examined against the background of economic, industrial, managerial and other changes accompanying the more recent Dengist reforms (see Warner, 1992).

3.2 EXTERNAL UNION STRUCTURE

The present structure of Chinese labour organization did not basically change in the four decades or so since 1949 (see Lee, 1984; 1986). The types of unions, as we shall see, remained roughly the same, although there had been an expansion of union membership as urbanization drew more workers into industry. Reform of the economy in the 1980s led however to rationalization of labour–management relations as:

> Deng ... introduced his own concept of 'democratic management' and abolished revolutionary committees as the enterprise level, on the grounds that they have fulfilled their 'historic duties' ... Certainly Deng has sought to rationalise the state planning system and the productive enterprise in order to achieve greater efficiency, while management is being evaluated according to economic as well as political criteria. The labour movement has also been restructured to harmonise with government ministries on industry lines, while regional federations of unions are linked with the Party structure on a geographical basis. (Lansbury et al, 1984, p.57)

The composition of union membership has resulted from a somewhat elastic definition of the term 'worker' and perforce 'workers' organizations'. Those who were involved in 'mental' as well as 'physical' labour were eligible, although the number of 'permanent' workers was less than the total labour force. In addition, apprentices and trainees were not enrolled. As Article I of the ACFTU Constitution (1988) states:

Membership in trade unions is open to all manual and non-manual workers in enterprises, undertakings and offices, whose wages constitute their principal means of livelihood.

Thus, the scope of recruitment of the Chinese labour movement has been rather wide as a result of its definition of workers. This characteristic has resulted from the fact that previously 80 per cent or more of the labour force worked on the land as peasants, with a minority in industrial employment, with an even smaller group in large enterprises, so the unions tended to be 'generous' in their categorization of who was eligible and who was excluded in order to expand their membership, although union members were attacked as a 'labour aristocracy' during the Cultural Revolution.

Trade unions in the People's Republic of China had long been organized on vertical lines, in keeping with Leninist ideology and Soviet 'industrial' principles of organization (see Brown, 1966; Banks, 1974; Littler and Lockett, 1983; Poole, 1986; Pravda and Ruble, 1987; Chiang, 1990). Craft and occupational structures were also based on an older 'guild' tradition which had traditionally characterized master–apprentice relations (see Ma, 1955; Chesneaux, 1969).

If in the early 1950s there were only around 100 000 primary trade union units, by the early 1990s there were over 600 000. There had been only just under two and a half million union members in 1949 when they were probably more of an 'industrial elite' than today, but this had grown to over 100 million (on paper, at least) with almost half-a-million full-time worker representatives.[2] There has in turn been a growth in the degree of nominal unionization of industrial 'staff and workers' from just over one in four, to over nine out of ten (*Beijing Review*, 13 February 1989, pp.27–31). There have been altogether 15 industrial unions and 29 provincial trade union councils in recent years. The ACFTU has remained the 'apex' organization which integrates the constituent parts. The 15 national unions have been respectively organized by trade in the following industries: railways, civil aviation, shipping, road transport, post and telecommunications, engineering and metallurgy, petrochemicals, coal mining and geology, water and electricity, textiles, light industry, urban development and building materials, agriculture and forestry, finance and trade, and education. The Federation's eight departments have been organized as follows: namely economy, technology and labour protection, labour and wages, women workers, propaganda and education, international liaison, organization, finance and accounts and auditing. The configuration of the ACFTU leadership is set out in Figure 3.1. The ACFTU 'advises' the

Government and the Party on new legislation, such as the Enterprise Reform Laws, and then helps to interpret their application. A new Trade Union Law to replace the older one of 1950 was adopted in 1992 to cover formal powers, rights and duties of trade unions and will be discussed later.

The organizational rationale of post-revolutionary Chinese unions was to set them up along industrial lines, but with a geographical principle which was introduced later when local union councils were given the power to run all local industrial unions except those already running under national industrial ones. The above move was spurred by the small percentage of industrial workers in the PRC's labour force, political considerations, and emulation of the Soviet model rather than any logic of union organization based on 'trades' (see Lee, 1984; 1986).

At the end of 1991, on 23 December, the 23rd session of the Standing Committee of the Seventh National People's Congress (NPC) started to amend the Trade Union Law formulated in 1950. At the chairman's request, Gu Angran, vice-chairman of the legislative affairs commission of the NPC Standing Committee, briefed the session on the draft amendments. He pointed out that:

The Trade Union Law formulated in 1950 has played an important role in establishing trade unions in new China, consolidating the political power of the people's democratic dictatorship; organizing and educating the large number of staff members and workers to participate actively, vigorously, and creatively in socialist revolution and construction; and

Figure 3.1 The organizational structure of the ACFTU leadership in the late 1980s

Chairman	1
Vice-Chairman	7
Presidium members	27
Secretariat members:	
First Secretary	1
Others	9
Members of the Executive Committee	299
Members of the Auditing Commission:	
Chairman	1
Vice-Chairman	2
Standing members	4

Source: ACFTU, 1988, pp.63–4.

safeguarding the legitimate rights and interests of the broad masses of
staff members and workers .... (SWB, 28 December 1991)

Since the Liberation, China has seen considerable political, economic and
social changes, and so has the labour force. To redefine the role of trade
unions in the economic reforms and to benefit from the experience gained
from their work over forty years or so, the leadership thought it necessary
to amend the 1950 Trade Union Law in an appropriate manner. The Trade
Union Law (draft amendments) was jointly designed by the All-China
Federation of Trade Unions (ACFTU) and the Legislative Affairs
Commission of the NPC Standing Committee, and was promulgated in
1992. Since 1978, the ACFTU and the Legislative Affairs Commission
had each conducted surveys and sought opinions by twice sending out
copies of draft amendments to provinces, autonomous regions,
municipalities and relevant central departments; and in turn had drawn up
the current draft amendments after repeated revisions (SWB, 28 December
1991).

A draft amendment to the law on trade unions was further discussed at
the Standing Committee. The Vice-Chairman of the NPC Standing
Committee, Ni Zhifu (also President of the All-China Federation of Trade
Unions) admitted on 21 February 1992 that China had undergone great
changes over the previous four decades, and some articles of the Law on
Trade Unions formulated in 1950 were now clearly out of date (SWB,
22 February 1992). The revised 1992 legislation is discussed in detail in
section 3.4 (and set out in full in Appendix 1).

In the same debate, the noted theorist of economic reform, the late Jiang
Yiwei, suggesting more worker-participation, advised that:

In the period of socialist construction after the victory of our revolution,
the primary or central task of our trade unions should be 'to educate
and organize, under the leadership of the CCP, the masses of workers to
learn how to exercise their democratic rights and fulfil their
responsibilities and obligations as masters of their own affairs' ...
The Party Central Committee has time and again stressed the policy
of 'relying on the working class wholeheartedly'. To carry out this
policy, first of all it is necessary to make the masses of workers feel
that in the enterprise where they work every day, they are truly the
masters; it is necessary to make the workers an integral part of the
enterprise ... Regrettably, under the old system, which was characterized
by a high degree of concentration and administrative command, workers
did not truly become the principal part of the enterprise; instead they

fell into a status resembling 'state employees'. This was one of the profound reasons why state-run enterprises lacked vitality. This question must be resolved in the course of carrying out in-depth reform. (SWB, 22 February 1992)

He argued that socialist enterprises were best equipped to develop the initiative of the workers. At present, efforts were being made to break the 'iron rice-bowl', and guaranteed wages and jobs. It was essential then that workers could be hired and dismissed, or promoted and demoted. At the same time, it was also necessary to adopt measures to encourage employees to 'regard the factory as their home' and to make enterprises 'their lifetime work'. At present, experiments in enterprise reform, he said, were being conducted in all parts of China. As to the balance between the state and the enterprise, many effective reforms had been introduced. On the other hand, he added, 'not enough attention had been paid to the relationship between the workers and the firm; as a result, few effective measures had been introduced in this vein' (ibid.).

The precise role the unions would play in the 'socialist market-economy' was even so yet to be clarified, but it was likely that they would follow the 'official' line as previously. One observer (Korzec, 1992) feared that the reforms were likely to fail because they broke the 'social contract' set up after 1949 between the state and the workers by introducing market forces. Under this arrangement, 'the enterprise, with its comprehensive welfare and political functions, is that state in miniature. Moreover, this identity based as it is on long-engrained habits of dependency remains popular' (Howe, 1992, p.ix). It was just this status quo that the Chinese trade unions institutionalized.

The main factors shaping the external union structure have thus been largely political, as indeed they were *vis-à-vis* the internal structure. The reader is referred to Figure 3.2 on the role of the State Bureaucracy, CPC and Trade Union Federation. Leung (1993, p.4) argues that 'without critical political transformation, it is difficult to find the basis of fundamental change in the nature of the union from that of a party administrative agency to that of a bargaining representative'.

3.3   INTERNAL UNION STRUCTURE

The way the union leadership is picked is broadly similar to that in other unions modelled on Leninist lines as described earlier (see Brown, 1966; Pravda and Ruble, 1987; Leung, 1993). The selection of union cadres and representatives takes place from the primary union level upwards. From time to time, 'mass participation' has been more or less emphasized. A combination of 'persuasion with coercion' (Lee, 1986, p.44) characterizes the system. The Party has consistently played a primary role in this process.

The trade union aided Workers' Congresses, of which there were said to be over 360 000 in the late 1980s (Zhang, 1988, p.35; Gong, 1989, p.3) supplement the formal 'representative function' of the unions. As Liu points out, enumerating its formal responsibilities in an officially sanctioned description promising more than may ultimately be fulfilled:

> According to the provisions of the Law of the People's Republic of China on Industrial Enterprises Owned by the Whole People, the Workers' Congress is the basic form of democratic management in enterprises and the organ for workers to exert such powers. It has the right to deliberate such major issues as the policy of operations, annual and long-term plans and programmes, contract and leasing responsibility systems of management; it may approve or reject plans on wage reforms and bonus distribution as well as on important rules and regulations; it may decide on major issues concerning workers' conditions and welfare; it may appraise and supervise the leading administrative cadres at various levels and put forward suggestions for awards and punishments and their appointment and approval; and it democratically elects the director. (Liu, 1989, pp.5–6)

The term 'oligarchic' might arguably be used by the critical observer to characterize the ACFTU, as opposed to 'democratic', in terms of the union democracy debate (see Edelstein and Warner, 1979). The degree of electoral competition is, to say the least, limited and alienation is now said to be widespread amongst many union members. A demand for direct elections of union officials surfaced again in the late 1980s (it had previously been a demand of the Democracy Movement of 1979) with a third of incumbent officials said to have been voted out of office in 100 enterprises sampled (Zhang, 1988, p.23).

Factionalism has long been endemic in union politics. This tendency has not resulted in membership opinion being more effectively represented for the most part, but largely reflects political waves external to labour–management relations *per se*. The main lines of cleavage are usually as in the Party, namely the rivalry between the old-style political conservatives and the reformers. There is probably a balance of forces in the Party Central Committee. An outright victory for the Party conservatives across the board would probably not now mean a return to a centralist, planned economy, however.

Union representation in the workplace – to make the workers 'masters of the country' – was formally built into the system, and has been so since the early 1950s (see Warner, 1987b). The institutional arrangements for this have evolved over four decades, although the changes in form may have overshadowed the shifts in function. The role of the Party Secretary in the enterprise, according to some observers (for example Walder, 1989), has long been and remains central whatever the changing institutional arrangements, whether managerial or representative. The Party controls the union's work and appointments in the trade union with the chairperson often holding the same rank as the deputy-director. Such officials have sometimes swapped roles with plant managers. The Party committee remains responsible to 'guarantee and supervise' policy implementation (Child and Xu, 1989, p.10). In this context, full-time union cadres may be seen as potentially still relatively influential compared with policy-making bodies in the enterprise, as they reflect the Party line, whether the factory director has officially more or less power (see Figure 3.2) although this may be changing, as we shall see in Part Two. On sensitive workforce issues however, such as dismissals, management in large enterprises often talks to the union officials representing the Workers' Congress rather than the Party Committee, according to this source (1989, p.28). Granick (1990, p.238) differs on this point:

Although the issue of dismissing workers for personal fault was mentioned in several of the sample enterprises, none of the informants suggested that the enterprise trade union was any obstacle to such dismissals. Instead, objections came solely from the local authorities of the area where the worker had his official residence. This is in sharp contrast to the situation in the Soviet Union, where no dismissal is legal unless it wins the prior explicit approval of the enterprise trade union committee ... Moreover, this system appears to be widely used ... [and] in Soviet industry of the 1957–65 period, [up] to 10 per cent of the Soviet industrial labor force was involved each year as plaintiffs in one or another aspect of the grievance procedure.

It is doubtful in any event if the unions have played much of an *independent* role in Chinese enterprises. The union officials traditionally supported increasing production if the Party wished this. The Workers' Congress was functionally not too distinct from the union and some sessions may be seen as just a formality. The workers elected to the

Workers' Congress were often drawn from the Party faithful: the traditional 'hard-liners' in the Party were usually the 'pro-worker' faction; the reformers would support the 'managerial' line. In the Special Economic Zones and joint ventures, there is often no Workers' Congress, although there may be a local union in the plant (see Warner, 1989) and in foreign-owned firms, there may be neither. The Joint Venture Implementation Regulations are said to recognize implicitly an adversarial role for unions (Henley and Nyaw, 1990, p.284). Union officials may deal directly with the overseas partners over disputes and attend top board meetings when labour-related policy issues are discussed (ibid.).

3.4   UNION GOALS, STRATEGY AND TACTICS

The formal goals of the ACFTU were from the very start 'to unite and promote the welfare of workers' (Lee, 1989, p.9). Its tasks included: (1) to develop workers' unions in China; (2) to unify the labour movement; (3) to set up an organization system; (4) to direct union activities; (5) to adjudicate interunion disputes; (6) to propagate the aims of class struggle; (7) to represent the Chinese workers in relations with outside countries; (8) to raise workers' educational levels; and (9) to protect workers' benefits. The opening paragraph of the Constitution of the ACFTU (1988) states:

> The trade unions of China are Chinese working class mass organizations led by the Chinese Communist Party and formed voluntarily by workers and staff members, and are important social and political organizations. Trade unions should conscientiously take economic construction as their central task and should faithfully reflect and safeguard the particular interests of workers and staff members while upholding the interests of the people as a whole, speak on behalf of workers and staff members, work for them, build up a dedicated, high-minded well-educated and disciplined contingent of workers and staff members and bring into full play the role of the Chinese working class as the main force in developing socialist material and cultural civilization.

The guiding principles of Chinese organized labour are described by Leung as:

> rallying around the four modernizations; to speak, to work and to defend the legitimate rights of workers; to strengthen political, cultural

Figure 3.2 A simplified diagram of the decision-making structure of a Chinese State Enterprise

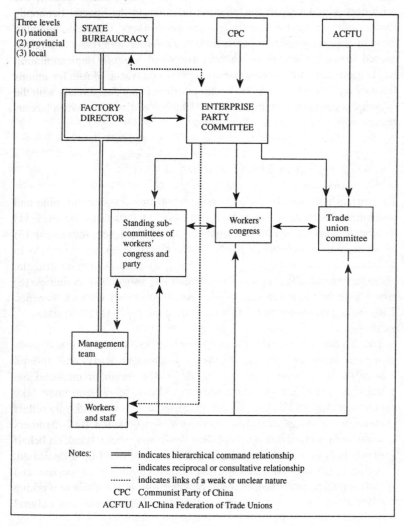

Source: Henley and Nyaw, 1986, p.642.

and technical education of workers; aiming to build a workforce with ideals, with high morals, culture and good discipline. (Leung, 1988, p.39)

More recently, Ni Zhifu, Chairman of the All-China Federation of Trade Unions and Vice-Chairman of the Standing Committee of the NPC told local trade union leaders in 1991 that:

> trade unions at all levels must actively participate in the country's reforms and protect the workers' interests on the basis of safeguarding the general interests of the state. He said that it is necessary to get the ordinary workers involved in the reforms in such areas as housing, social security and medical care for the success of the reforms lies in the support of the workers. He urged enterprises, especially the large and medium-sized state enterprises, to set much store by the initiative and wisdom of the workers in revitalizing their management and improving economic performances. He also urged the full implementation of the 'enterprise law' which provides the power of the workers' representative congresses. Democratic management is not merely a form, but an important system that calls for the full reliance on the workers and ensures their rights as masters of the enterprises, he stressed. (SWB, 7 August 1991)

Trade unions in China in the new formulation are organized around four main functions, according to the most recent official (and legal) definition. First, they must protect the interest of the whole country, but at the same time *safeguard* the legitimate rights and interests of the workers. Second, they must help their members *participate* in the management of their own work units. Third, they should *mobilize* the labour-force to raise productivity and the economy's performance. Fourth, they should *educate* the workers to be better members of society (Interviews, at ACFTU Headquarters, July 1993). These four functions are clearly set out in the Trade Union Law as revised in 1992, and are set out in the first chapter, Law's which covers Articles 1–10 describing the general provisions of the legislation (see Appendix 1 below for the full text).

The 1992 revised law does not differ however in its essentials from that of 1950, and is replete with similar ideological terminology. Key words, like 'mass organizations', 'working-class'. 'masters of the country', 'socialist labour emulation', 'collectivism and socialism', 'democratic centralism' and so on, set the tone of the document. Rights and obligations are stressed, but the right to work and the right to strike do not feature. The latter, which featured in the 1975 Constitution, was removed by constitutional amendments in 1982. Rights are also qualified by the terms 'legitimate' and 'democratic'. The phrase 'voluntary basis' also appears, as does 'work in an independent and autonomous way'.

The term 'workers' is normally expressed as 'workers and staff members', linked to 'alliance of workers and peasants'. The ultimate goal is to 'turn them into well-educated and self-disciplined labourers with lofty ideals and moral integrity'. All actions must conform to the 'Constitution', the 'law', and 'patriotism'. There is obeisance to other countries' trade unions on the basis of 'non-interference' in 'each others' internal affairs'. Much is included; very little is excluded. The circle is thus squared.

While 'socialist modernization' is set out as a goal, the terms 'economic reform', 'four modernizations' or 'open door' are not noted. Previous clauses about representing and protecting employees in private firms have been deleted. However, 'labour-contracts', 'joint ventures', 'foreign-capital enterprises', but not 'Special Economic Zones' and 'Open Cities', enter the scene. The tone of the document still remains in the 1950s, but the detail has been extended to cover the economic and political realities of the 1990s, to a degree, at least. Labour legislation in the PRC was paradoxically weak (see Josephs, 1990, Xia, 1991, Korzec, 1992, Leung, 1993) and most laws mainly protected the employees of SOEs. Even in early 1993, there were still no ordinances setting out minimum wages, working hours, industrial safety, collective bargaining and so on. The eventual national 1994 Labour Law was published on 6 July of that year, to be effective 1 January 1995 (see Appendix 2).

Many consequences of the economic reforms now directly concern the trade unions, such as dealing with workers made redundant, the new labour contracts and payment systems. Issues involving social and unemployment insurance have now to be tackled, as well as dealing with joint ventures where foreign multinational companies are involved, or other sources of overseas investment. Not all of these problems can be dealt with at national level, so provisional and municipal level labour organizations have to be shown how to respond (Interviews, at ACFTU Headquarters, July 1993). It looks as if the trade unions are still at best reactive *vis-à-vis* the momentum of rapid economic change. It should also be noted that an embryonic employer's body, the All-China Federation of Industry and Commerce (ACFIC) was founded in 1984, and had approximately 182 000 members by the early 1990s.

Such a momentum also carries its dangers, for the trade unions as the sectors in which it is weakest or sometimes non-existent are the very ones which are the fastest growing, such as township industries, privately owned firms and joint ventures and overseas owned companies. Conversely, precisely the sector they are strongest in, while remaining pivotal in the economy, represents a shrinking area of membership, namely the state-owned enterprises.

Another feature of the changing economic scene is the large number of temporary, casual and part-time workers, especially those rural migrants flooding into the cities and townships, as well as into the SEZs, mostly unprotected by labour legislation. While a few may obtain union membership, most will not. The total number of non-union members will probably rise as a percentage of the urban work-force. It is therefore clear why the ACFTU has revised its terms of reference to include a much wider range of firms to target than hitherto, although its chances of recovering ground remain debatable.

Plant-level 'industrial relations' functions, in the widest sense of the term, were normally carried out both by the trade unions and the elected Workers' Congresses, as described above, which represent the work-force and staff in the enterprise on the basis of one representative for ten or twelve persons. In big plants, the basic unit was the union team centred on the work-group, which met once a fortnight, or monthly, as needed. The Workers' Congress in an enterprise was convened between one and four times a year depending on 'custom and practice'. The union committee in the work-place through its full-time cadres provided continuity of contact when the Congress was in abeyance. The union was thus unavoidable in the *danwei*, the all-important official place of work and the building-block of Chinese society, as noted earlier. It had for years controlled workers' lives both inside and outside work (see Walder, 1986). These work establishments not only provided 'cradle-to-grave' welfare services, but also helped to shape the worker's sense of identity. Given the part trade unions play in the modernization process, according to Lee (1986) they first stressed production values rather than consumption ones, but second, had to look after the everyday welfare interests of their members (see the *Gongren Ribao* (Workers' Daily) 19 July 1988, p.2). The unions also played other social roles, such as enforcing and monitoring birth-control policies, by their surveillance of women workers in the factories and offices. As Leung (1993, p.9) puts it:

Trade unionism in China had been dominated by 'welfarism, surveillance and control of the working population rather than political representation of the working class. At best, trade unions are looked upon as 'caretaker' of the workers, channeling their grievance to the higher authorities.

The 1986 ACFTU survey (pp.103–6) had found that the overriding number of replies put 'livelihood and welfare' at the top of the list of members' priorities.

To achieve these objectives, the trade unions have long operated a 'check-off' system to finance their activities and members paid 0.5 per cent of their wages each month to the union, with the enterprise contributing another 2 per cent of the wage-bill to supplement this deduction. About 5 per cent of all union subscriptions went to the ACFTU.

Union effectiveness, as far as official policy was concerned, took the form of the unions helping the government achieve economic growth and modernization, as well as protecting workers' interest in the welfare field, providing educational facilities and so on. The union was expected to cooperate with management. Its role centred on 'labour productivity, worker morale and welfare rather than the interpretation of national policy' (Henley and Nyaw, 1986, p.648). The trade union did not bargain freely, or fix wage levels, but in contracted or leased enterprises they helped determine the allocation of funds and the arrangement of working schedules. Normally, they were supposed to implement the resolutions passed by the Workers' Congress in these areas. In the everyday work of the enterprise, the unions were also expected to defuse conflicts between the work-force and management, if the latter acted out of order, for example by reducing bonuses or by cancelling labour insurance if there was a stoppage by the workers involved. The union tried to intervene informally to sort out the grievance and get production restored. Chinese workers still retained 'a *de facto* shop floor bargaining power', in so far as they can raise the productivity level by working harder if they choose to do so (Littler and Palmer, 1987, pp.268–9).

In recent years, Chinese trade unions, on the central government's initiative, have promoted a system of 'collective agreements' (Gong, 1989). These accords are based on individual enterprises in order to anchor labour–management relations.[3] An officially sponsored trade union publication describes their characteristics, perhaps rather over-optimistically, as follows:

> Clearly defined in the collective agreements are the director's objectives during his term of office, annual targets in production and management, plans to improve workers conditions and welfare and specific measures to achieve the above-mentioned objectives and targets as well as responsibilities on the part of the director, the trade union and the Workers Congress. Then the director and the trade union chairman sign the agreement respectively on behalf of the administration and the

workers and employees. This practice is well received by the workers for it links up the workers and the management in a community of interest in which obligations, risks and benefits are shared by both sides. (Gong, 1989, pp.7–8)

It was claimed by the above commentator that such agreements boosted production significantly compared to enterprises that do not have them.

The Party nonetheless usually had the final say as it appointed union officials and organized and even manipulated the Workers' Congresses (Walder, 1989, p.247). It also screened the nominations list for all offices in the work-place, union and otherwise: (a situation not unlike the KMT in Taiwan). Workers therefore often turned to the Party when they had grievances about bonuses or discipline, although the union was formally supposed to voice them on their behalf.

More recently, the union's role was (yet again) reformulated by trade union officials at the 1994 meetings of the National People's Congress and Political Consultative Committee:

With the emergence of the labour market and the upgrading of the enterprise system, trade unions in China will surely play a bigger role in the market economy. All trade unionists attending ... were aware of their own new role: being the 'mouthpiece' of the interests of staff members and workers. They presented their views vehemently on numerous issues ranging from staff and worker ability to withstand the strains that should be given consideration in the course of reform, the status of workers and trade unions after the introduction of 'a company system' to state-owned enterprises, protection of the legitimate rights and interests of Chinese personnel of foreign-funded enterprises and perfection of a social security mechanism. Under the planned economy characterized by single ownership, the main role of trade unions was to care for staff and worker well-being and to ensure production. Thus the work of the then trade unions was figuratively summarized into 'issuing film tickets, managing meal coupons and collecting bathing tickets'.

China's trade unions are now becoming 'anti-shock valves' enabling reform to progress in a stable society.

At present, the problem of Chinese enterprises suffering losses in operation and suspending or partially suspending production remains pronounced. In many localities, prices have gone up quite rapidly, making life difficult for some staff members and workers.

Many deputies to the National People's Congress and members of the National Committee of the Chinese People's Political Consultative

Conference who were trade union members appealed to the government to give full consideration to the economic and mental ability of the general public to withstand the resulting strains of the various major reform measures to be taken. Meanwhile, they also briefed the sessions on moves taken by the trade unions in various localities to alleviate contradictions and reduce friction. Sun Hongrong, president of the China Textile Trade Union, said: As Shanghai's textile industry was confronted with structural readjustment, staff and workers would have to leave their current posts and seek new jobs. The trade union of the municipality's textile departments sponsored all types of training courses to pass on job-seeking knowledge free of charge to staff members and workers who had quit their current posts and ran job introduction centres and undertakings in the tertiary industry to find jobs for them. (SWB, 8 April 1994)

3.5 DISCUSSION

A sociological theory of trade union organization has highlighted their twin rationales of 'administrative' and 'representative' functioning (see Child et al., 1973). Using such analytical tools, we can see that trade unions in the PRC were disproportionately geared to the 'administrative' function, although it would be foolish to wholly disregard their 'representative' function, especially at shop-floor level.[4] The critical observer is, however, forced to view the macro-political (and even more so the macro-economic) role of Chinese unions as relatively removed from the life of the ordinary worker they claimed to represent. According to an ACFTU survey in 1986, fewer than 30 per cent of workers had a positive view of Workers' Congresses, less than 40 per cent viewed the unions with enthusiasm, and 21 per cent said they had no idea what unions do (Li, 1989, p.78). The ACFTU National Conferences echoed Party thinking for so long that it is hard to imagine them reflecting, let alone initiating, independent ideas or policies.

Workers' concerns about their jobs, wages and standard of living generally, working conditions, and, even more urgently, price-stability, ought to have been articulated more explicitly if the trade unions were to live up to their prescribed roles in communist society. For example, when important changes were introduced during 1986 to undermine the 'iron rice-bowl' system, with its former guarantee of job security for life, the union leadership, it was felt, should have spoken up more loudly on the workers' behalf (see Rosen, 1989).

The new policy was based on the introduction of tighter labour discipline, to be discussed in detail in Chapters 4, 7 and 8:

> The system involves open recruitment through examinations. No longer are the children of retired workers allowed to fill their parents' positions automatically, nor are employees' children guaranteed a job, as was previously the case. At the same time, factory directors have been given the right to dismiss workers for breach of discipline. (*Beijing Review*, 24 October 1988, p.25)

Clearly, trade unions in communist societies present conceptual difficulties for industrial relations analysts (see Littler and Palmer 1987). If trade unions were defined as organizations of workers which bargain freely and collectively, then they might not be considered as unions at all (see Banks, 1974, pp.37ff; Poole, 1986, pp.90ff). In so far as unions with rather more differentiated functions developed in the fast-changing Eastern European economies, such as Hungary, Poland and the former Soviet Union, a simplistic view of unions in communist or socialist societies is now much less tenable than previously (see Littler and Palmer, 1987, pp.265–70; Borisov et al., 1994, pp.15–25).

In the middle 1950s, the trade union committees in factories were clearly subordinated to the Party Committee, even merged with it in some cases (see Zhang, 1988, p.41). In this context, union officials were appointed by the Party Committee in the enterprise. This development probably represented the high point of integration of Party and union. Lee for example, dealing with this point, concludes that:

> Chinese trade unions are fundamentally different from the unions in Western democracies. To use the analytical concept of structural-functional analysis, Chinese unions have little or no 'sub-system autonomy'. Chinese union leaders also make no pretence about this ... The reconstructed trade unions after the Cultural Revolution were similarly controlled by the Party. Chinese unions are essentially an arm of the executive to mobilise the resources of the society. (1986, p.159)

Any 'representative' function of trade unions for the labour-force was however mitigated by their 'exclusive' membership requirement, as 'only permanent workers could join unions and were eligible to the medical care, unemployment, housing and other welfare benefits administered by trade unions' (ibid., p.115). Temporary and contract workers had been kept out of union protection and indeed this was one reason amongst others for the 'fall' of the ACFTU during the Cultural Revolution. Curiously enough, temporary contract labour was a 'socialist' idea imported from the Soviet Union during the 1950s when top officials had been sent to the USSR to study their contract system in order to reduce overhead costs and to gain greater labour flexibility (ibid.).

The failure of Chinese trade unions to cater for *all* workers was a weakness which represented a grievance that periodically surfaced during the Great Leap Forward in the late 1950s and again in the early 1960s when the labour contract system was initially used (ibid.). In the early 1980s, the unions asked local committees to help recruit contract workers (Wilson, 1987, p.229). Clearly, the growing use of such contracts during the later period of economic reforms was to fuel the dissatisfaction with the official trade unions as the contract system was extended nationally (see Leung, 1988, p.61).

The Chairman of the ACFTU, Ni Zhifu, outlined the official position on 22 October 1988 to the Eleventh National Congress of Chinese Trade Unions:

It is necessary to introduce the mechanism of competition in reforming the labour system, to grant the enterprises the autonomy in selecting workers and vice-versa, and to set up an employment system which allows a reasonable flow, together with a relative stability of the labour force. Rational labour reorganization should be carried out in accordance with the principles of openness, equality, competition and optimum selection, while trade unions should organize democratic supervision by the workers and staff. At the same time, they should urge and assist enterprises to diversify their operations, open up new avenues of employment, make proper arrangements for the placement of redundant personnel and reduce the rate of unemployment in society. (ACFTU, 1988, p.17)

The latter part of this statement appears intended to 'sweeten the pill' for the workers potentially threatened by such changes.[5]

Contracts may be for varying periods, even for ten years, although some may be for a duration of less than one year, as we shall see in greater detail in Part Two. They have legal validity, and state the obligations of the enterprise with regard to safety, training, remuneration, insurance and welfare and so on. As the contracts are for fixed periods, they may help recruitment as well as training.

A Mediation Committee may be set up to resolve disputes which crop up when contracts are introduced. There are nine members in such a body, full-time leaders of the union committee, part-time worker-representatives, and the personnel director. When a dispute arises, the union is supposed to look after their members' interests. If mediation does not work, the case may go to the 'municipal labour arbitration committee' (Dong, 1989, pp.28–9). Details regarding contracts, mediation and the like will be set out in Chapters 5 and 7.

It may be hypothesised that the greater the extent and speed of the modernization policies, the deeper the level of dissatisfaction with the official trade unions in their present form (see *Gongren Ribao*, 28 December 1988, p.1). Yet, for the permanent labour-force, the collusive nature of the enterprise socio-political coalition ensured an increasing standard of living and improved working conditions over much of the last decade according to a leading Western authority on Chinese industry (Walder, 1989). If 'the party leads the union organization, appoints its officials, and organizes even manipulates congresses of workers and staff' (1989, p.247), then it can make sure it looks after the faithful. The ACFTU survey carried out in 1986, noted earlier, reported that over 80 per cent of those interviewed (in fact nearly 650 000 members) believed their standard of living had improved since 1979 (see He et al., 1989, pp.32–8).

The critic, at this point, may well ask 'why study trade unions in communist societies?' given their often *subordinate* importance to the decision-making process. It is also not clear what their long-term future role might be. As the economic reforms are extended further in the PRC, the role of trade unions has to change substantially. In this context, the Party leadership is not keen to see the unions linking up with other social groups. An alliance of workers and students, as had been the case with the Polish Solidarity movement, was precisely what the Chinese authorities had been preoccupied with since the early 1980s (see Littler and Lockett, 1983). Until spring 1989, the twin streams of potential dissent have been kept as segregated as possible. Student marches, where they occurred, were keenly screened by the police for any workers who dared to throw in their lot with the protesters. Industrial strikes had already been spreading in the late 1980s, many reported, even more unreported. Chan (1993, p.43) believes it is the SOE employees who would register the most vocal reaction if their privileges were threatened by the reforms.

One feature of the Tiananmen Square protests in late spring 1989, if perhaps on the fringes of student-led dissent, had been the presence of the Workers' Autonomous Federation.[6] Its appearance has been well-documented (Fathers and Higgins, 1989; Lu, 1991; Walder and Gong, 1993) as were examples elsewhere, and indeed its leaders were prominently featured in the subsequent official crackdown, being severely sentenced for their apparent audacity. The guiding principles of the Workers' Autonomous Federation are set out in Figure 3.3, clearly showing their wish to be outside Party control.

Dissident staff of the ACFTU were said to have given out leaflets in the Square in May 1989 calling for greater union autonomy and asking that 'Trade unions should work and speak for the workers and masses' (Fathers and Higgins, 1989, p.66). In addition, the headquarters of the ACFTU donated 100 000 yuan (27 000 US dollars) to the Red Cross for the student hunger-strikers on 18 May – a remarkable step (SWB, 2 June 1989). There had even been rumours of an unofficial one-day general strike in Beijing. The activities of the 'free' trade union organizations were also reported in Chengdu, Guangzhou, Hangzhou, Hefei and Shanghai, amongst other places (*Echoes from Tiananmen*, nos 1 and 2, June and August 1989). As late as 9 June, at least a thousand workers were reported marching behind the Workers' Autonomous Federation banner in the demonstrations in Shanghai. The autonomous trade unions were accused of usurping the name of the working class, fabricating rumours and attempting to overthrow the people's government in the official press. Such illegal organizations, it was said, 'will certainly become the rubbish abandoned by history' (*Gongren Ribao*, 18 June 1989, p.1).

On 25 July, the official Chinese news agency reasserted that:

China's trade unions must work under the leadership of the CCP and no trade unions opposed to the CCP are allowed to be established [according to] Ni Zhifu, President of the All-China Federation of Trade Unions (ACFTU). (Xinhua report in SWB, 28 July 1989)

Addressing the third meeting of the 11th ACFTU presidium which opened there on that day, Ni stressed that any attempt to work outside the CCP leadership and put the trade unions into an opposition role must be resisted. 'Otherwise, we will miss the correct political orientation of trade union reform and construction, leading to great errors' (ibid). Ni then stressed the trade unions' role in representing and safeguarding workers' rights and interests and then went on to argue that:

The trade unions must avoid simply acting as agents of the government and work independently so as to increase the attraction to workers and enjoy more confidence from the workers, leaving no opportunity to those who attempt to organize 'independent trade unions'. Otherwise we will also make great errors. (Ibid.)

Worker discontent due to the adverse consequences of the economic reforms was a major problem (see Mirsky, 1989, p.3). According to some accounts, only workers (rather than students) had been executed in the reaction to the events of June 1989 including some associated with the Workers' Autonomous Federation (see Goldman, 1989, p.5) but it is hard to confirm whether students were thus protected. (Thousands of *both* groups went to prison, even so.) In the early spring, they had physically tried to stop the workers marching with them, fearing they would only be joining for the pursuit of materialistic goals. But later they relented, as a million people marched in Beijing on 17 May. The fear of a Solidarity-style movement was in the end unfounded.[7] Deng nonetheless appeared to mistrust Soviet and Eastern European reforms more than Western ideas:

> Those people who have been influenced by the free elements of Yugoslavia, Poland, Hungary and the Soviet Union have a reason to create turmoil. Their motive is to overthrow the Party. (Cited in Goldman, 1989, p.5)

By February 1992, an underground labour union network, the 'Free Trade Unions of China' was reported as distributing pamphlets in many factories in Beijing (Reuters' News Agency report, 5 February 1992).

Two years later, in April 1992, an account of clandestine trade union activity described:

> Serious outbreaks of industrial unrest [which] have flared in parts of China as a result of Dickensian factory conditions and widespread abuse of workers' rights. The problem, disclosed in the normally tame official press, suggests that many workers – deemed 'masters of the country' under communist rule – are in danger of becoming an underclass. ... An official report says 250,000 labour disputes have broken out since 1988, including 1,100 during the past two years in the prosperous economic zone of Shenzhen, near Hong Kong. They include strikes and incidents of shop-floor violence. ... A survey of foreign-funded companies published in the official magazine 'Outlook' shows that exploitation of labour has returned on the scale of Shanghai in the 1920s and 30s – the worst period in communist demonology. [It] reported on a series of abuses, ranging from illegal employment contracts to arbitrary fines imposed on workers and non-payment for overtime. Many firms had 'disregarded China's labour laws ... or simply ignored workers' safety, and wantonly infringed on the workers' legitimate rights and interests' ... More than 800 underground unions had been formed in

Figure 3.3 Beijing Workers' Autonomous Federation provisional memorandum

Based on the initial guiding principles, prepared by the preparatory committee of the Beijing Workers' Autonomous Federation, issued on 25 May 1989.

Preamble:

In the entire People's Patriotic Democracy Movement, led by the students in mid-April, the majority of the Chinese workers have demonstrated a strong wish to take part in politics. At the same time, they also realize that there is not yet an organization which can truly represent the wishes expressed by the working masses. Therefore, we recognize there is a need to set up an autonomous organization which will speak for the workers and which will organized the realization of workers' participation and consultation in political affairs. For this purpose, we put forward the following preparatory guiding principles.

1. The organization should be an entirely independent, autonomous organization, built up by the workers on a voluntary basis, through democratic processes, and should not be controlled by other organizations.

2. The fundamental principle of the organization should be to address political and economic demands, based on the wishes of the majority of the workers, and should not just remain a welfare organization.

3. The organization should possess the function of monitoring the party of the proletariat – the Chinese Communist Party.

4. The organization should have the power, through every legal and effective means, to monitor the legal representatives of all state and collective enterprises, guaranteeing that the workers become the real masters of the enterprise. In other enterprises, through negotiation with the owners and other legal means, the organization should be able to safeguard the rights of the workers.

5. Within the bounds of the constitution and the law, the organization should be able to safeguard all legal rights of its members.

6. Membership of the organization should come from individuals on a voluntary basis, and also group or collective membership in branches of various enterprises.

Tiananmen Square, 28 May 1989

Source: Echoes from Tiananmen, 15 June 1989, p.1.

Guangdong, China's most developed province. Many had the characteristics of secret societies. They were based on personal loyalties, and lacked formal rules, but were feared by employers and government. (*Daily Telegraph*, 1 April 1994, p.6)

3.6   CONCLUDING REMARKS

To sum up, Chinese trade unions have long played a key role in the mobilization process. They have not, however, bargained collectively like Western unions; instead they have tried to discipline and ensure the production commitment of the labour force (Lee, 1986, p.160), a role not unlike their counterparts for many years in little Dragon economies, like South Korea, Taiwan and so on. To do this, they were organized in the PRC case on both a geographical and an industrial basis. The ACFTU was and still is a 'transmission belt' of government policy and has played its part in whatever current campaign the Party delegated to it, such as attempting to seek out corrupt officials or being a watch-dog about excessive price increases. It has, since 1949, mainly been allowed to act in a *consultative* manner and to shape official policy goals and targets only broadly, in so far as they affect wages and conditions of work, welfare matters, worker education, and labour protection (see Wilson, 1987, p.243). The effectiveness of trade unions in these tasks has depended on how far that could mobilize worker support for official policies in these areas and appear to credibly represent workers' interests, at the same time possibly promoting a form of 'societal corporatism' (Chan, 1993), but this view may not be logically consistent with the premise of the 'transmission-belt' function.[8] As long as the Party's role is predominant, we must conclude that the role of the ACFTU will continue to be subordinate.

   In Part Two, we go on to look at the ongoing, subsequent wave of reforms attempting to change the personnel, wages and social insurance systems, with their implications for labour–management relations in enterprises in the state-owned sector.

4 Economic Reforms and their Implications for Labour

4.1 INTRODUCTION

As the linchpin of the labour–management system, China's 'iron rice-bowl' employment policy mainly had its roots in the early 1950s, as we have already seen in earlier chapters. It was originally intended to protect skilled workers, but eventually spread to cover the majority of the urban labour-force, who now number over 150 million workers, with just over 100 million in industry (see Tables 4.1 and 4.2). After leaving school, young Chinese workers were allocated jobs by the local labour bureau, in most cases with little reference as to where they wanted to work and in which kinds of tasks. They were assigned to a work-unit (or *danwei*) which registered their citizenship status (or *hukou*) (see Cheng and Selden, 1994). Employment for life for those in the state sector was until recently more or less assured. The *danwei* constituted a 'mini welfare state', providing housing, medical care, pensions and so on (see Leung, 1988, p.55) as noted in Chapter 1. It was, in these respects, not unlike its state enterprise counterparts in the former Soviet Union.[1]

The classic *danwei* model resembled the 'total institution' as characterized by Western social scientists (for example, Goffman, 1959; 1961). Shenkar and von Glinow set the scene:

Like total institutions, the typical Chinese work unit is situated within a walled, gated and guarded compound. Its employees depend on the unit for everything from social insurance and medical care to provision of ration cards for basic food staples and various 'industrial goods'. They are also subject to strict entry and exit barriers. Though in theory, individuals are not committed to work units against their will, refusal to join an officially assigned *danwei* can have serious repercussions, ranging from failure to find a permanent work place to a politically tainted record. However disgruntled they may be, employees are reluctant to leave the work unit to which they have been assigned out of fear of remaining unaffiliated in a society in which major necessities

45

are supplied only through organizational affiliation. (Shenkar and von Glinow, 1994, p.13)

Rewards were based on the Wage Grade system – usually eight levels for factory workers – which as we have seen had itself been taken over mainly from the Soviet model (see Howe, 1973 and Takahara, 1992 for background). Citizenship registration was anchored in the *danwei* and labour mobility was minimal. Urban dwellers without their *hukou* were non-persons. Dismissals were rare; motivation was low. As has been said of other communist economies, 'they [the cadres] pretended to pay us, and we [the workers] pretended to work' (anon.). For much of the time, and especially during the Cultural Revolution, an egalitarian wage-payment system was common, incentives were limited, and over-manning was rife.

The orthodox Soviet rewards system evolved in the late 1920s under Stalin's policy of stressing the development of heavy industry. There were three basic props to the Chinese copy:

- wage standards (*gongzi biaozhun*)
- wage grades table (*gongzi dengji biao*)
- technical grades standards (*jishu dengji biaozhun*)

Wage standards defined the reward for a given period of work, usually a month, and piece-rates based on dividing wage standards by set norms; *the wage grades table* defined the ladder of wage grades and differentials; *technical grade standards* defined the skill benchmarks of the workers, which helped define the wage grades (see Takahara, 1992, pp.9–12 for further details).

There was a conflict of interest on wages from the very beginning:

> In the initial attempt to spread the Soviet system conflict can already be observed between staff/workers and managers on the one hand, and members of the policy elite on the other. Staff and workers preferred stability and relative equality of real earnings, and managers were reluctant to implement policies which their own workforce resented. The policy elite was eager to enhance productivity by setting up a wage system with wide wage differentials, which they considered a better reflection of the principle, 'to each according to one's work'. (Ibid, p.13)

The 1956 reforms were a key event in devising a national rewards system. Most industrial enterprises introduced the eight grades, although some (like construction) kept to seven, while others (like textiles) pursued the position-wage system. Technical standards were to be used in grade-promotion. Differentials in wages were widened. Political ideology and seniority were largely put to one side (ibid., p.32).

Between 1957 and 1976, the Soviet-style wage grade system was transformed by a number of factors associated with (amongst others) the 'Great Leap Forward' and the 'Cultural Revolution'. In these long years of the 'rational low wage system', the *de facto* underminings included half-grade promotions, complicating the wage system further, the encroachment of the seniority factor and central, unified control of most wage adjustments. Urban wages were held down and 'production' became *de rigueur*. 'All in all' concludes Takahara (1992, p.64) 'China's wage system became one that only weakly embodied the principle of "to each according to one's work"'.

An interesting, but by no means unique, feature of the post-1950s Chinese employment system was the practice of 'occupational inheritance' (or *dingti*). When a worker retired, he or she could recommend a close relative for his or her job. This practice most likely led to overmanning on an extensive scale (Howe, 1992, p.ix). A classic case of such job inheritance was at the Anshan Iron and Steel Corporation (Byrd and Tidrick, 1987). Over 17 000 children had replaced their parents over 1980–3, some of the latter retiring early. The corporation mainly used collective enterprises to provide dependents of their workers with jobs.[2] In the mid-1980s, the main enterprise employing over 220 000 workers in its mining and steel operations set up collectives to provide jobs for another 160 000 of their family-members, spread over 20 industries and constituting over 170 units. It also used 8000 such workers in its main plants (ibid., pp.71–2).

Overmanning has long been common in a labour-surplus economy like China's. In the late 1980s, the *People's Daily* alleged that around one in four urban workers were not productive in most enterprises, up to 30 million out of 130 million in this estimate (see Leung, 1988, p.58). At the time, one in five state enterprises was said to be 'in the red'; now, possibly as many as one in two. The reformers claimed that this state of affairs led to 'gross inefficiency, inflexibility and over-staffing' (ibid., p.59). Given that there were at least 150 million surplus rural workers, it was not surprising that there was reluctance to increase the level of unemployment, as we shall see later.

In contrast to this state of affairs, the former Soviet Union has been described as having a 'genuine' labour-market (Granick, 1987, p.109) with over two-thirds of labour hired directly by enterprises. It was an active market, with a 'quit-rate' said to be commensurable with US enterprises.

Table 4.1   Population and labour-force statistics for PRC, 1993

	Total	*Increase over 1992*
Population	1185m	13.46m
Urban labour force	150m	2.84m
Total wage bill	477 bn yuan	21.1%
Average urban wage	3236 yuan	19.4%
Net per capita income	2337 yuan	10.4%*
Net rural per capita income	921 yuan	17.5%*

* allowing for price increases
Source: SSB, 1994.

Table 4.2   Change in labour force 1978–92

Unit:	1978	1992
Total national labour force	401.5	594.3
of which:		
industrial	60.9	102.2

Source: SSB, 1993.

Employees left their jobs on their own initiative rather than that of state agencies or on enterprise decisions. Separations were in the order of almost one in three workers per year. Employment norms were therefore quite different from those found in Chinese enterprises.

Granick notes that:

> The distinction between Chinese and Soviet labor conditions originates in the radical differences between the two countries in the number of urban citizens with both the capability and the desire to work in the state sector, in relation to the feasibility of the state's providing such work given the capital resources of each country. (1987, p.113)

He surmised that as long as social arrangements kept the number of dismissals low by world standards, 'an active labor market in the state sector will not be possible' (ibid., p.114). The same author later elaborated the above:

The Chinese urban labor market in the state sector is similar to the Soviet and East European in two major respects. The first is that there is the common assumption that governments, rather than enterprises, should have the prime authority in determining the size of an individual factory's work force. The second is that social mores are observed which greatly restrict the ability to dismiss workers on any grounds.

The differences in the treatment of employment are threefold. (1) The Chinese labor turnover rate is negligible in the state sector, in contrast to the Soviet which has long been at much the same high level as is observed in the West under conditions of low unemployment. ... (2) The creation of additional urban jobs has been a major objective both for enterprises and for local authorities in China. ... (3) A multitier system of nonprivate job opportunities within the same industrial sector is a prominent feature of Chinese enterprises, in contrast to the situation in European socialist countries. Engagement as a regular state employee is the preferred employment status in China, and such employment is controlled by national authorities. ... This multitier system is the mechanism used to reconcile the constraints on hirings, imposed by the national authorities, with the job-creation objectives of both enterprises and local (including provincial) governments ... (Granick, 1990, pp.253–4)

The root problem according to this view was that the criterion from the mid-1950s onwards was neither the labour market nor job evaluation, even personal favouritism: it was rather promotion by seniority, with such status accumulated prior to the mid-point of that decade carrying weight (Granick, 1987, p.114). Thus, the Maoist legacy was one of substantial income-inequality unrelated to effort, responsibility, or skill-level. It was however possible for individual managers sometimes to avoid the constraints of the system by subterfuge, but this was not generally the case.

Steps to scale down this system have met with mixed results, as Chinese state enterprises have been pressed to adopt the labour contract system, with more open job recruitment (see Figure 4.1). As early as 1984, the present writer (see Warner, 1986, p.361) found the number of apprenticeships cut back in many large firms visited and raw recruits put on contracts.[3]

On the other hand, Granick (1991, p.274) found that open inheritance of jobs was still very common in the early and mid-1980s, with over 90 per cent of posts in this category. It was, as he put it, 'automatic', 'legal' and 'real' (1991, p.274). If the *dingti* arrangements were formally cancelled in 1986, later reports still indicated the practice was prevalent through labour-service companies set up by local labour bureaux. With rising youth unemployment, it was said to be likely to continue 'in legal or semi-legal guise' (Korzec, 1992, p.25).

4.2   MARKET MECHANISMS

Given the scale of the problems, the rationale of Dengist reforms was to introduce greater efficiency into the system by the use of market mechanisms. There was to be trade-off between efficiency and equality (see Hsu, 1991, pp.106ff). Efficiency was to be seen not only as *technical* efficiency in terms of the best input-output rations, but also *allocative* efficiency in terms of optimizing use of resources. The Chinese leadership had seen China at a primary stage of economic development and was therefore willing to see increasing inequality continue for some time. Equality has thus been reinterpreted 'flexibly' for the while (1991, p.112). Discussions of wage-related issues had long focused on the Marxist dictum of 'distribution according to labour', but some now argue that differentials were not too great, once other factor contributions were taken into account. Reforms had to be designed to give both enterprises and individuals the greatest autonomy and initiatives possible as a strategy of development, although the state was still left as a player in the new game (Jiang, 1980; Jiang and Zhou, 1992). Economists like Dong Fureng tried at the time, for example, to set out plausible efficiency-centred strategies.

Figure 4.1   Direction of labour–management reforms

	System characteristic	Status quo	Experimental
1.	Strategy	Hard-line	Reformist
2.	Employment	Iron rice-bowl	Labour market
3.	Conditions	Job security	Labour contracts
4.	Mobility	Job assignment	Job flexibility
5.	Rewards	Egalitarian	Meritocratic
6.	Wage system	Eight-grade labour	Material incentives
7.	Promotion	Seniority	Skill-related
8.	Factory union role	Consultative	Co-ordinative
9.	Management	Economic cadres	Professional management
10.	Factory party role	Central	Ancillary, in principle
11.	Work organization	Taylorist	Flexible
12.	Efficiency	Technical	Allocative

Dong raised the following key questions:

> Labor is not a commodity in a socialist economy, so how can there be a labor market? Yet if there is no labor market, how can labor supply and demand be regulated? Planned allocation of the labor force cannot become the universal mode of regulation; regulation of labor should include market regulation of labor supply and demand. ... How is a socialist labor market to be organized? What differences will there be from a capitalist labor market? (Dong Fureng, 1987, p.56)

Another basic question concerned labour's role both as a factor-input and a stakeholder in the enterprise (see Byrd and Tidrick, 1987, pp.67ff). Workers want secure employment as well as decent rewards and benefits. Managers have their own agenda, seeking flexibility in the internal labour market in the enterprise. The desires of both parties sometimes match, sometimes conflict. However, the wishes of each were not conclusive in that labour allocation and rewards had been long controlled by *external* forces. Job assignments, as we have seen, were decided by the labour bureaux. Wage-scales were national; discretion was low.

In a major World Bank/CASS study (Tidrick and Chen, 1987) few managers or workers admitted to overmanning. Workers wanted employment for their offspring. Managers hoarded labour for fear of staff shortages or because they want to please their work-force and their political masters. Labour quotas could sometimes be evaded, by contract labour for example. Such contracts could add to managerial autonomy as well as discipline.

As a result of the labour system, state enterprises had consequently become 'mini welfare states' buttressed by hereditary job practices and work-force intermarriage. Such entities constituted 'small societies' (*xiao shehui*) as White described them (1987, p.366). Not only state enterprises, but also large collectives exemplified these characteristics. As a result, very few workers ever moved either jobs (or residences) between firms, sectors or regions. Clearly, such factor-immobility could not continue if market forces were to be introduced into the Chinese economy (see Han and Morishima, 1992).

Even as late as 1988, a polemic ensued regarding a proposal to create a 'labour market'[4] since not all economists agreed that labour was a commodity under socialism (Hsu, 1991, p.162). Earlier, the Maoist proposition that 'distribution according to labour', conditional on 'each according to his labour', became eagerly contested. Later, Marxist principle as such was no longer to be sacred. The contribution of the late

Jiang Yiwei (1980) a leading reform economist, had been crucial in such debates leading to labour reform. He had argued that an individual's labour could only become society's labour through the enterprise. Enterprises in turn should only be rewarded according to their performance.

Some Chinese economists in the late 1980s began to support the notion that the total wage-fund of the enterprise should be a reflection of its performance on both macro- and micro-grounds. Growth of aggregate wages ought not to go beyond national income and productivity; at the micro-level, the new approach was intended to increase the incentives of both firms and employees. For this to happen, however, other changes must take place such as price reforms, so that enterprise profits could reflect their performance. Some reform economists went on to argue that it was wiser to open up the labour market and let the market determine wage levels. The caveat was advanced however, that profits were not created by labour alone. If wages were geared to profits rather than labour productivity, workers might become work-shy and seek illicit ways to boost profits to increase their wages. Other economists wanted a half-way house, with a fixed wage plus a bonus reflecting increases in enterprise profits. One idea was to merge the wage-fund, bonus-fund and welfare-fund as a 'labour contract-fund' which would be part of the costs of production. When total production costs fell, with higher labour productivity, the fund would increase and vice-versa (see Hsu, 1991, p.167).

As price reforms were introduced, food for example became more expensive. Allocative efficiency was enhanced, and if wages were indexed, at least this was an *overt* rather than a *covert* subsidy. Some economists did not want national indexation, but rather a selective subsidy or a local adjustment. There was – to sum up – no consensus among leading Chinese economists on price and wage reforms. Because China's price reform was postponed, so was serious wage reform. However, as Hsu points out:

> China's recent price-wage discussion does illustrate functional economics at work – its attempt to include wide-ranging micro- and macro-concerns and its pragmatic pros and cons weighing approach with greater sophistication. (1991, p.169)

Partly as a result of such thinking, material incentives were reintroduced. Bonuses soon became more important as a method of rewarding effort and productivity. While such new practices were welcomed by some workers who stood to benefit, potential losers were resentful. Many managers paid all their employees a bonus in order to placate them and to avoid any disruption to production. 'Red-eye disease', as jealousy is sometimes called in Chinese, became quite general as a result of the economic reform policy. Greater economic rationality led to discrepancies in rewards between groups of workers in the same firm or between firms but these were not perceived as a return for greater effort (see Thompson, 1992, pp.241–4).

Another consequence of the reforms was to move away from the Soviet-style grading system and to build-in greater rewards for flexibility. Promotion was previously by seniority and political fidelity rather than acquired expertise and motivation: it was better to be 'red' rather than 'expert'. Previously, all wage levels were fixed by the state (Leung, 1988, p.69). In principle, the system was based on 'to each according to their labour'; there had long been a minimum wage system based on the cost of subsistence for two people. The actual wage levels for each grade for each enterprise had been worked out by the local district labour bureau, following provincial and industrial-level guidelines. Fringe benefits, housing subsidies and the like were ascertained accordingly. The system was criticized for 'low wages, high employment', but fundamentally meant gross overmanning. It was seen as being inefficient not only by internal critics, but also by foreign investors. Consequently rewards were to be linked to performance and in principle at least the 'iron rice-bowl' was to be 'smashed' (Leung, 1988; Wedley, 1992).

The moves to 'marketization' continued in fits and starts, as the Chinese economic reforms were implemented in the 1980s. Low labour productivity was perceived as a bottle-neck and an obstacle to modernization. At bottom, it was seen as a result of 'irrationalities' in existing economic systems (Korzec, 1992, p.55). By 1987, the State Economic Commission launched extensive wage reforms; state enterprises were to decide their own reward levels. There would be a basic wage, topped up by bonuses and productivity deals (see Chapter 7, later), but not to exceed incremental changes in productivity. Such reforms were not however welcomed by economic conservatives, whether lobbying at macro- or micro-levels, and were not well received in official trade union circles. Piece-work, which had been used a great deal in the 1950s in state enterprises and then banned in the Cultural Revolution, was reintroduced, but it never reached its incidence in the earlier period. Covering only one in ten state enterprise employees by the mid-1980s (Granick, 1991, p.283), it was particularly common practice in coal-mining and the docks. Piece-work rates were mostly used to compensate for low bonuses and because they could be paid out of costs rather than profits.

Under the old labour system, dismissals were very rare. They are now easier in principle but are in reality minimal – less than 1 or 2 per cent, with several forms of dismissal, varying in severity and depending on the gravity of the offence (ibid., p.275). They vary from temporary suspension to outright sacking (see Korzec, 1992, for further details). Sometimes workers who perform poorly may be transferred to a 'labour-service' company owned by the same enterprise group, even on the same site. This arrangement may be referred to as 'one factory, two systems'.

Redundancies are another novel feature of the economic reforms. As state enterprises are made more economically responsible, the less productive ones are shedding labour, particularly on 'pilot' or 'experimental' sites selected for trying out the new enterprise contract responsibility schemes, as we shall see in Part Two. In such instances, older workers, or the less competent, are shed, transferred or retrained. Precise numbers of such industrial redevelopments are not available, but are likely to be small overall. Similarly, large numbers in agricultural labour have left the countryside. Estimates running into tens of millions, even as many as 100 million (see Thompson, 1992/93) have been made of such mobility in the whole economy. Any cursory inspection of all forms of transport in the PRC, particularly trains and buses, reveals a vast number of people in transit. It is mobility in that part of the 'dual' labour-market where job security is weakest or non-existent (see Granick, 1991; *China Labour Bulletin*, April 1994, p.2).

Disguised unemployment is a common feature of economic development. Overmanning in both the rural and urban sectors in China testifies to this phenomenon. *Frictional* unemployment, due to changes in jobs, would be possible in low incidence in the relatively more mobile part of the labour market referred to in the last paragraph, and until the early 1990s was very low in the state sector where job allocation built-in rigidities. The rate of job transfer is however now increasing for professionals and technically skilled personnel in state-owned firms (see *Beijing Review*, 1 February 1993, p.12). *Premature* unemployment also exists, especially where perhaps as many as one in ten young people in cities may be 'awaiting assignment', as the phrase goes.

Indeed,

All over China, millions of workers born into the 'iron rice bowl' system, of cradle-to-grave employment and state social services are discovering that life no longer offers the certainties it once did. Socialism 'with Chinese characteristics' means that managers of state-owned enterprises have now been told by central government that their factories must stop losing money. They have looked at their over-manned production lines, and for the first time have been allowed to conclude that fewer people, working properly, could get the job done.

New foreign management partners have brought in notions of productivity and profitability. They insist on the right to sack people who do not work hard. China's underemployed workforces, who had grown lazy on the knowledge that – under communism – a job was for life, are now facing a new scourge: unemployment. And the authorities are facing up to the social unrest this may cause. (Poole, 1993, p.14)

The regime had inherited a not insignificant degree of urban unemployment after the 'Liberation', which was not easily dealt with, estimated at between five and 12.5 million in 1950 (Riskin, 1987, p.60). The labour bureaux had jurisdiction of this area as well as welfare and labour mediation. The jobless total swelled again when the pressures of the private sector mounted. Policies in the 1950s to deal with the problem ranged from temporary assignment to public works, help in starting small businesses, aid in returning to the worker's home village, or pure relief (Howe, 1971, p.93). Urban employment in the mid-1950s was said to be as high as 7.8 million or 20 per cent of the urban labour force at the time (see Riskin, 1987, p.111).

The persistence of urban unemployment ensured pressures to institutionalize job security.[5] The labour movement had fought for the elimination of unemployment, but industrialization did not reduce it drastically as the First Five-Year Plan (1953–7) was capital-intensive. Rural migration into the cities due to poverty, disasters and collectivization added to the problems in the 1950s as it was to do later. Estimates vary for the urban jobless percentage over the decades of lurching economic policies, but by the mid-1980s, officially stated to be 2 per cent, it was in reality much higher, at least 5 per cent (Korzec, 1992, p.50, note 140) and even higher for young workers.

The return of rusticated youth after the Cultural Revolution had fuelled anxiety about joblessness in the towns. Unemployed young people openly demonstrated and such acts even spilled over into violence. Groups of such youths were said to have paid 'collective visits' to labour-bureaux to harass staff there. Delinquency became a talking-point. As young people flocked from rural areas into the towns in increasing numbers because of contemporary pressures in the country on the one hand, and the attractions of the cities on the other, social stability was under stress. An angry former army cadre complained in a press interview that:

There are now more prostitutes, more rapes and more robberies. A large part of them have been committed by unemployed young people. Many youths now dare to kill people, steal guns and even rob state banks! (Cited in Leung, 1988, p.60).

Social instability was, therefore, a fear of defenders of the status quo. It is also likely that a contributory factor to the political turmoil preceding the Tiananmen Square massacre in June 1989 was linked to uncertainty regarding employment and favouritism regarding job opportunities and continues into the present (see *China Labour Bulletin*, April 1994, pp.1–3).

Urban unemployment generally became a widely discussed issue in the early 1980s. By 1981 the Central Committee and State Council decided to act on the problem:

> The new policy sought to expand employment: first by changing the structure of the urban economy – expanding the commercial and service sectors and encouraging collectives and private enterprises; and secondly, by establishing more job channels – for example allowing enterprise managers to recruit their own labour, developing the role of labour service companies and encouraging individuals and groups to create their own jobs by setting up co-operative, household or individual businesses. (White, 1987, p.370)

Initially, dealing with joblessness was given priority status but eventually confronting the problem of low labour productivity took precedence, hence the shift to a contract-based strategy.

White believes this proposal was first raised at an inaugural meeting of a new body, namely the Chinese Society for the Study of Labour Problems. He thinks it is probably the same as the Chinese National Society of Labour Science set up in January 1982. It was said to have the Ministry of Labour, the Economics Institute of the State Planning Commission, the Institute of Economics of CASS and the All-China Federation of Trade Unions as institutional supporters. It was advised by well-known economists, Yu Guangyuan and Xue Muqiao, as well as sociologist Fei Xiaotong (White, 1987, p.372).

The policy was launched in 1982–3 and initially piloted in several large cities such as Beijing, as well as in the Shenzen SEZ. A press campaign against the 'iron rice-bowl' was drummed up at the same time. Official opinion was divided and between 1983 and 1986 a pragmatic approach was adopted to gain both official and public acquiesence, if not acceptance of the proposals.

As White sums up:

The main elements of the labour contract system were as follows: (1) the contract is to be signed between the worker and the enterprise and formally approved by a local state labour agency. The contract specifies the duration of the agreement, the 'responsibilities, powers and benefits' (*zi, quan, li*) of the respective parties including wages, welfare benefits, labour insurance, nature of the work required and productivity standards, and terms for renewal or cancellation. Contracts can vary in length from two or three years to as long as twenty. Reformers tend to favour shorter ones, from two to five years, but recognize that the duration can vary according to specific production needs. (2) The enterprise's previous responsibility for providing welfare benefits should be shifted to labour insurance companies and state welfare agencies outside the firm. It is hoped that this would allow enterprises to concentrate on production and reduce workers' dependence on their enterprise. (3) Renewal of the contract would depend upon the performance of the worker and the labour requirements of the enterprise. If the enterprise decides to let a worker go, or the worker him-herself decides to leave voluntarily at the end of the contract, state labour agencies can provide temporary financial assistance, retraining and help in finding another job. (Ibid., p.367)

The notion of contracts as an incentive is contained in the Chinese pun, 'Fixed workers look (*kan*), contract workers act (*gan*)' (cited in White, 1987, p.367).

Contracts, in theory at least, would represent freedom of choice for both workers and managers. Workers could seek new jobs and leave when their period of contract ended. Personnel managers could choose new employees and monitor their progress before offering extended employment. Social costs such as welfare could be externalized to labour insurance companies or state agencies.

A major 'political' argument against such a move was advanced to the effect that one of objects of the Revolution had been to create the very work-place security that the 'iron rice-bowl' implied. A cautionary note was sounded by a reform economist, noted earlier, the late Jiang Yiwei:

In his words, workers would become 'hired labourers' instead of 'masters' of the enterprise – managers would become the real 'masters'. Jiang proposes a three-tiered system of fixed, contract and temporary workers which would achieve greater labour flexibility without these political costs and would embody what he considers the key element of reform, that the welfare of workers be linked with the fate of their enterprise. (White, 1987, p.380)

Managerial opinion was however divided as to the merits of labour contracts. Where skills were at a premium, say in capital-intensive enterprises, managers were loath to let workers go and many preferred the old system. They were even keener to hold onto professional staff. In less skill-intensive firms like textile mills, managers tended to prefer contracts. Older managers were anxious to keep the labour system they had grown used to; younger managers were keen to change it (ibid., p.381–2). Reaction on the workers' side was mixed. As White suggests:

> Many state workers see job security as an achievement of socialism and the contract system as a step towards capitalist 'wage labour' which traps workers between the Scylla of authoritarian managers and the Charybdis of urban employment. (1987, p.384)

Those in a seller's market, like trained graduates, were keener to take their chances with the new system.[6]

In order to put the role of *danwei* job security into perspective, it is necessary to analyse the many employment statuses which have evolved in the PRC. Most workers in state and urban collective units have had *de jure* and *de facto* 'life-long employment by one unit' (Korzec, 1992, p.30). Other categories are contract workers (*hetong gong*); temporary workers (*linshi gong*); seasonal workers (*jijie gong*); peasant workers (*yi gong yi nong*); and workers contracted from the countryside (*nongcun xieyi gong*).

Since the mid-1980s, it has been official policy to introduce greater flexibility into the Chinese surrogate labour-market. Critics of the new system see it as the phasing out of the 'right to work', heralded since the 'Liberation' as one of the main achievements of the regime, and enshrined in Article 42 of the Constitution. Korzec (1992, p.27) sees this as undermining the very 'social contract' holding Chinese society together, with ominous consequences for both the economy and the polity. Given the previous lack of effective personal job mobility, public attitudes remain ambiguous, with the young and talented particularly favouring greater occupational choice.

In this respect, such criticism is premature and less indicative of policy initiative than accommodation to pressures from below, and outside parties such as joint-venture partners. Events have, however, moved faster than most observers, pessimistic or optimistic, would have imagined.

There are now signs that the labour system is evolving much more rapidly in the early 1990s than in the middle and late 1980s, as we shall see in Part Two.

The main vehicle of such change was the 'Temporary Regulations on the Use of Labour Contracts in State-run Enterprises' set out by the State Council in July 1986, enacted in October of that year. Henceforth, new recruits would not hold jobs for life, but contracts for defined periods of employment. Other 'Temporary Regulations' originating at the same time covered employment in state enterprises, discharges of personnel violating labour discipline, and insurance of employees 'waiting for employment' in state firms. The four 'Temporary Regulations' clearly added up to a new policy on jobs.

These so-called 'Temporary Regulations' grew out of earlier reforms in Shanghai and the Shenzen Special Economic Zone after 1980, where in the latter case new workers had at first been given jobs for life, but this was changed in 1982 to contract employment (Korzec, 1992, p.65). Wages were accordingly raised to a higher level to compensate for the loss of security and other perks. The basic wage constituted a decreasing proportion of total 'take-home' pay, with inactive payments predominating (a point to be elaborated in Chapters 7 and 8).

None the less, these changes built new injustices into the system. As Leung notes:

> As employment and wage systems are drastically reformed, welfare provisions, which for decades have provided fairly standardized benefits for the ill, the old and those bearing children, have been thrown into uncertainty. Reformers have attempted to lay the burden of welfare directly on the shoulders of each enterprise. This, however, would make the quantity and quality of welfare dependent upon the economic performance of the unit and the individual priorities identified by the managers or the work-force, to the serious detriment of older workers, women or the sick. (Leung, 1988, p.206)

The upshot of these developments was an increasing degree of variation in the wage system, particularly as the SEZ areas grew more rapidly than those with the traditional state-sector industries, such as those in the North-East, notwithstanding the burgeoning township industries especially in the coastal regions and South-East of China.[7]

Job mobility in the past had been very limited, as we have seen earlier. Hiring had long been based on annual quotas, nationally determined. School-leavers 'awaiting assignment' (*dai ye*) were allocated to posts available. Those in state enterprises who wanted to move needed permission from both inside and above the unit to gain a 'transfer' (*diao dong*). Those in the Party needed special approval. In urban collective units, there was greater flexibility in principle but not much evidence in practice. Few were dismissed; few were free to resign. There was little incentive to move as wages varied very little from firm to firm; in addition, housing and welfare benefits were at risk if workers were permitted to move (Davis, 1993, p.1062).

In the early 1980s, the employment system became relatively more flexible, but only by degrees. Wage inducements were made possible, labour exchanges were set up and private firms were free to recruit freely. By 1986, labour contracts had been introduced on a three to five year basis. While in 1980, 63.5 per cent of new entrants went to state enterprise jobs, by 1990 this had only dropped to 60.5 per cent (Davis, 1993, p.1065). Job transfers were lower than in Western countries, but were, broadly speaking, still comparable with Japanese experience. Arbitration boards were set up in major cities to deal with appeals against enterprises refusing individual transfers but few employee plaintiffs won their case (1993, p.1066). Davis's research however reveals an increase in job mobility; for men, having been in the army helped; and for women, age was an important factor. It indeed took time for offered transfers to be approved. Men benefited from the reforms, with educational credentials and job seniority noteworthy determinants. Women's job moves were often horizontal to accommodate domestic priorities after marriage. Davis's conclusions are that there were no obvious or immediate increases in inter-firm mobility or unambiguous advantages in status for those who moved successfully. If a 'real' labour-market does emerge, she conjectures, the outcomes might be rather different (1993, p.1085).

Officially, China has had a 'three-in-one' policy, using established labour bureaux, labour service firms and a mixture of informally organized networks that encourage exchange in sectors like self-employment (Thompson, 1992, p.246). A pioneer in the last of these categories has been the Beijing Talent Exchange Centre. In 1989, it launched the Spring Labour Fair, bringing together 130 firms and 6000 potential workers. By 1992, attendance had grown tenfold. By 1993, even greater numbers, possibly over 100 000, attended a National Talent Fair. There are also unofficial labour markets for rural migrants such as young women seeking jobs as domestic servants (1992, p.246). In the early 1990s, job transfers became easier. In 1992, nearly one million technical and managerial personnel registered at personnel exchange centres in order to seek relocation. According to a recent estimate, as many as one in three professionals would like to move their place of employment: even so, the actual transfer rate is probably around two and a half per cent. Many qualified young graduates would like to work in joint ventures. In Shanghai, which has nearly 1000 substantially-sized foreign-funded enterprises, half their employees were hired by such personnel agencies (see *Beijing Review*, 1 February 1993, p.13).

The extension of the notion of contracts for jobs has been a feature of the 1980s changes in the labour-market.[8] By the end of the decade, it was estimated that at least one in ten workers in the labour-force was employed on a contract-basis rather than having jobs for life, perceiving themselves in effect with a second-class status in a 'dual' labour-market (White, 1987; Leung, 1988; Granick, 1991). A figure of 13 per cent of all state enterprise employees (then around 100 million) had been suggested by one source (Korzec, 1992, p.29). Official SSB estimates reported over 19 per cent in total in 1993 (see Table 4.3). Part-time employment had also grown, with more urban workers taking on second jobs (*Beijing Review*, 8 March 1993, pp.27–29).

Whilst labour contracts are to be found in the state enterprises, they are even more common in other forms of economic organizations, such as township industries, joint ventures and privately and/or foreign-owned firms. The labour-force in these instances is more likely to be young, and/or female, as well as of recent rural origin (see Jacka, 1992). Less high overhead social costs mean lower labour costs for enterprises, but where higher money-wages are on offer for such recruits (not always the case) this may compensate for such limited tenure. The notion of using temporary 'contract-labour' in contrast to most industrial workers in permanent jobs was originally imported from the former Soviet Union in the mid-1950s, as noted earlier. It was used quite extensively on construction projects, but also spread to other kinds of sites. Contract-labourers had reduced status in that they did not have the security, privileges and perks of the employed in the state enterprises. In the mid-1960s, the resentment felt by these contract-labourers made them ready recruits for the Red Guards during the Cultural Revolution. Currently, temporary short-term contracts coexist with labour-contracts of medium or longer-term duration. Such personnel practices reflect a greater degree of convergence with other East Asian labour-markets.[9] It enables the PRC to take advantage of its plentiful supply of people to offer cheap labour to foreign firms, such as Hong Kong entrepreneurs, who are thus willing to bring their capital as well as their managerial expertise to bear on the problems of low productivity and poor quality control and to rectify these. In theory, such joint ventures or wholly-owned enterprises provide an export base along the coastal periphery of China (see Vogel, 1991). In reality, many foreign-funded firms ignore health and safety regulations and have a high level of industrial accidents. According to Chinese official statistics, there were over 65 000 deaths overall at work-places in the PRC in 1993 (*The Independent on Sunday*, 29 May 1994, p.8).

4.3   STATE OWNED ENTERPRISES

A major part of the policy shift signalled in early 1992, confirmed by the late spring and legitimated in the autumn of that year, has been the reform of the state industrial sector. This part of the economy had been the favoured recipient of government support, heavily subsidized and staunchly protected. The reason for this special treatment was its vanguard role in the modernization process since 1949. It was also a major contributor to state funds, as tax revenues could be gathered from the more productive sub-sectors.

State-owned enterprises ('owned by the whole people', in the official jargon) have long been the work-horse of Chinese industry, employing over 100 million workers and staff. Large and medium-sized firms in this sector number over 100 000 and used to produce the bulk of total gross value of industrial output: by the end of 1992 it was just under 50 per cent of this total (see Table 4.4). These larger factories employed over 45 million workers by this date (see SSB, 1993) and were seen as

Table 4.3   Contract staff/workers (unit: millions)

	1983	1992
Total	0.65	25.41
of which:		
State	0.57	20.58
Urban collectives	0.08	3.99
Others	–	0.84
Percentage of total staff/workers		
Total	0.6	17.2
State	0.6	18.9

Source: SSB, 1993.

Table 4.4   China: share of gross industrial output value by ownership 1979–92

	State-owned %	Non-state-owned %	collectives %	Of which: individuals %	others %
1979	78.5	21.5	21.5	n.a.	n.a.
1980	76.0	24.0	23.5	0.0	0.5
1981	74.8	25.2	24.6	0.0	0.6
1982	74.4	25.6	24.8	0.1	0.7
1983	73.4	26.6	25.7	0.1	0.8
1984	69.1	30.9	29.7	0.2	1.0
1985	64.9	35.1	32.1	1.9	1.2
1986	62.3	37.7	33.5	2.8	1.5
1987	59.7	40.3	34.6	3.6	2.0
1988	56.1	43.2	36.2	4.3	2.7
1989	56.1	43.9	35.7	4.8	3.4
1990	54.6	45.4	35.6	5.4	4.4
1991	52.5	47.2	35.7	5.7	5.7
1992	48.1	51.9	38.0	6.8	7.1

Source: SSB, 1993.

inefficient and overmanned. It was not uncommon to find an enterprise with scores of thousands people on site. Such large firms have the full stereotypical apparatus of Chinese labour–management relations with a consistent set of personnel practices (see Warner, 1991, pp.210ff). They have also almost complete unionization: Workers' Congresses as well as branch union committees. Examples of these large state enterprises are to be found in the North-Eastern cities like Shenyang, or in Shanghai, Wuhan and so on. In the 1980s, 42 per cent of state industrial output was derived from factories in 17 large cities (see Leeming, 1992, p.115).

Since 1986, they have only grown at around 7.5 per cent a year and the volume of state subsidy has become not only a drain on resources that could be best used elsewhere, but also anomalous in an emergent, if still regulated, market economy 'with Chinese characteristics'. Previously, this sector had not been appreciably open to market forces. By spring 1992, the government had decided, on the basis of policies formulated in May and September of the previous year, to steer these enterprises into the market, holding them responsible for their profits and losses, even to the point of bankruptcy (see *Beijing Review*, 30 March 1992, p.4). A reform of the labour and personnel system was announced at the same time, for 60 000 enterprises, involving 30 million workers or just under 30 per cent of the nation's total industrial sector employees.

The Commission for Restructuring the Economy, the Ministry of Personnel and the All-China Federation of Trade Unions put forward a 12-point proposal for deepening reform of the system of administration of labour and personnel, wage distribution and social insurance in enterprises in early 1992. The gist of this document was as follows:

1. Earnestly follow the guidelines of the State Council circular on stopping unnecessary inspection and appraisal of enterprises, and non-interference in the internal structure of enterprises. A comprehensive review of the various regulations and policies governing enterprises, formulated in recent years, should be conducted. Any contents which do not conform to the enterprise law and other relevant state provisions concerning improving enterprises should be revised or abolished. It is necessary to take effective measures to resolutely do away with unnecessary activities on inspection, appraisal, target-fulfilment, promotion and examinations; thus enabling enterprises to devote their undivided attention and efforts to improving production and operation.

2. Strengthen in a practical way the internal economic responsibility system in enterprises, and strive to establish and perfect various rules and regulations.

3. Carry out reform of the personnel system in enterprises, and gradually implement an appointment system for management and technical personnel.

4. Consolidate and improve the labour contract system.

5. Gradually implement a full-time labour contract system.

6. Strengthen wage management and improve the method of linking total wages to economic efficiency, and gradually switch linking wages with a single target performance to multiple-target performance. It is necessary to pay attention to maintaining and enhancing the values of state-owned assets, technological advancement and productivity, as well as to improving other comprehensive economic performance indices including the ratio between capital invested and profits delivered, and taxes paid to the state.

7. Implement and independent distribution system with distribution according to work, and overcome egalitarianism. It is necessary to gradually practise a wage system based on the skills of a certain

section on a production line, provided it is within the limit of the total wages determined by the state, and carried out on a voluntary basis among enterprises.

8. Make strenuous efforts to improve the quality of labour contingents in enterprises, and adhere to the principle of training before employment and training before promotion. Newly-recruited technical workers should undergo professional training and strict assessment.

9. Continue to implement the reform of pension and social insurance systems, and gradually establish a multi-tier insurance system, integrating basic insurance provided by the state and supplementary insurance provided by enterprises with personal savings in insurance.

10. Continue to expand the scope of existing insurance and improve the system of on-the-job insurance.

11. Speed up reform of the labour planning system and implement autonomy in personnel appointments and wage distribution among enterprises.

12. Strengthen democratic management among enterprises and bring the role of the Workers' Congress into play. (SWB, 13 February 1992)

In order to deal with the mounting losses of the state industrial sector, an initial reduction of the work-force was announced, and the establishment of a social security system (that is, unemployment insurance) to cushion the blow to the displaced workers (to be discussed at length in Part Two). The state would at the same time develop employment in the service industries to absorb surplus labour and raise wages for both workers and government employees. The goal of these cuts was to deal with the low levels of economic efficiency, excessive overmanning and unduly high indirect employment costs due to the generous welfare provisions provided in state industrial enterprises, referred to, as we saw earlier, as 'the iron rice-bowl' (see Figure 4.1).

In order to deal with the human costs of bankruptcy (see Poole, 1994, for example), retraining was also proposed. Over 500 enterprises were designated as experimental plants in 1991. Greater competition was introduced and lifetime tenure for cadres abolished to encourage freer transfer of workers and performance-based remuneration. Some enterprises are even experimenting with letting employees buy shares in the company. Enterprises with long-term losses were to be merged, shut down or made bankrupt. Of a survey of 1097 plants, it was said that 39 were shut down, 417 ordered to suspend, 229 switched to other lines of manufacture, 410 merged and two declared bankrupt (*Beijing Review*, 15 June 1992, p.20). In 1992, there were 675 bankruptcies in the state sector. (*ibid.*, 7 February 1994, p.21) By 1993, it was reported that over 900 000 workers were made redundant in cities due to restructuring (*China Labour Bulletin*, April 1994, p.2).

To mitigate the effects of change, a reform of welfare provision was set out:

> The focus of deepened reform of the social welfare system is to straighten out the administrative system and to set up a social insurance system involving the state, the enterprise and individuals so that the funds can be used rationally and increase their value effectively. The current social welfare system has two weaknesses ... This year, along with the reform of the enterprise labour system and the readjustment of enterprise organizational structure, reform of the insurance system for workers in transition must be placed on the agenda. Insurance funds for those workers should be used effectively. The basic needs of the workers in enterprises which are bankrupt or which have been annexed or scrapped should be secured. (*Beijing Review*, 15 June 1992, p.18).

The new regulations enable state enterprises to decide 'the time, conditions, methods and numbers when living new employees' and to adopt 'the contracted management or all-personnel labour contract system' (*Beijing Review*, 16 November 1992, p.14). Firms would hire through examinations: senior staff who failed the tests would be assigned menial jobs, and junior employees would be promoted. Enterprises could even hire from abroad, an unprecedented innovation. Wages would be fixed by enterprises according both to performance-levels and regulations, with freedom to arrive at the total sum for bonuses. According to a survey carried out by the ACFTU, claiming a sample of 210 000 workers from over 400 enterprises, only around one in eight (12.2 per cent) were able to display a high level of 'enthusiasm' in their work because of the labour contract system.[10] Seven out of eight (87.8 per cent) responded that they could only have mediocre or inadequate levels of motivation. Over one in three (36.3 per cent) thought they had no sense of being 'masters' in their enterprises; half (51.5 per cent) thought workers' status was unduly low; and the rest believed they had virtually become 'hired hands' (SWB, 21 March 1992). Low enthusiasm among workers, it was claimed, was principally reflected in the following: (1) low attendance rates; (2) low utilization rate of working hours, which is not above 50 per cent; (3) low labour enthusiasm and unwillingness to learn professional skills; (4) low labour productivity; and (5) low political enthusiasm where workers are not eager to join the youth league or the party, but only pursue material interests. The official union interpretation of such data, which must however be critically regarded, may be summed up as follows:

> The system of labour contracts has affected the enthusiasm of workers and staff members ... With a sense of being 'second-class workers', workers employed under labour contracts generally consider themselves inferior to others, feel insecure and lack the sense of having a stable job. As a result, their initiative and creativity in work are declining.
>
> The unfair distribution has hurt the enthusiasm of workers and staff members. The sharp contrast between the high income of self-employed businessmen and the low income of workers in state-owned enterprises has had a great impact on workers. Moreover, state-owned enterprise workers also earn much less than those working in joint ventures or foreign-invested enterprise...
>
> The improper management of enterprise leaders has also impaired the enthusiasm of workers and staff members ... (SWB, 21 March 1992).

4.4 COLLECTIVELY AND PRIVATELY OWNED ENTERPRISES

Collectively owned (that is by major administrative units and municipalities) industrial enterprises in urban and rural areas employing well over 50 million workers produced over 38 per cent of total gross value of industrial output (see Table 4.4) and were growing fast at the end of 1992 (see SSB, 1993). Since 1986, they have grown at around 18 per cent per annum in such terms. In principle, they may recruit freely according to their production needs, but the larger collectively owned ones are often like state-sector enterprises, as they may be controlled by lower-level government bodies. They may now also reward workers and managers more flexibly, but this may vary.[11] Township enterprises have nearly 20 000 trade union branches with nearly three million members (SWB, 6 May 1992) but worker-representation is relatively limited. It is not known, however, how many enterprises described as 'collective' are indeed 'private'. Some entrepreneurs find it 'politic' to turn over a minority of the shares to staff members, or pay substantial bonus payments, registering their firms as 'collective' enterprises (see Young, 1992, p.66).

In 1987, there were only 150 000 licensed individually owned firms (although many more were illicitly run); by 1992, there were over 15 million of them (*Beijing Review*, 15 February 1992, p.4). Most of these are in small-scale commercial trade, or in services, such as catering or repairs. Little capital, labour or level of skills is needed. Many operate either in 'grey' or even 'black' markets, and have a dubious reputation. Safety regulations are, for example, often neglected and factory accidents rife, as noted earlier. Yet, they probably account for over 20 per cent of retail sales (see Young 1992 for further details). Individually owned firms, in both urban and rural areas, are now said to employ just under 25 million workers and make nearly 7 per cent of the nation's goods measured by gross value of industrial output (see Table 4.4). Small family concerns are registered as *getihu* (*geti gongshanghu*) that is individual industrial and commercial households, and were initially supposed to employ no more than seven people and five who are apprentices. By 1988 larger examples of *siying qiye* (privately run enterprises) were legalized, being defined as having more than eight employees (Young, 1992, p.64). They have greater leeway in their employment practices and in effect operate in more flexible ways than the state-owned and collective enterprises, although small firms are less well researched empirically than the latter (for a clear exception, see Nee, 1992).

4.5   JOINT VENTURES

Joint ventures and wholly foreign-owned firms are increasingly numerous, at least on paper. By the end of 1993, one source estimates that there are more than 140 000 joint ventures (Wang, 1994, p.8). Since 1986, their output (together with that of private firms) has grown at over 50 per cent a year. They only produce a minor percentage of the value of industrial output but are important for technology and knowledge transfer. Joint ventures and wholly foreign-owned firms now account for over five per cent of gross industrial output by value. They are able to recruit their own workers, by examination and selection techniques, in theory at least; but in the early days labour was allocated. Some of these firms may have trade unions, but not necessarily Workers' Congresses.[12] In Shenzen, and other large coastal cities like Dalian and Shanghai, it was claimed more than half the foreign-funded firms had trade union representation in the early 1990s (SWB, 6 May 1992) although many have been described as little more than 'sweat shops' (see Jacka, 1992, p.136). Situated mostly in coastal cities (see Vogel, 1991), joint ventures may have however to pay more to attract better qualified workers and to compensate for the higher cost of living there, but many workers receive low wages. These enterprises have greater autonomy in their labour–management policies than state enterprises.[13] They can 'hire and fire', enforce their own disciplinary measures and work practices. Stricter supervision and greater 'one-man' control by overseas managers is common in such firms (see Howell, 1992), but many local Chinese managers still used collective decision-making (see Wang, 1992; 1994).

The presidium of the second session of the 12th All-China Federation of Trade Unions recently analysed labour relations in foreign-invested enterprises:

> They felt deep concern about how some foreign-invested enterprises had violated relevant Chinese laws and regulations and had seriously encroached on the legitimate rights and interests of workers. ...
>
> [There are] 47 000 enterprises, employing more than five million workers, [which] have been completed and put into operation. On the whole, the labour relations in foreign-invested enterprises are stable and most foreign-invested enterprises operate and organize production according to the law, but there are some quite serious labour-relations problems in some foreign-invested enterprises. (SWB, 8 April 1994)

There are however clearly attractions in working in some foreign-funded ventures:

> In the summer of 1991, the Hangzhou BC Foods Co Ltd, a joint venture with the UD Coca Cola Co, advertised for four secretaries. Unexpectedly, more than 500 people applied for the positions. A situation where one person is to be selected from 100-plus applicants is quite common now in foreign-funded businesses, namely Sino-foreign joint ventures co-operative and exclusively foreign-owned enterprises. (*Beijing Review*, 16 November 1992, p.21)

The relatively high income of such employees gives them a standard of living well above their counterparts in other fields of work. However, there are drawbacks, for unsatisfactory performance may lead to a drop in wages, demotion or dismissal.

Wages and bonuses are generally higher in monetary terms in the Special Economic Zones than in many firms inland. Higher wage-costs are none the less mostly balanced by higher productivity. Additional labour costs are incurred by the foreign investor, but these are not paid to the worker. The local labour-service company takes this percentage of total labour costs in order to cover both direct and indirect costs of labour supply, such as social insurance and so on (see Howell, 1992, p.219). Joint ventures also often supply dormitory accommodation, often cramped, in order to house these mainly rural migrants, who may only be temporary and/or contract employees, as they have traditionally done in the initial days of industrialization in both China and Japan.

Acceptance of Western management practices in joint ventures has not been universally welcomed. Apparently, the foreign managers of a joint-venture enterprise in Tianjin, for example, had widened salary-differentials and abolished some living and service facilities for employees. The latter's response was to become 'slack' in their work (SWB, 21 November 1991).

Yanh Zhijun, the Vice-General Manager of the Babcock & Wilcox Joint Venture in Beijing argued that

> overseas management methods could not be copied as easily as technology. Foreign partners should not disregard China's traditional culture and ways of work. ... the Western style of management has its advantages, but the Chinese style is good at fostering enthusiasm among employees. Ideally a blend of the two will be sought. Initially, the overseas partners doubted the purpose and effectiveness of China's trade unions, but later they changed their attitude to support the work of the unions. ... Some enterprises have wrested final authority from the foreign-side managers and instituted agreements called for advice and consent from Chinese managers on all major decisions. (SWB, 21 November 1991)

4.6   CONCLUDING REMARKS

As the enterprise reforms unfold, the nature of industrial relations and possibly nascent HRM in Chinese factories will no doubt change further as state-owned firms become less representative (see Figure 4.2). Since the trade unions have traditionally complied with shifts of national policy, it is likely that they will continue to do so. In all areas outlined in this chapter, trade unions and Worker Congresses (where one or both are actually present) will no doubt have had their say, but may increasingly be bypassed or overridden where there is genuine discretion for enterprise directors, as we shall shortly see in Part Two. If Party influence relatively diminishes in industrial affairs at the macro-level, the role of the national

Figure 4.2 Industrial relations and different forms of ownership

Variable	State-owned enterprises	Collectively owned	Privately owned	Joint ventures and foreign-owned
1. Scale of production	Large/medium	Medium/small	Small	Varies
2. Degree of unionization	Virtually complete	Moderate	Minimal	Moderate to zero
3. Trade unions	Present	Present	Absent	Sometimes in joint ventures
4. Worker Congresses	Present	Present	Absent	Sometimes in joint ventures
5. Wage determination	Previously fixed	Variable	Variable	Variable
6. Hiring and firing	Constrained	Variable	Unconstrained	Variable
7. Labour contracts	Newly-recruited	Most	Most	Most
8. Training	Extensive	Limited	Minimal	Extensive

trade union federation will weaken, as the one follows the other. If the Party's role relatively lessens at enterprise and work-place level, then the official union role will be similarly attenuated, for the same reason. It is, however, uncertain as to when this might happen or how precisely it will work out in detail. I hope to suggest in the subsequent chapters in Parts Two and Three, probable lines of development in labour-management relations.

Part Two
Old Wine, New Bottles?

(Xinpin zhuang jiu jiu?)

We must integrate theory closely with practice, be consistent in what we do and what we say, oppose empty show and reject all boasting. There must be less empty talk and more hard work.

(Deng Xiao-ping, Speech, 18 August 1977)

5 Labour Reforms at City Level: Background

5.1 INTRODUCTION

In order to understand the labour reforms in China in greater depth, we need to look at their implementation in greater detail. Data collected at first hand will be set out as follows. First, the general background of the reforms in the cities concerned will be set out in Chapter 5. Second, the enterprise contexts will be outlined in Chapter 6. Third, the specific 'three-system' reforms (*san xiang zhidu gaige*) covering personnel, wages and social insurance, will be characterized in Chapter 7.

The field investigation was carried out in Beijing and the North-East of China (in Heilongjiang and Liaoning provinces). It covered ten large to medium-sized state industrial enterprises (the main focus of the study – see Figure 5.1) although reference will be made to other relevant sites.[1] The firms were located in the cities of Beijing, Dalian, Harbin and Shenyang. In addition, background data were collected via discussions with experts at the Chinese Academy of Social Sciences (CASS) and three provincial academies, four major municipal and provincial labour bureaux, five university departments, six economic and social science research institutes, as well as one economic development zone and one trade union federation headquarters. Semi-structured interviews were undertaken with senior managers, employees at different levels, labour bureaux personnel, union officials and researchers, using junior colleagues from the CASS Institute of Industrial Economics as research assistants and interpreters. Documents and statistics were also collected and translated by the latter. The field work was completed during July and August 1993. The research was sponsored by the British Academy/Economic and Social Research Council Joint Exchange Programme, in collaboration with CASS.

The sample was selected from an originally longer list set out by myself and narrowed down in collaboration with my colleagues at the CASS Institute of Industrial Economics. They were intended to be typical of large state enterprises chosen by the State Council as being at the leading edge of the economic reforms, and as pilot experimental sites in the North-

Figure 5.1   Enterprises in the sample (in alphabetical order)

1. Beijing Iron and Steel Corporation (*Shougang*)
2. Dalian Port Authority
3. Dalian Locomotive and Rolling-Stock Works
4. Dalian Shipyard
5. Harbin Pharmaceutical Factory
6. Harbin Power-Equipment Company
7. Shenyang Area/Anshan Iron and Steel Complex (*Angang*)
8. Shenyang Gold Cup (*Jin Bei*) Auto Company
9. Shenyang Smelting Works
10. Shenyang Transformer Works

East (see Figure 5.1). Out of the ten enterprises investigated, two were in the original World Bank/CASS study undertaken in the late eighties (see Tidrick and Chen, 1987).

5.2   RATIONALE OF THE REFORMS

As we have seen earlier, the major backdrop to reform of the employment system in China is the attempt to change the nature of enterprise-management. At the beginning of July 1992, the State Council issued new regulations pushing state enterprises to change their management systems towards a more market-oriented model (as described in Chapter 4). In order to pinpoint the key issues in the current debate on both enterprise and labour reform, we now summarize the range of views at hand.

The problem, according to one informed source, was that of ownership. For the enterprise to stand on its own two feet, there must be the threat of bankruptcy, but this is not always possible if the State is the 'owner', and therefore the challenge is to create a legal entity, whereby ownership and management are separated. The confusion between the boundaries of the State and the enterprise bedevilled clarification of the above issue during the earlier phases of the economic reforms, it was argued. Further, the unequal environments facing firms did not help the implementation of price and taxation reforms. The same applied to labour and employment system reforms. If any one factor-market is unreformed, the overall enterprise reforms will not work. Suggestions as to how to resolve the problem include making the employment system an autonomous one, with greater freedom for personnel decisions. The so-called 'iron rice-bowl', it was concluded, would have to go (Interview with Professor Zhou Shaopeng, CASS Institute of Industrial Economics, Beijing, July 1993).

In recent years, new policies were introduced to depose the 'three irons', namely the 'iron chair, bowl and salary'. From 1981 onwards, there was an attempt to implement a system based on contracts in industries like building, ports and so on. After 1986, state enterprises were required to set up such a system. Newcomers were to be put on contracts, in the spirit of 'old man, old method; new man, new method.' Such additions to the labour-force were, by definition, in a minority. The challenge was how to change the system writ large, namely how to reform the employment of the bulk of the work-force in the enterprise, how to separate the surplus workers from that group and how to make provision for helping them. One solution had been to set up 'labour service companies' to employ young people coming back to the cities after having been rusticated, and similarly catering for older cadres and workers displaced during the Cultural Revolution.

In 1984, the system of hereditary jobs (*dingti*) began to be phased out (as we have seen in Chapter 4) and this provided another excluded employment group to be found work, as in the above groups. If a worker was 'released' but was found a better job and salary, this then led to resentment for those left in the enterprise. If the worker took an inferior job and salary, then he or she was demotivated. To obtain greater co-operation to boost the skills and effort of those left, greater choice was a boon. Some believe that the undermining of the old employment system helped to stir up the 1989 troubles. In any event, such reforms were frozen after the 4 June events because of 'the danger to society' from such changes.

Up to 1991, around 85 per cent of workers in large state enterprises were still permanent employees. From this date, the State Council pushed for comprehensive reform with both old and new workers on contracts up to five years in duration. Such changes in employment status were not without problems. If workers signed contracts, were they still 'masters of their country'? Did they become 'employees'? Who then was their employer, the enterprise director, or general managers and so on? Was he or she an 'employee'? One expert believes contracts to be double-edged. Employees, including enterprise directors, could leave for a higher salary. Managers might not be able to offer higher rewards to retain key personnel. Keeping organizational or commercial secrets safe might be a problem in such a situation. Cadres were clearly differentiated from workers in the past, but the latest reforms seek to blur the differences. Beijing Iron and Steel has not only fired workers but also demoted cadres to worker level (Interview with Professor Zhou Shaopeng, July 1993).

Early steps have been taken to create a labour-market but there was not much inter-firm mobility. For the average worker, there are 'Job Placement Centres' where they can register, especially the migrants who come to the city from rural areas. If someone from another town finds a job elsewhere, he or she can have their job frozen but have their salary stopped. They can also keep their old citizen registration. A major drawback is that if everyone signs a contract, and if these are easily renewable, then there is no change from the *status quo ante*. Further reform really should implement the principles of 'employees can go in and can go out', 'every employee can go up and can go down', 'employees can change jobs inside and outside the enterprise', and 'workers can choose enterprise and enterprise can choose workers', slogans ascribed to the present Mayor of Beijing.

The latest reforms were predicated upon creating four employment statuses:

1. fixed workers
2. contract workers
3. short-term or temporary workers
4. part-time workers.

The above assume social security provisions of employment, retirement, and medical insurance. There are two basic principles underlying these reforms; first, one of *equity*; second, of *efficiency*. The outcome depends on reconciling these (see Jiang and Zhou, 1992). Another fundamental problem facing the labour-market reformers was that much of the economy is itself in a transitional phase. One recent estimate was that one third of the economy was amenable to state control, another third was market-oriented, but a further one-third was a 'middle ground' (Interview with Professor Dong Fureng, CASS Institute of Economics, Beijing, July 1993).

In the labour system reforms, there was a similar situation, with the attempt to bring in the contract system. Where there has been any change, it was a change in *form* but not in kind. Contracts are renewed as a formality and most are paid the same level of bonus. In principle, state-owned enterprises are supposed to generate jobs if the business is viable but in fact few enterprises fail because the state or local government provide subsidies to enable them to meet their wage-bills and preserve employment levels. When the reform of the employment system was first debated (as we have seen in Chapter 4) there was a widespread reluctance to use the term 'labour-market', because of the strait-jacket of Marxist terminology. The official line was that such a term implied that labour was a 'commodity', a term only used under capitalism. Party-line economists believed that if there was to be a 'labour market', the worker would become an 'employee', not a 'master'.

Against this view, critical Chinese economists argued that labour is a kind of resource and that in a market economy, the market best distributes resources. In the end, the official sources spoke only of a 'labour-service market', but in theory, services are not the same as the concept of 'labour'. Marx, it was said, only used the term 'wage-labour' and never mentioned 'employed' or 'hired' labour. There is consequently a theoretical problem involved when rendering Marxist 'labour-theory' compatible with the needs of a market-oriented economy, even one 'with Chinese characteristics'. A further problem was that of the workers' status as 'masters' in both enterprise and society. In principle, the Workers' Congress was said to be the highest decision-making organ in the enterprise, but if the top managers can hire and fire, then there is a 'contradiction'. At the international representational level, too, the enterprise directors are now put forward as 'employers' in the ILO meetings in Geneva, and the workers as 'employees', although *de jure* the unions retain their role to assist the workers and staff in their role as 'masters of the country' in China (Article 5, Trade Union Law of the PRC, 3 April 1992).[2] By contrast, attitudes towards employment in joint ventures are less problematic. Jobs in such enterprises are very much in demand. Hirings are selective and firings are less disputed. Dismissals are even thought reasonable. Thus, one solution may involve the expansion of joint ventures (Interview with Professor Dong Fureng, July 1993).

On the other hand, workers' rights were not always enforced in such kinds of firms:

Some foreign-invested enterprises do not sign labour contracts with workers. As a result, workers' jobs are not safeguarded, the workers are not insured against unemployment and workers' legitimate rights and interests are not protected by law. The Qingdao City Federation of Trade Unions carried out a survey in 48 foreign-invested enterprises and found that 11 had signed labour contracts with only some workers and four had not signed any labour contracts at all. In 1992, Shenzhen carried out a general inspection on enforcing labour laws, made selective examinations among 280 000 workers and labour formalities. The number of foreign-invested enterprises in the Shantou SEZ and Zhuhai which have not signed labour contracts accounts for 70 and 90 per cent respectively, of the total of such enterprises. (SWB, 8 April 1994)

A major group of workers caught in the 'middle ground' of the labour-market are the temporary contract-workers, as we have seen earlier. A good number of the 'dirty jobs' in the cities are done by peasants who have migrated to the cities from rural areas. Such workers are unrecognized by the state and do not have welfare provision. They are found in construction, refuse-collection and so on. In the mining industry, the largely temporary work-force is turned over every three years. The workers have many social problems, such as finding housing, a suitable marriage-partner and the like. They are often competing with the registered jobless for work (see *China Daily*, 13 May 1993, p.2).

5.3   BEIJING: GENERAL

Labour contract reform was implemented in the Beijing area from the mid-1980s onwards. By 1993, about 15 per cent of the total labour-force of two million workers in the main city-districts was covered, with wider coverage planned (Beijing has over ten million inhabitants in all, around half living in the central area). In 1992, the State Council had extended labour reforms in state-owned enterprises. Initial steps were taken in 'selected' large enterprises, where workers were said to be 'more eager' for reform, with formal approval of their Workers' Congresses. After reform, job mobility was said to be enhanced, but not remarkably so. These firms could now also fire personnel, if overstaffed. In a study of 23 such enterprises, however, only three per cent had left their jobs for employment elsewhere (Interviews, Beijing Municipal Labour Bureau, July-August 1993).

A *standard labour contract* existed in the Beijing area, as in other cities and provinces. It covered the basic employment conditions, length of contract, medical care, pensions and so on and could be adapted to specific enterprise circumstances, after formal approval by the respective Workers' Congress. Enterprises and workers signed the contract, which was then checked by the local Labour Bureau against the appropriate regulations. If the worker disagreed with the terms offered, he or she could refuse to sign it and/or change their job, or go to the so-called 'labour-service market'. If disputed, labour contracts could go to arbitration by the local labour bureaux. In principle, further adjudication could be made by a Court of Law, although this was queried by the Beijing Municipal Labour Bureau officials interviewed. In any case, they claimed that there had been no such cases to date. If the contract format was passed by the Workers' Congress, 'there was no need to go to Court'.

Dismissal procedure was specified in the contract and was mostly related to poor work performance and/or discipline. If offences were minor, the enterprise should re-educate the worker; if major, it should fire the individual concerned. If the above behaviour was satisfactory, the worker could still leave if he or she wanted another job elsewhere. In practice, it was claimed very few people were fired in Beijing enterprises, probably less than 1 per cent. In a case-study cited by the Beijing Municipal Labour Bureau, less than 50 workers were fired out of around 7000 in a large state-owned mechanical engineering plant they had studied in 1992 (Interviews, July-August 1993).

Wage reform was piloted in 60 or so enterprises in the Beijing area in the late 1980s. Wage and salary levels were to be linked to enterprise efficiency. The market would determine profits or losses and the enterprise would decide how to distribute appropriate rewards. By 1990, it was claimed that 96 per cent of workers in the Beijing area were covered by such procedures. The 'labour-service market' would deal with those changing jobs or who were unemployed. If workers had to leave their jobs, they could claim labour insurance since 1986 depending on their previous wage-level and how much the enterprise had paid to the fund. It could be as low as 97 yuan per month as a basic payment, or as high as 75 per cent of their original basic wage.[3] The number affected was estimated to be no more than 1 per cent of the Beijing labour-force. No labour insurance benefits would be paid to workers who left their job of their own accord, or who were dismissed for bad conduct. Several labour bureau officials were of the opinion that benefits should only be paid to 'those waiting for work' if they agreed to undergo retraining.

Vocational training was to be provided for those outside the enterprises as well as those inside, and those 'in the labour market'. Intra-enterprise training was to be geared to those aspiring to higher qualifications by passing skill examinations or for those coming to terms with new technology and new products. Extra-enterprise training was to be mostly related to preparing school-leavers for employment or for those 'in the labour market' who needed retraining. The labour bureaux were mostly not directly involved in training: their main role was 'supervisory' and they organized and accredited training schools by sector, which were paid for out of public funds.[4] There were no tuition fees, except for computer training. If a worker wanted new skills to change their job, they had to pay for these. In-house training was paid for by the enterprises (Interviews, July-August 1993).

The move towards greater flexibility in labour supply posed new problems, as a recent press report indicates:

The government recently ordered state companies to find jobs for any workers they lay off in order to prevent social unrest. The layoffs are the result of a new government policy that state companies can no longer expect bailouts and must turn a profit or shut down. However, the *China Daily* said a survey by the All-China Federation of Trade Unions in nine cities found that companies could find new jobs for only 40 percent of their laid-off workers. Many companies set up restaurants, hotels and other 'service companies' and reassign laid-off assembly-line workers there, often at lower wages.

'Because the country's social security system is not well-developed yet, it is impossible for the state to shoulder the remaining 60 per cent', the paper said. (Associated Press, quoting *China Daily*, 13 May 1993, p.1)

This picture must be placed against a national backdrop which feature at the time of writing was said to be over 2000 training centres dealing with around 3 million clients and nearly 10 000 job placement agencies (see *Beijing Review*, 21 February 1994, p.6).

5.4   DALIAN: GENERAL

Dalian, the most northerly major port in China, has a total population of over five million, of whom one and three-quarter million are city residents (with a working population there of over 800 000). The main economic activities, formerly dominated by the Russians and then the Japanese are, in order of importance, the port, trade, industry and tourism. There were over 2000 joint ventures and foreign companies located there employed over 40 000 workers in 1993. There were nearly 250 large state enterprises and 3500 township industries (with over 330 000 employees). Heavy chemical industries and high-quality engineering stand out. Over 80 per cent of products are shipped to other parts of China or exported. There are over 120 research institutes in enterprises and 17 major colleges and universities (with approximately 40 000 students). Dalian has been an 'Open City' since 1984 and in 1992 exported goods to the value of 2 billion US dollars; Dalian's Economic Development Zone aspires to be 'a second Hong Kong'. Tourism is also a major industry (around 8.5 million visitors, with over 100 000 from abroad) – not surprisingly, given its scenic and, to date, relatively unspoilt coastline and moderate climate.

Dalian was therefore chosen as an 'experimental' site for labour-system reform because of its strategic location, and several major conferences on the policy-change were held there, principally in 1991 and 1992. By mid-

1993, nearly 200 enterprises in Dalian had introduced the latest reforms, employing nearly one-third of the city's workforce. In the state-owned enterprises, it was claimed that over 70 per cent of workers were on contracts of different duration (either short, medium or long). Labour contracts varied in their detail between institutions, but there were basic laws (and a model contract available locally). Fundamental rights were preserved, such as maternity leave and so on. Contracts had to be approved by the trade unions and stamped by the enterprises and the certification officer in the Bureau.

The problem of surplus labour has been extensively studied in Dalian. Estimates differed, varying from 10 to 30 per cent. By mid-1993, it was estimated that over 25 000 workers had left their enterprises since the labour contract reforms were introduced. Enterprises were left to solve the problem, but the state (that is, government agencies) also has to play a major role, by providing and paying for retraining and helping to set up small businesses. There was assistance for workers in Dalian's enterprises to transfer workers to firms where they are needed. For example, in 1992 over 6000 workers were helped in this way. The residual displaced labour-force had to go directly to the 'labour-service market'. By 1995, all mobile workers will be allocated by this mechanism. Already, joint ventures and collective enterprises have adopted this policy (as well as the 200 or so 'experimental' enterprises in the city).

At the beginning, it was claimed that there was some reluctance on the workers' side in Dalian to accept the reforms of the labour system. Later, there was greater interest as the increase in rewards was said to improve motivation especially in heavy and dirty work. It enabled blue-collar workers to stay in production-line jobs, as it was claimed that they could earn up to 1000 yuan per month. The old eight-grade wage system went, as did automatic promotion. Enterprises now had greater autonomy and out of the 14 areas of discretion, those over wages and personnel arrangement were set out as amongst the most important.

Under the recent labour system reforms, every town and city will have its own 'labour-service market'. The Dalian office has 86 employees and 14 departments (soon to be reduced to 10) of which the most important ones deal with the following:

1. labour protection
2. job-placement
3. assessment
4. training
5. contracts
6. arbitration

There are also specialized labour-service market service organizations dealing with house and office cleaning, construction, disabled workers, individual and small businesses, and temporary labour. Cadres could also use such labour-market services as well as workers, but not many did. The service tried to provide alternative jobs for the labour surplus in government departments estimated at 10 per cent at least. Official figures put the unemployment rate in Dalian at a very low level (1.2 per cent in 1992 and graduates at 1.5 per cent – *vis-à-vis* the national official average but not necessarily meaningful figure of 2.6 per cent).

Social insurance reform in Dalian started in 1985 and was moving to an integrated system by the early 1990s. All forms of enterprise must now have social (including labour) insurance (notwithstanding foreign-owned and joint-venture companies) in order to facilitate job mobility. All employees are to be covered wherever they work; pensions are to be paid by enterprise contributions based on 19 per cent of an individual's income to the State fund and 1.5 per cent to be paid by the worker. Unemployment insurance is covered by a 1 per cent contribution to the state fund by the enterprise only, based on 1 per cent of its turnover.[5] Before the reforms, enterprises paid all doctors' and hospital bills for their employees; now the individual has to make some contribution to the cost of medical care (Interviews, Dalian Municipal Labour Bureau, July–August 1992).

While Dalian did not have Special Economic Zone status, it had an 'Economic Development Zone', the difference being that the latter was under the jurisdiction of local government and not a (relatively) autonomous administrative entity. The Development Zone aspires to be the 'Hong Kong of the North-East', with over 850 foreign firms signed-up and around 200 in actual operation. Over three billion yuan of investments had been agreed, and over 800 million US dollars already placed. There were approximately 40 000 employees in the firms on site, of which around 55 per cent were joint ventures. Compared with other such zones, the DEDZ had a greater number of large investments, with over 70 firms investing over 10 million US dollars each, and with the average placement of all foreign firms in the region of five million US dollars by 1993. Products covered included electrical goods, machinery, clothing, food and chemicals. Forty per cent of all companies located there were from Hong Kong and a similar number from Japan, with US, Taiwan and South Korea amongst the remainder.

The average wage level for production workers in the Development Zone was said to be over one hundred US dollars per month (which was over 600 yuan at the mid-1993 tourist rate and higher at the 'swap' rate) but the government took over 25 per cent for welfare benefits, leaving 400 yuan per month to be paid to the worker. The official regulations in the case specified that joint-venture salaries should not be less than 120 per cent of those of state-owned enterprise workers to cover this imposition.[6] Incomes of Chinese managers in such foreign-owned or joint-venture firms were said to be in the region of 1000 yuan per month. The labour contract system was reportedly enforced in all such firms and it was claimed that many were unionized, although up to a third were not. The unions could only discuss conditions outside working hours. There were also often Party committees and Workers' Congresses, as in state-owned enterprises (Interviews, Dalian Economic Development Zone, August 1993). Xinhua News Agency claimed later in the year that 'most labour disputes have occurred where there are no unions, while employee–employer relations are "good" in most enterprises with unions. Last year, strikes and sit-ins were reported in five enterprises in northeast China's Dalian Development Zone designated to attract foreign investment, of these, four had no unions.' (SWB, 1 November 1993)

The case-studies' average monthly earnings in Dalian should be set against the following figures (given by the Economic Research Institute there): (1) state enterprises, over 270 yuan; (2) rural industries, over 500 yuan; (3) joint ventures, over 800 yuan.

The average earnings in Shenzen were, however, estimated to be double those of Dalian. The average worker and professional paid virtually no tax unless earnings were over 800 yuan per month, when 10 per cent income tax was deducted. The average GNP per capita in the city, it was claimed, was just under 200 yuan per month, one of the highest in China. The quality of life was deemed to be of a high standard, notwithstanding the longevity of its citizens which exceeded 72 years (Interviews, Dalian Economic Research Institute, July–August 1993).

5.5 HARBIN: GENERAL

Harbin, located near the Sino-Russian border, has long been a major industrial centre, and was a Treaty city after 1896 under Russian influence. It experiences very severe winters and mild summers (see Leeming, 1992, p.174). It had a population of 3.5 million in 1993, out of a total of 36 million in Heilongjiang province. The work-force in the city numbered over 1.2 million, with around 8.5 million in collective and state enterprises in the province as a whole, with over 80 000 (and, in the province, 300 000) newcomers respectively coming into the labour market each year, excluding university graduates. About ten million peasants were said to be 'waiting for employment' locally. There were over 3000 state enterprises in Harbin and over 15 000 in the province, with around 150 large ones in the city and 300 elsewhere. Around one-third of these made a loss, it was estimated (Interviews, Heilongjiang Provincial Labour Bureau, Harbin, August 1993). About 80 per cent of the province's industries were in state sector hands, a quarter of output depends on prices and quotas set by central government *vis-à-vis* 5 per cent for China as a whole (see Poole, 1994, p.15).

Increasing numbers of employees in state enterprises in Harbin were now becoming part of the labour-contract system. All newcomers to work-units since 1986 have had to sign a contract, but only 20 per cent of older employees overall. In large state enterprises in Harbin, the Provincial Labour Bureau claimed that all employees had to sign as part of the comprehensive 'all-in' or 'three systems' reforms, covering labour contracts (*laodong renshi zhidu*), wages (*gongzi fenpei zhidu gaige*) and social insurance (*shehui baoxian zhidu gaige*) reforms. The implementation of labour reform in Harbin, however, varied from enterprise to enterprise. The largest state firms, which had contracts with the government, tried to enforce 'comprehensive' labour contract reforms with mixed degrees of success.[7] They could decide how many employees they needed and how they recruited them. (There was even more variation in small and medium-sized enterprises.) In 'profit and loss' enterprises, it was claimed that workers could refuse to sign a contract and hence leave or retire early. In large state firms, it was uncontestable that newcomers had to sign, some enforced the new system for all or most employees, and still others (a minority) kept the old system. Not very many had the 'comprehensive' contract system, according to local experts (Interviews, Heilongjiang Academy of Social Sciences, Institute of Economics, Harbin, August 1993).

In fact, only one-third of all state-owned enterprises in the city had adopted such the 'all-in' reforms; however, in 1992, 45 of large ones, and in 1993 over 100 were included. The 'three systems' reforms, it was claimed, represented a move from a permanent to a flexible employment model. All employees would be on three to five-year contracts. If needed, contracts could be renewed. The principles covering such contracts in the city and province are as elsewhere in Dalian and Shenyang, namely also based on a sample contract. Workers could become cadres and vice versa, as in other pilot enterprises (Interviews, Provincial Labour Bureau, August 1993).

Wage-system reform was also being implemented. Average annual wages in Harbin in 1992 were estimated at around 2400 yuan and 2295 in the province, according to labour bureaux sources. Enterprises had been given autonomy to set up their own wage-systems, the state controlling only the aggregate wage-fund. Incomes would be determined by contractual agreements and efficiency levels. They might vary according to profits or losses of enterprises. The basic wage is weighted by around 50 per cent, welfare by 25 per cent and the bonus by another 25 per cent. The social insurance reforms are also to be introduced into all cities, townships and then eventually rural areas. As yet, they are only being fully implemented in the cities, based on enterprise payments of 20–22 per cent of employees' incomes and 2 per cent as individual contributors (Interviews, August, 1993).

5.6 SHENYANG: GENERAL

Shenyang, the largest industrial conurbation in the North-East, had a total population of over 6.5 million people, of whom 2.3 million are workers (with 1.9 million in factories) in 1993. It has a harsh winter climate and muggy summers compounded by air pollution. Liaoning province, as a whole, has about 10 per cent of all capital investment in China. It had the largest share of foreign government loans, mainly in large-scale construction projects (Leeming, 1992, p.173). There were over 20 000 enterprises active in the city's economic life. It is worth noting, however, that four out of ten large state firms were said to be loss-making. The average annual adult wage (including bonus) was estimated to be in the region of 2860 yuan in 1992. Under the economic reforms, Shenyang was the first city to introduce the management contract system in 1986 (see Thomas 1993, p 46) and the labour contract system from 1982 onwards. By 1988, over 2000 enterprises had introduced labour contracts for newcomers, and around 20 000 workers had left their units. In early 1991, the *comprehensive* labour contract reforms were introduced in 12 pilot enterprises.[8] Later, over 50 enterprises were implementing the system. By 1993, all sizeable enterprises (nearly 6000) had adopted the system after consulting with worker representative bodies, to cover approximately 1.4 million workers.

There was a standard labour contract on offer from the Shenyang Municipal Labour Bureau (see Figure 5.2: English translation by Ding Yi). The individual enterprises could, however, tailor these to their own specific requirements. The contracts were two-sided, setting out mutual responsibilities, such as nature of the post, period of employment, rewards and benefits, welfare, arbitration and so on. All new employees had to sign such contracts, and many existing managers and workers had to move on to the new arrangements. The impact of the labour contract reforms in

Figure 5.2   Sample contract: Shenyang Municipal Labour Bureau, 1992

No ....

LABOUR CONTRACT

Name of Employing Company
....
Name of Worker
....

Shenyang Labour Bureau

On the company side,
Nature of Ownership

With regard to production and job requirements, and after entry-examination, the company will employ .... on the workers' side to make a labour contract. Both sides willing to obey the State Labour Contract System regulations after discussion have made the following agreement.

I   Company will employ .... in .... post for
         .... months from .... to .... including
         probation period.

II   *Rights and Responsibilities*

1.   For the Company side, according to production needs and regulations of the Company and according to the regulations of the contract, the Company will make the regulations regarding managements' procedures.

2.   The Company will take safety precautions before the Worker takes his or her post and provide safe conditions for work and study.

3.   The Company will protect the Worker's benefits.

4.   The Company has the right to give bonus and enforce sanctions according to the Worker's performance.

For the Worker's side,

1.   The Worker has the right and obligation to receive benefits from the Company.

2.   To obey the policies of the State and the regulations and discipline of the Company.

3.   To follow the regulations of safety operations and to make sure of safety in his or her work.

4.   To complete the economic targets set by the Company.

III   Production Targets ....

IV   Total Payments ....

V Labour Safety Gear ....

VI Labour Insurance and Welfare ....

VII Contract Enforcement Conditions ....

VIII *Special Conditions* ....

IX Two copies of the contract; for the Company one copy, for the Worker the other. Both sides will sign their name and go to a special office for Contract Enforcement regarding possible disagreement at a future date. Both sides must conform to the contract. If one side has a disagreement, he or she can go to the Labour Arbitration Department.

Signed (on the Company side) ....
Signed (on the Worker side) ....

Seal .... by Registry of Certificate
          (If contract is not stamped and sealed, it is null and void)

Year   Month   Day

Shenyang were allegedly extensive. Between 1991 and 1993, over 150 000 workers were said to have switched jobs within their enterprises, and a further 15 000 displaced, going to other enterprises, setting up their own business or taking early retirement (Interviews, Shenyang Municipal Labour Bureau, August 1993).

The Shenyang Municipal Labour Bureau was relatively large. Before the economic reforms, there were 18 departments, but by 1993 there were eight.

1. administration and personnel
2. training
3. wages
4. insurance and welfare
5. arbitration
6. health and safety
7. environmental and pollution control
8. safety in mines.

There were 136 employees before re-organization; now there were 93 in total.

Labour mobility was a major goal of the new system. The Municipal Labour Bureau had to act as a labour-exchange for job-seekers. In the first six months of 1993, over 40 000 applicants came to the Bureau to seek new jobs, of which one-third were successful. Many came because their existing place of employment was closing down, or shedding labour; in addition, newly set up firms were looking for new employees.

The Shenyang Bureau's new roles are now planned in the following *four* key areas of activity:

1. labour employment service   3. social insurance
2. wages-monitoring   4. labour law enforcement.

1. The *Labour Employment Service* activities include helping new or displaced members of the work-force to find work; setting up a computerized database of available jobs; retraining for the unemployed; and helping the unemployed to set up new business ventures.

2. The *Wages-Monitoring* system involves macro-control of the parameters of employees' incomes. Since enterprise autonomy has been introduced and firms can determine their distribution of profits, the Bureau can enforce rules restricting increases of wages to growth of output and productivity. Within enterprises, managers can decide who gets individual rewards according to the 'post plus skills' system. Where the firm does not make a surplus, the state can sign guarantee regarding wages set in labour contracts.

3. The *Social Insurance* system covers pensions, unemployment and sickness insurance. It was started in 1986 and by 1993 over half a million received state pensions as opposed to company ones. In October 1992, a 2 per cent levy on workers' incomes was introduced to pay for universal social insurance benefits.

4. The *Labour Law Enforcement* function is a relatively novel activity and is not yet very well-developed. It deals with guide-lines laid down in Temporary Regulations of the State Council in the labour field. These are not exactly 'laws' in the Western sense, but are directives relating to such matters as contracts, conditions of employment, arbitration and so on.

Workers' attitudes to the labour contract reforms vary. According to a study carried out by the Institute of Sociology in Shenyang, younger workers were keener on the changes than older workers, but were resentful of their lower salaries. They were also more mobile, using the more successful enterprises which offered higher wages as their reference-point. In loss-making enterprises, the researchers reported that morale was lower but there were few strikes. The biggest concerns of workers, according to the study, related to employment rights and social security. As Shenyang was the industrial base of China *par excellence*, this finding was critical (see Thomas, 1993). Most enterprises in the above study were state-owned and either large or medium sized. The data were collected from interest-groups in the factories such as women's, youth and minority organizations (Interviews, Liaoning Provincial Academy of Social Sciences, Institute of Sociology, July-August 1993).

5.7 CONCLUDING REMARKS

In this chapter, we have described the rationale of the economic reforms up to 1992–3, and set out the background to changes in the labour system in four cities, Beijing, Dalian, Harbin and Shenyang. The role of intermediary institution, the Municipal (or in one case, the Provincial) Labour Bureau was examined *vis-à-vis* the specific implementation of the reforms at enterprise-level. A redefinition of the goals and structure of each was also discussed. Managers now had greater powers, at least on paper, to hire and fire: the slang expression for sacking staff, *chao youyu* (derived from the Cantonese) literally 'to fry the squid', has become common parlance.[9] Prior to this change, depriving workers of their livelihood had been a measure of last resort.[10] In the next chapter, we go on to look at the specific characteristics of the enterprises where we studied the 'three-systems reforms' in detail.

6 Selected Case-Studies at Enterprise Level

In this chapter, we set out the characteristics of the ten state-owned enterprises which were among the experimental sites selected for the implementation of the 'all-in reforms' (most located in the North-East, with a bench-mark case included in Beijing). Data were collected relating to the *foundation of the enterprise*, its *main products*, *sales revenues*, *profits and tax*, *work-force size*, and details relating to its *personnel*, *wages* and *welfare structures* and *policies*. We thus hope to set the company-context of the specific labour and personnel reforms in each case.

6.1 BEIJING CAPITAL IRON AND STEEL COMPANY

Capital Iron and Steel (the *Shougang* Corporation) is one of the flagship enterprises of the Chinese state sector. It employed over 220 000 employees overall (around 120 000 in Beijing, 60 000 on the main production site) 1992. It had 120 plants, 40 domestic affiliates, 27 joint ventures and 18 equity joint ventures.[1] Its turnover was over 12.6 billion RMB at the time, with profits and tax of 5.1 billion yuan (for a summary see Figure 6.1). It had an annual output of 4.42 million tons of iron, 5.75 million tons of steel and 4.4 million tons of steel products respectively. Its target annual output of steel production of Beijing area was 10 million tons by the year 1994. It describes itself as follows:

> Beijing Iron and Steel Corporation of Shougang is one of the largest metallurgical enterprises in China. Its equipment and facilities have, through modification, come up to world advanced standards and measured on major economic and technological indices are taking a lead . . . 90 per cent of products are made in accordance with international standards. The Special Steel Corporation of Shougang, with an annual output of 627 thousand tons of qualified carbon steel and various alloy steel, is one of the major enterprises in China to produce special steel. Its steel products, precision casting, steel shot and graphite electrodes have found a good market both at home and abroad. . . . The annual output of steel of Shougang is expected to pass 20 million tons by the year of 2000. (Company brochure, 1993, p.3)

Figure 6.1   Case Study No.1: Beijing Capital Iron and Steel (*Shougang*). Summary

---

1. Location . . . Beijing outskirts

2. Product(s) . . . Iron and Steel, plus diversified range of products

3. Sales (1992) . . . > 12.6 billion yuan

4. Profit + tax (1992) . . . > 5.2 billion yuan

5. Workforce size (1992) . . . >220 000 aggregate (incl. 120 000 in Beijing area and 60 000 in plant)

6. Employee income (1992) . . . > 5000 yuan

7. Labour contract system . . . Only 10 per cent, mostly newcomers

8. Wage system . . . Performance-related, 16 grades for both workers as staff together

9. Social insurance system . . . Pension and unemployment insurance according to government regulations

10. Training . . . Highly developed from primary to university level

---

It had started to reform its labour and personnel system from 1979 onwards, and after 14 years had promoted its own style of reform.

6.2   DALIAN PORT AUTHORITY

Dalian Port was built in 1898 by the Russians and after 1905 was run by the Japanese. In 1945, the Soviet Army invaded Manchuria and ran its strategic facilities. The Chinese, that is the local Dalian Municipal Government, took it over in 1951. Over forty years later, it comprised 62 berths with a capacity of 60 million tons, accommodating over 200 000 container-units per year.[2] It handles imported grain, chemical fertilizers, manufactured products and so on, as well as exported corn, crude oil, chemicals, etc. These goods were dealt with by eight loading-companies and there were over 25 000 employees in the port authority, of whom four in five were male workers (for a summary, see Figure 6.2). The port, the largest employer in Dalian, is run by the Ministry of Transportation and the City Government, with around 800 administrators in the authority's office. The eight companies work on an 'enterprise contract' basis and these are signed with the DPA. The length of these are discretionary and there are bonuses and penalties, depending on profits or losses. The Authority describe its activities as follows:

Figure 6.2   Case Study No.2: Dalian Port Authority. Summary

1.	Location . . . Dalian centre and outskirts
2.	Product(s) . . . Goods-handling; 62 berths
3.	Sales (1992) . . . n.a. (Value of 60 million tons)
4.	Profit + tax (1992) . . . n.a.
5.	Workforce size (1992) . . . > 25 000
6.	Employee income (1992) . . . > 3600 yuan
7.	Labour contract system . . . 100 per cent of employees claimed to be covered
8.	Wage system . . . Basic, period of service, welfare plus bonus
9.	Social insurance system . . . Pensions paid by DPA; unemployment insurance comes out of profits
10.	Training . . . Technical school on-site

The port has 62 production berths with comprehensive ability, complete facilities and fully equipped machinery. It handles the loading and discharging of crude oil, refined oil, minerals, coal, timber, grain, containers, complete sets of equipment and other sundry goods. At the same time, the duty-free warehouse and services like replenishing oil and fresh water, tally and ship repair, washing-holds and container-repairing are all available in the port. All kinds of foreign trade institutions, the Ocean Shipping Agency, Seamen's Club and Friendship Store are all close to the port providing excellent services for both domestic and foreign businessmen and ships calling at the port. (Company brochure, 1993, p.1)

A new port was under construction in Dayao bay, a location only six kilometres away from Dalian Economic Development Zone, listed as one of the four main deep-water international transit ports in China. The four berths of the first phase project were completed by 1992, with a further six berths to be built after that. The overall plan of the port was to build 20 berths, by which time, the handling facilities of the port would be greatly increased.

6.3   DALIAN LOCOMOTIVE AND ROLLING-STOCK WORKS

Dalian Locomotive and Rolling-Stock Works is a long-established enterprise, set up by the Russians in 1901. From 1905 to 1945, it was run

Figure 6.3   Case Study No.3: Dalian Locomotive and Rolling-Stock Works. Summary

1.	Location . . . Dalian suburbs
2.	Product(s) . . .Locomotives and rolling-stock
3.	Sales (1992) . . . > 500 million yuan
4.	Profit + tax (1992) . . . > 60 million yuan
5.	Workforce size (1992) . . . > 12 000
6.	Employee income (1992) . . . > 3800 yuan
7.	Labour contract system . . . Newcomers only, since 1990
8.	Wage system . . . Post, skills, service plus bonus
9.	Social insurance system . . . As per government regulations
10.	Training . . . Training department

by the Japanese as a repair works. After the Liberation, it became the biggest producer of locomotives and rolling-stock in the PRC, making over 50 per cent of total production, and is controlled by the Ministry of Transportation. In 1992 it made over 200 locomotives and 1800 rolling-stock per year. Its turnover then was over 500 million yuan, with profits plus tax of around 60 million yuan. There were over 12 000 employees on the payroll, in 23 workshops, with 70 per cent of components produced in-house (for a summary, see Figure 6.3). It had the normal state enterprise welfare infrastructure of crèches, hospitals and so on, with a middle, high and technical school.

Affiliated with China National Railway Locomotive and Rolling-Stock Industry Corporation, the Dalian Works is the largest locomotive manufacturer in China, with approximately half of the locomotive fleet in use on Chinese railways produced there. It extends over an area of 93.76 hectares and includes 4355 various machines in 23 workshops including foundry, welding, machining and assembly shops. During the 10 years from 1954 to 1964, the Works designed and produced 10 types of steam locomotives. It began to produce diesel locomotives in 1964, and to the present time has developed more than 10 types of locomotives, (including DR, DF3, DF4, DF5, DF6 and DF10 models) and produced more than 3000 diesel locomotives of various classes of horsepower and multiple uses. In addition, the Works has designed and produced more than 40 types of railway cars.

Figure 6.4   Case Study No.4: Dalian Shipyard. Summary

---

1. Location . . . Dalian central

2. Product(s) . . . Merchant ships, oil tankers, etc.

3. Sales (1992) . . . > 45 million yuan

4. Profit + tax (1992) . . . > 6 million yuan

5. Workforce size (1992) . . . > 17 000

6. Employee income (1992) . . . > 4700 yuan

7. Labour contract system . . . > 20 per cent, mostly newcomers since 1984

8. Wage system . . . Post, skill, efficiency, years of service plus bonus

9. Social insurance system . . . As per government regulations

10. Training . . . Cited as model for PRC: devotes 14 per cent of total revenue

---

Dalian Locomotive and Rolling-Stock Works employed 1045 various technical employees, including 273 senior engineers and 721 engineers in 1993. In conformity with its management strategy, summed-up as 'basing itself on technology and winning by quality', the Works pays much attention to enhancing its technical level and adopting new techniques. In addition to the special-purpose and high-efficiency automated equipment produced in-house by its own engineering employees, the Works has also introduced machines and high precision instruments imported from the United States, Germany, Britain, Switzerland, Sweden and Japan (company brochure, 1993, p.2).

6.4   DALIAN SHIPYARD

The original company out of which the contemporary Dalian Shipyard emerged was set up by the Russians in 1898, taken over subsequently by the Japanese in 1905 and after the Liberation became a Chinese state enterprise. In the 1980s, it underwent restructuring during the economic reforms, and most of the workshops were divided from the main yard. In 1984, it had around 17 000 employees, but the work-force is now reduced somewhat.[4] In 1990, the enterprise was divided into two parts, an old one with over 10 000 employees and a new one with over 4500. Its fixed assets in 1992 were approximately 0.28 billion yuan, its turnover around 45 million yuan, and its total profits and tax over 6 million yuan (for a summary, see Figure 6.4). As a result of the reforms, it had to respond to market forces and consequently offer a higher quality product. Its management were given greater autonomy, not the least in the area of labour and personnel.

The enterprise describes its activities as follows:

> With a long history and rich in experience, Dalian Shipyard is now one of the most important shipbuilding enterprises and the main export-base of the China State Shipbuilding Corporation (CSSC), and is the first yard authorized with the privilege of independent foreign trading. Dalian Shipyard is experienced in building, repairing and converting merchant and naval ships of various types and sizes as well as offshore structures in compliance with the rules of major classification societies such as ZC, LR, DnV, ABSm GL, NK and relevant international regulations and standards. (Company brochure, 1993, p.1)

The Shipyard has contracts to build, repair and convert various kinds of ships, marine equipments, offshore platforms and modules and their accessory equipments; as well as to manufacture electrical and mechanical installations and large equipment used in civil engineering, petrochemical, energy, transportation and metallurgical industries, and associated projects. It offers packages for the design, installation, supply and service of such projects, as well as technical consultation services.

6.5   HARBIN PHARMACEUTICAL FACTORY

Unlike most of the other state enterprises studied here, Harbin Pharmaceuticals is a relatively recent establishment. Set up in 1958, producing a restricted range of products on a small scale, it is now a leader in its field with over 5000 employees (about half women) and one of the top four such firms in China (for a useful comparison on a similar company, Northeast General Pharmaceuticals, see Thomas 1993, p.51). It was one of the first firms to issue shares (in 1990 to the value of over 100 million yuan) with most held by the state, and some held by the managers and employees (less than 10 per cent). In 1992, its turnover was over 500 million yuan, with profits and tax of 38 million yuan (see Figure 6.5). Having introduced the 'comprehensive' reforms in 1990, the company left the Bureau of Pharmaceuticals to set itself up as an industrial grouping, and the enterprise had became part of this.[5]

One of the key enterprises in China and also the largest production base of semi-finished antibiotics in Heilongjiang Province, Harbin Pharmaceuticals covers an area of 420 000 square metres, with a building

Figure 6.5   Case Study No.5: Harbin Pharmaceuticals. Summary

```
1.   Location . . . Harbin outskirts
2.   Product(s) . . . Various: penicillin, amphicillin, etc.
3.   Sales (1992) . . . > 500 million yuan
4.   Profit + tax (1992) . . . > 38 million yuan
5.   Workforce size (1992) . . . > 5000
6.   Employee income (1992) . . . > 3800 yuan
7.   Labour contract system . . . 100 per cent described as on contracts
8.   Wage system . . . Post, skill, service plus bonus
9.   Social insurance system . . . As per government regulations
10.  Training . . . Technical school on-site
```

area occupying 140 000 square metres and over 5000 staff and workers. It has ten production workshops, a quality-inspection centre, a pharmaceutical research institute and a power station with a capacity of 12 000 kilowatts. Its main products include semi-synthetic antibiotics and cephalosporin, as well as injection and capsules. These have won BP 80 and USPXX awards and enjoy high prestige on domestic the market. It has also exported to countries in Western Europe, North America and South-East Asia. (Company brochure, 1993, p.1)

6.6   HARBIN POWER EQUIPMENT COMPANY

Set up in 1959, Harbin Power Equipment Company originally started making components, but now makes full systems, with over 1300 employees.[6] Its turnover was around 20 million yuan in 1992, with neither profit nor loss (subsequently expected to be in credit to the tune of one million yuan on turnover of over 35 million yuan). In 1992 the average worker's income was around 3200 yuan per year, expected to rise to over 4000 in 1993 (see Figure 6.6). Harbin Power Equipment is part of a broader grouping, namely Heilongjiang's Electricity Industrial Bureau. It is also a key manufacturing firm certified by the Electricity Industry Ministry for high-temperature and high-pressure valves. Of the 1300 employees in 1993, 146 were experts, five senior engineers; 62 engineers, and 10 technicians. It has 30 million yuan fixed assets and 380 sets of machinery, of which 245 are main manufacturing facilities. There are

Figure 6.6   Case Study No.6: Harbin Power Equipment. Summary

---

1. Location . . . Harbin outskirts

2. Product(s) . . . Power equipment, transformers and compressors

3. Sales (1992) . . . > 20 million yuan

4. Profit + tax (1992) . . . Neither profit nor loss

5. Workforce size (1992) . . . > 1300

6. Employee income (1992) . . . > 3200 yuan

7. Labour contract system . . . 100 per cent of employees covered

8. Wage system . . . Partial post plus skills system

9. Social insurance system . . . Covered by local Power Equipment Bureau

10. Training . . . As above, plus own training department

---

three main product-categories: high-temperature and high-pressure valves, pressure containers, and coal loading/unloading equipment for power station. (see Company brochure, 1993, p.1)

6.7   SHENYANG AREA: ANSHAN IRON AND STEEL COMPANY

The Anshan Iron and Steel Company (the *Angang* Corporation) is one of the largest companies of its kind in China. It was set up in 1919 by the Japanese but was not a steel producer at that time. In October 1949 it took on its new name, the Anshan Steel Complex. Today, it is an integrated steel company, from the extraction of iron ore to finished production. It dominates the city of over one million people, with 109 plants, 90 per cent in Anshan, about one hour's drive from Shenyang. It has over 220 000 employees and a capacity of around 8.6 million tons of steel.

Steel is in very short supply in China: Anshan produces a wide range of products to meet these needs, including steel for construction, railways, and so on. It has a steel capacity of 8.6 million tons, for pig-iron 8.4 million tons and for steel plant 6.6 million tons (1992 figures). Its turnover in 1992 was over 20 billion yuan, with profits and tax about 20 per cent of that figure, and fixed assets valued at around 20 billion yuan (see Figure 6.7). Among the top enterprises in China in turnover and profitability, it described its technical activities as follows:

The AISC is rich in technical expertise and has comprehensive scientific and technical research facilities. They include the Design and Research Institute, the Iron and Steel Research Institute, the Mining Design Institute, the Automation Research Institute, the Environmental Protection Research Institute, the Machine-Building Research Institute, the Refractories Research Institute, the Information Research Institute, and the Economic Research Institute. (Company brochure, 1993, p.3)

The Anshan complex produced around 25 million tonnes of iron ore, 7.8 million tonnes of iron, 8 million tonnes of steel and 5.6 million tonnes of rolled products in 1992. It also makes rolled products of over 600 grades and more than 20 000 sizes, and serves over 30 industries such as metallurgy, coal, hydro-electricity, railways, construction, electronics, aviation, space industry, light industry, etc. Many of the products are exported to over 20 countries including Australia, Japan, Thailand, and the United States.

Of the 220 000 employees in 1993, over 40 000 are cadres (including 26 000 engineers and technicians). Since the enterprise-reforms, the company is free to select its workers by public entry-examinations, but had previously often recruited from the offspring of existing employees since Anshan was in many ways a 'company town'.[7] This practice of occupational inheritance (*dingti*) was discontinued in 1984. Anshan Iron and Steel was also selected as one of the 20 state enterprises studied in the earlier World Bank/CASS study of the reforms (see Tidrick and Chen, 1987, ch.1).

Figure 6.7   Case Study No. 7: Shenyang Area/Anshan Iron and Steel. Summary

1. Location ... Anshan city, 60 miles from Shenyang
2. Product(s) ... Iron & steel and associated products
3. Sales (1992) ... > 20 billion yuan
4. Profit + tax (1992) ... > 2 billion yuan
5. Workforce size (1992) ... > 220 000 employees
6. Employee income (1992) ... > 4200 yuan
7. Labour contract system ... < 10 per cent, mostly newcomers
8. Wage system ... Post, skills, efficiency, service plus bonus
9. Social insurance system ... Highly developed, from primary to university level
10. Training ... Highly developed, from primary to university level

6.8   SHENYANG GOLD CUP AUTO CORPORATION

Gold Cup (*Jin Bei*) Auto Corporation was set up in 1984 in its modern form, although the original factory dated from 1949 (its earlier years are described in Thomas, 1993, p.50) and as one of the eight largest such enterprises of its kind in China (there were 19 in the country as a whole). Its total production in 1992 was 41 000 units. It had over 29 000 employees and its turnover was 3.6 billion yuan, with 300 million yuan profit. It was founded as a corporation in 1988; and became the first limited company in China.[8] Before it became a group enterprise, it was state-owned and known as the Shenyang Auto Company.

By 1993, Gold Cup's products included light trucks and transit vehicles, based on KDK from Toyota of Japan (10 000 p.a.); one to two-ton trucks (30 000 p.a.), one model developed by themselves and another based on Japanese parts; and a one-ton truck (51 000 p.a.) in collaboration with General Motors. (There had, however, been no joint venture agreements with either Toyota or GM.) The enterprise comprised 19 production factories, with light trucks made in one and another producing the GM-sourced trucks, with the rest of the 17 producing parts for the former two. The total of 39 000 employees breaks down into over 6300 managers and professionals, around 2600 engineers and technicians, with the rest production workers (see Figure 6.8).

Figure 6.8   Case Study No.8: Shenyang Gold Cup (*Jin Bei*) Auto Corporation. Summary

1. Location . . . Shenyang: various sites
2. Product(s) . . . Small vans and commercial vehicles
3. Sales (1992) . . . 3.6 billion yuan
4. Profit + tax (1992) . . . 300 million yuan
5. Workforce size (1992) . . . > 39 000
6. Employee income (1992) . . . > 3800 yuan
7. Labour contract system . . . 100 per cent of employees said to be covered
8. Wage system . . . Workers on basic and hourly rates plus bonus; cadres on 'post plus skills' system
9. Social insurance system . . . As per government regulations
10. Training . . . Local plus other sent to Japan, plus TQM training

Since the reforms, the Corporation had been organized as a core Headquarters Centre, plus myriad branches in which each enterprise manager has a high degree of autonomy, replicated at factory-level. In 1988, the reform of leasing state-owned and collective enterprises was introduced. The enterprise contract-system was the first of its kind in China, and the share-ownership system was introduced. Both managers and workers could be rewarded if profits rose. Basic income rose as targets were fulfilled and increments could be paid if targets were overfulfilled.

There was no currently available company brochure of its activities or products in English.

6.9   SHENYANG SMELTING WORKS

Shenyang Smelting Works was founded in 1936 by the Japanese and is today run by the Ministry of Metallurgy. It is one of the biggest plants of its kind in China. Among its products are copper, zinc and gold. The quality of its non-ferrous metals is well known all over China. It employed over 7000 workers and had annual sales of over 1.2 billion yuan in 1992, with profits and tax of over 100 million yuan (see Figure 6.9). Before the economic reforms the company produced everything according to the State plan; it now have to respond to the market. It earned over 30 million US dollars in foreign exchange, the second largest in Shenyang.

Figure 6.9   Case Study No.9: Shenyang Smelting Works. Summary

```
┌─────────────────────────────────────────────────────────────────────┐
│                                                                     │
│    1.  Location . . . Shenyang Industrial District                  │
│                                                                     │
│    2.  Product(s) . . . Non-ferrous plus precious metals            │
│                                                                     │
│    3.  Sales (1992) . . . > 1.2 billion yuan                        │
│                                                                     │
│    4.  Profit + tax (1992) . . . > 100 million yuan                 │
│                                                                     │
│    5.  Workforce size (1992) . . . > 7000                           │
│                                                                     │
│    6.  Employee income (1992) . . . > 3700 yuan                     │
│                                                                     │
│    7.  Labour contract system . . . Almost 100 per cent of employees covered │
│                                                                     │
│    8.  Wage system . . . Post, skills, efficiency, service plus bonus │
│                                                                     │
│    9.  Social insurance system . . . As per government regulations  │
│                                                                     │
│   10.  Training . . . Technical school on-site                      │
│                                                                     │
└─────────────────────────────────────────────────────────────────────┘
```

The company describes its activities as follows: It has six production systems dealing with copper, lead, zinc, gold and silver, sulphuric acid, semiconductor materials and high purity metals. The total output of these combined reaches around 260 000 tons per annum. Its lead ingot and zinc ingot products have won national gold medals, and electrolytic copper the national silver medal. In addition, the other 19 kinds of products such as gold and silver are rated as high quality. It describes itself as follows:

> Shenyang Smelting possesses strong technical capabilities, excellent scientific research equipment and advanced assay and measurement. . . . [It] is willing to provide all kinds of technical service and supply a variety of products of high quality, according to the demand of customers both at home and abroad. (Company brochure, 1993, p.1)

Shenyang Smelting was another of the 20 enterprises selected by the earlier study of China's industrial reforms carried out by the World Bank/CASS research team (see Tidrick and Chen 1987, ch.1).[9]

6.10   SHENYANG TRANSFORMER WORKS

Shenyang Transformer Works was established in 1938 by the Japanese. It started as a repair shop, but gradually emerged as a principal producer of transformers after the Liberation. It had over 12 500 employees (including 1000 engineers) of whom around 8500 are state employees and 4000 work for collective enterprises in the group, with a turnover of over 500 million yuan in 1992 and profits and tax of approximately 40 million yuan. It is the biggest producer of transformers in China, contributing over 50 per cent of total national production (for a summary, see Figure 6.10). The company brochure described its activities as follows:

> Shenyang Transformer Works – the largest and most famous professional manufacturer with fifty years experience in China – mainly produces EHV transformers, EHV instrument transformers, all kinds of special transformers and reactors which have served well domestically as well as over 32 countries and regions in the world. (Company brochure, 1993, p.2)

The enterprise was one of 12 which were selected to carry out the 'comprehensive' labour reforms.[10] It had also reduced its workforce by

Figure 6.10   Case Study No.10: Shenyang Transformer Works. Summary

---

1. Location . . . Shenyang Industrial District

2. Product(s) . . . Transformers and related products

3. Sales (1992) . . . 500 million yuan

4. Profit + tax . . . (1992) 40 million yuan

5. Workforce size (1992) . . . > 12 500

6. Employee income (1992) . . . > 4500 yuan

7. Labour contract system . . . 100 per cent of employees covered

8. Wage system . . . 10 grade 'post' system plus bonus

9. Social insurance system . . . As per government regulations

10. Training . . . Via training department

600–700 employees who had been found jobs in the service sector, or who had taken early retirement.

6.11   CONCLUDING REMARKS

The 'sample' has depicted the 'leading-edge' reform enterprises in the region, with a balance of older and newer sites. We can, however, contrast it with Tidrick and Chen's observation (1987, p.19) when discussing their own CASS/World Bank 'sample' that the enterprises were 'typical of Chinese enterprises in that they were only partly reformed' (in the early 1980s) in that the firms in the present investigation were now further along the reform path by a considerable degree. We now move on in Chapter 7, to discuss the 'three systems' reforms in greater detail.

7 The 'Three Systems' Reforms

7.1 LABOUR AND PERSONNEL REFORMS

This chapter deals in detail with the implementation of the *'three-systems reforms'* (*san xiang zhidu gaige*) in the mostly North-East state-owned enterprises investigated. It describes, for example, the reform of *labour contracts* (*laodong renshi zhidu gaige*), how many employees were covered and so on. We then examine changes in the *wages system and rewards* (*gongzi fanpei zhidu gaige*) to employees. The section also deals with *promotions* (and *dismissals*) as well as *training* and the role of the trade unions and Workers' Congress in the reform process. Lastly, we turn to the changes in *welfare benefits* and the implementation of a *social insurance reform* (*shehui baoxian zhidu gaige*).

7.1.1 Beijing Capital Iron and Steel

The labour contract system in Capital Iron and Steel is (rather surprisingly) not very extensively developed; only 10 per cent of the employees have such contracts and these only newcomers.[1] The view of the Personnel Department was that the new system was 'not a good idea' because there was no proper social insurance yet in China and the new labour laws were not fully implemented. When there was such insurance, they would change but are 'not in a hurry'. They claimed that they never hindered people from leaving their job to work elsewhere. They have fired people but very few. The company policy according to the Personnel Department was to make the workers feel they were 'masters of the country' (Interviews, Capital Iron and Steel Corporation, August 1993).

In order to implement the labour and personnel reforms, the use of formal examinations in Capital Steel was extensive and it was claimed that this system was company-specific. There was an Examinations Committee which recommended employees to be promoted or demoted, based on their opinions of employees' abilities after interviewing and their exam results. Individuals could not be either promoted or demoted, or dismissed, 'by their boss alone'. The Chairman of the committee was elected by the Workers' Congress, and the other members elected from the different departments involved. Anybody could apply to the committee to change their job or apply for a specific position.

Labour-management relations in Capital Iron and Steel had its distinct part to play in the implementation of the labour reforms. The Workers' Congress met once a year to review last year's performance and to discuss the coming year's plans. In between, every section had to report to the General Manager, who was formally elected by the Congress. The trade unions were described as 'active' in supervising the work of the different departments. The grievance-channel was, first, to the trade union; second, to the 'Supervisory Committee'– set up 'like a court to hear workers' complaints' including those regarding contracts, with the same membership as the Examinations Committee; third, directly to the General Manager.

7.1.2 Dalian Port Authority

Every employee of the Dalian Port Authority signs a labour contract and these range from one to ten years. They are normally of three kinds: one-year; five-year; ten-year. The contracts depend on the 'posts' or positions filled by the employee. They do not say anything about payments, which is somewhat unusual. The rewards are now based on individual responsibilities.[2]

Since the economic reforms, the labour force has been reduced by a modest number (less than 5 per cent). The loading companies have autonomy to fire only if workers are in serious breach of discipline. There is one trade union for the whole DPA, with each of the eight loading companies having its own branch vetting the implementation of the 'three systems reforms'. The port-wide Workers' Congress meets every two years, but each company has its own congress which meets when needed, as in the case of the labour contract's formal approval. Managers have some discretion *vis-à-vis* hiring from the labour-market but are not free to decide basic wage-levels. If they wish to increase wages, they have to seek the approval of the City Government. However, bonuses depend entirely on profits generated by the company. Profits are also a source of funds for unemployment insurance. Pensions are paid by the DPA and are between 75 and 100 per cent of former basic wages. The Authority has its own training-school, requiring three years', study before work, and recruits around 100 university graduates per year.

7.1.3 Dalian Locomotive and Rolling-Stock Works

In 1990, Dalian Locomotive and Rolling-Stock introduced the labour contract system for newcomers, including university graduates. Older workers remained under the previous arrangements.[3] The renewable contract specifies the mutual responsibilities of the enterprise, period of employment (usually three years) and so on. The worker is free to leave after the contract expires, but few do. The enterprise also signs a contract with the Ministry, concerning profits, wages and productivity.

Personnel reforms had been relatively extensively implemented in Dalian Rolling-Stock. The company was free to hire as it saw fit. It mainly recruited new workers from its own technical school or from the labour market, the numbers depending on how many retired. Apprenticeships varied in duration depending on the technology; if unskilled, it was one year, with wages of at least 100 yuan per month. The rules on dismissal were as elsewhere, for example on breaches of labour discipline. The role of the trade unions in the implementation of the reform was mentioned only briefly here and its main work involved joint consultation on production plans and welfare. The Workers' Congress met three or four times a year.

Promotion for technician or engineer rank now strictly depended on examination and other achievements like developing material-saving technologies or new technologies. For cadres, promotion hinged on introducing significant improvement in the organization of their departments, and workers were upgraded according to the state regulations. Training with the new system was via a special department of the enterprise. In the case of newcomers, they were trained before they started work; others were trained on-the-job, and if they wanted to broaden their studies, they could take outside classes.

7.1.4 Dalian Shipyard

Two types of employment coexist in the shipyard. Workers recruited under the older system have fixed employment status, but after 1984 newcomers had to sign labour contracts as elsewhere. These could be ten-year, between three and ten years, and under three. Over 2000 workers have contracts, and around 8000 have fixed status. The goal was to have 'all-round' contract reform by 1995, with everyone under the same, that is, the new system, covering responsibilities, duration of contract, rewards, sanctions and so on.

The personnel system in Dalian Shipyard had been reformed but recruitment was not yet drawn from the labour market. They had their own technical school, recruiting middle-school leavers for two or three years of study combined with an apprenticeship system. The latter lasted up to three years' duration, with half a year probation, but this was not needed if the young workers had attained level-three technician grade. There were over 2000 professionally qualified staff in the yard and around 100 university graduates were hired each year as trainees. Promotion for cadres was now through an appraisal committee, consulting their peers; for assistant engineers, there was an examination and appraisal; for workers, examinations and review of work performance. Dismissals were few and according to state regulations, for example for unauthorized absence greater than two weeks, or running their own business on the side.[4]

The role of the trade union and Workers' Congress in Dalian Shipyard was assumed to be a formality in the implementation of the latest reforms. The state regulations specified the union's role as consultative in decision-making. It had been involved in the approval of systems reforms, as well as in traditional areas such as welfare and leisure, as well as labour protection. It also helped in discussions of production-levels and promotions. There were two meetings of the Workers' Congress, one to review last year's progress and the plan for the coming year, with the second one to monitor the half-yearly achievements of the enterprise (Interviews, Dalian Shipyard, August 1993).

As part and parcel of the reform-package, training in the shipyard was well supported, with over two million yuan spent on it in 1992. State policy was to invest up to 14 per cent annually in this area of human resource development. Cadre and professional training depended on the level of technology and the products made. Workers received initial training in the technical school and at the apprenticeship stage, with in-post training. If higher-level preparation was needed, outside courses were used to enhance theoretical knowledge as well as advanced techniques. The company was regarded as a 'model' for training and education practices in China.

7.1.5   Harbin Pharmaceuticals

Personnel reforms were recently introduced in Harbin Pharmaceuticals and all employees were on contracts, even the directors. As the enterprise was expanding, it needed another 800 workers, a clear contrast with most other state firms.[5] The contracts covered the required items such as labour protection, responsibilities of workers, duration of contract, wages and so on. There was a standard contract as approved by the local labour bureau.

Promotion was based on achievement, skill, and attitude. Dismissals criteria were on the lines described for other state firms.

Fringe-benefits were still an important factor in remuneration, with housing, education, health and welfare covered. Rents were very cheap, still less than one per cent of workers' incomes. All levels of schools were provided from kindergarten to technical level. The Director said his job was 'like that of running a small city'.

Training was well provided for in a company with a highly trained workforce (about 15 per cent were professionals and technicians). Workers were trained in their own technical school and about one in three attended courses there. Cadres and technicians underwent periodic retraining. There were no apprenticeships, but 40–50 new trainees were recruited each year. (Interviews, Harbin Pharmaceutical Works, August 1993)

7.1.6   Harbin Power Equipment

The new 'comprehensive' reforms were introduced in Harbin Power Equipment in 1991. Income-distribution was now to be linked to profitability. All employees were now on contracts. State employees were on five to ten-year contracts (and could move to other such enterprises), state contract workers were on one-year arrangements and temporary contract workers were on a six-month to one-year basis. There were separate contracts for cadres and workers, but university graduates had to sign up too. Promotion for cadres depended on educational, achievement and attitude; for workers, level of output, quality of work, discipline and training were important. Dismissals followed a probationary period if there was a breach of labour discipline. In 1992, only nine workers were dismissed.

The role of the trade unions and Workers' Congress in Harbin Power Equipment was emphasized relatively more sharply than elsewhere.[6] There were frequent 'model worker' and 'emulation' schemes organized by the trade union which also was active in soliciting ideas for productivity improvements. The Workers' Congress met regularly four times a year to discuss important decisions such as the system reforms, income distribution and dismissals. The Party Secretary was also the Factory Director, described as 'combining the party and leadership as one' (Interviews, Harbin Power Equipment Factory, August 1993).

7.1.7   Shenyang Area: Anshan Iron and Steel

Limited implementation of the labour contract system was apparent. Older workers did not need contracts, it was said, but most newcomers had to have them.[7] About 2000 contracts a year were offered. About one in ten workers were on a contract, although the 1500 or so graduates hired a year did not require them. The contracts covered the customary areas such as responsibilities, rewards and benefits, social insurance and so on. Anshan Iron and Steel now had greater power to fire workers for matters like disobeying safety regulations, absences and damage to plant or materials. In the final analysis, very few were fired: most were 're-educated' and 're-employed'. In 1992, a policy of labour reorganization was introduced with the goal of an overall cut of 20 per cent in the workforce and 40 per cent of administrative staff. Two out of ten workers have been made redundant in several steel plants, but most were said to have found new jobs in the service sector.

Anshan Iron and Steel has extensive training facilities with a Deputy Director in charge of the Training Department. Its activities are broken down into technical, vocational, cadre and worker training. It has its own Industrial College, Medical School, Metallurgical Cadre School, Steel Technical School, Vocational and High School. Elementary education is however the responsibility of the municipality. University graduates mostly obtain on-the-job training in their first year on production sites.

7.1.8   Shenyang Gold Cup (*Jin Bei*) Auto Company

All employees of the Gold Cup Auto enterprises were now on contracts, including university graduates. The company contract covered:

1. length of employment period
2. wages and salaries
3. responsibilities of the job
4. termination of contract
5. welfare arrangements, such as housing, education, medical, etc.

With the reforms, several benefits will be paid for by the state rather than the company, such as pensions and in due course, medical care. In Gold Cup Auto, very few workers had been dismissed or made redundant. They were reluctant to fire people because of the difficulty they would have finding other jobs. However, contravention of production operations regulations constituted definite grounds for dismissal.

The company had an automotive design college and a technical school (in collaboration with their Japanese partners). Employees were also sent to Japan to Toyota or Isuzu for technical training. If retraining was needed, workers could be released to study foreign languages or accountancy, externally.

Gold Cup had been linked with Toyota since 1988 in the use of Japanese technology. Japanese technicians had been invited over to train Chinese workers to use Toyota's production management methods, including just-in-time techniques and *Kanban*.[8] Each production line has three technicians in charge of quality control. Quality-Circles are also used: 'they are not just a slogan on the wall'. At the beginning, Gold Cup employees were reluctant to adopt such methods, especially in the personnel field, but later acceptance became more general, 'after training and persuasion'. Similarly, joint training efforts were carried out with General Motors. (Interviews, Shenyang Gold Cup Auto Company, August 1993)

7.1.9 Shenyang Smelting Works

Almost all the workers and cadres at Shenyang Smelting Works were now on contracts; only a small percentage transferred from the army were on temporary arrangements. Selection was based on an entrance examination and interviews. Successful workers were offered a contract, detailing its duration (normally two years), the terms of employment, nature of the job, salary and conditions of work, and so on. If employees' performance was satisfactory, the contracts were renewed. Problems were said to arise only in 0.3 to 0.5 per cent of cases.

The enterprise employed more than 7000 employees (of which 63 per cent were production workers and 21 per cent were cadres) in 1993. The General Manager was appointed by the Ministry of Metallurgy, but the employees were able to have their say and voted to approve the choice. He then selected the Deputy General Managers. Technicians need a higher degree; if they do not work hard they can be engineers but do not get promoted to senior engineer rank. Annual assessments are made for promotion and salary increases. Senior-level engineers need a degree and five years' professional experience. Promotion at professional level has to be approved by the Ministry. Apart from a professional exam, they also need to pass one in a foreign language. Middle-level engineers need to have a degree and around four years' lower management experience. The enterprise has the freedom to promote at this level. Lower-level engineer appointments for assistant engineer require a degree plus one year's experience or technical-school qualifications plus four years' experience in order to seek promotion to middle-level posts. Under the new arrangements, the group-leaders selected the best eight of each level of workers for promotion each year; a similar system applied to cadres.

Since the beginning of 1992, over 30 per cent of the workforce had been displaced. Most of these had gone into the service industries, retired, taken early retirement or suffered poor health. Around 350 had been put on a retraining programme. For the first three months, they received 100 per cent of the previous salary, then for the next three months 75 per cent, and after that 75 yuan per month.[9] If they performed well, they could replace a non-performing worker. In 1986, the new policy on enterprise autonomy, it was claimed, gave managers in Shenyang Smelting greater freedom to fire workers. The following grounds were cited as causes for dismissal:

1. breaches of labour discipline
2. contravention of operating regulations
3. poor performance
4. rejection of job-transfer
5. corruption and theft
6. bad behaviour.

The State lays down the overall regulations regarding dismissals, but each enterprise, it was said, could apply their own version. If they wish to do this, they must discuss it with the trade unions and send their reasons in writing to them. If personnel are fairly dismissed, they must be paid social insurance. If the worker disagrees with the grounds for dismissal, the matter can go to arbitration. Specific reasons for dismissal at Shenyang Smelting included:

1. lateness, more than five times per month
2. unauthorized absence, greater than ten days continuously
3. unfinished work, more than three months
4. accepting transfer, not taking-up within five days
5. 'moonlighting' if on sick-leave
6. disregarding superiors, such as group-leader
7. drinking at work
8. wasting materials greater than 1000 yuan in value
9. poor quality of work
10. corruption.

Training in Shenyang Smelting was principally carried out in their own Technicians' School, or on-the-job working under a Master. Senior engineers in the firm would also provide lectures. If the trainees did not pass the appropriate exam, they were not allowed to do the job. If they passed, they could move to the higher grade. Every worker had to take such exams and the results were filed in case of possible later promotion (Interviews, July-August 1993).

7.1.10 Shenyang Transformer Works

Every employee in Shenyang Transformers had a labour contract, of varying length. Engineers held five or ten-year contracts. Cadres might not be reappointed, and workers could now be made cadres. Contracts had to specify the nature of the job requirements, rewards, conditions of work, welfare, social insurance and so on.

The normal reasons for dismissals were found, such as labour indiscipline and unauthorized absence. If people wanted to leave voluntarily, this was permitted. Some were paid to leave, or found another job. If they could not get another within three weeks, they continued to receive their former salary but without the bonus. After a year, they would be paid 70 per cent of this base.[10]

7.2 WAGE SYSTEM REFORM

This section deals with the wage-system reforms introduced in the early 1990s (for background see Howe, 1973 and Takahara, 1992). It examines how far the old grade system has been replaced by a more flexible, efficiency-based one, and the weighting factors like *post* (responsibilities) and *skills* in their new mix (*gongzi fenpei zhidu gaige*) are balanced with other elements such as individual *bonuses*.[11]

7.2.1 Beijing Capital Iron and Steel

The wage system in Capital Iron and Steel has been reformed since 1985. Rewards became more performance related, so a worker on a given grade could earn more money. Over a third of the workforce were paid on this 'floating' system. If workers performed well they could go up a few grades; if they made mistakes they could be demoted to a lower grade. If they achieved targets, they could get 11 per cent more. Bonuses were related to the worker's monthly performance record, using a points system. They had introduced a unified 16-grade system, with graduates starting on the sixth. The old eight-grade system was phased out in 1984. The new one produced a greater variation in income: if workers worked well, they could be rewarded. If the company made more profits, wages could go up.

Capital Iron and Steel was one of the top ten iron and steel companies in China; in fact, second for profits and third for wages. It did not pay the highest wages in Beijing but its rewards were above the average level for the city. The average annual level of wages in the corporation in 1992 was over 5000 yuan, rising to 7000 in the subsequent year. The wage levels in the other North-East cases are set out in Table 7.1. The national average wage across all sectors of industry was around 2700 yuan per year (with bonuses of 564 yuan) (see Table 7.2). This standard was higher than Anshan Steel, but less than the Shanghai or Wuhan Iron and Steel companies. The wage system set managers' pay at 10 per cent above the average level of incomes, but a production worker could earn more than that if earning danger money and the like. Capital's policy was to break down the barrier between cadres and workers ('workers can be cadres, cadres can be workers' was the slogan invoked). All employees worked on a points system, and could aim to get more than their norm. Examinations were held each year for promotion to a higher grade. Rewards were related to the responsibilities of the post and the individual's performance level.

Table 7.1   Annual average level of wages (including bonuses) in 1992 in the selected case studies (in rank-order of magnitude)

Rank order	Enterprise	Yuan per annum*
1.	Capital Iron and Steel	5000
2.	Dalian Ship Yard	4700
3.	Shenyang Transformers	4500
4.	Anshan Iron and Steel	4200
5.	Dalian Locomotive	3800
5.	Gold Cup Auto	3800
5.	Harbin Pharmaceuticals	3800
8.	Shenyang Smelting	3700
9.	Dalian Port	3600
10.	Harbin Power Equipment	3200

Source: Interviews, summer 1993
*rounded-up to nearest 100 yuan. At the time of the investigation, one US dollar was worth approximately 6 yuan at the tourist rate, and just over 8 yuan at the 'free market' rate. Using the latter, the lowest wage in our sample for example would be worth US$450 per annum, but purchasing power parity estimates have projected the 'true' level at several times this, up to 6 times the nominal value (see Wedley, 1992).

Table 7.2   Wages of staff/workers in Chinese industry (current yuan)

	1978	1992
Average annual wages	615	2710
of which: state enterprises	644	2878
urban collectives	506	2109
others	–	3966
Averages annual bonuses	12	564
Average annual subsidies	neglig.	607

Source: SSB, 1993

7.2.2   Dalian Port Authority

There are eight grades as in the old system, namely:

1. a basic income (of about 200 yuan a month average)
2. an hourly rate
3. a period of service payment
4. a welfare provision (housing, education, etc)
5. a bonus.

The average wage was about 300 yuan a month (1992) – 3600 yuan a year – with cadres said to earn slightly less, by about 50 yuan. (Interviews, Dalian Port Authority, August 1993).

7.2.3   Dalian Locomotive and Rolling-Stock

Wages and conditions in Dalian Locomotive and Rolling-Stock were above the average level for state employees in the city, with average wages plus bonus of over 320 yuan a month, or around 3800 yuan a year in 1993. The old wage grade system has gone. Although special workers were on 1–8 grades, most are on 1–6, with earnings depending on the following factors: *post*; *skills*; *period of service*; *individual bonus*.
    Retirement is normally at 60 for men and 55 for women.

7.2.4 Dalian Shipyard

Wages in Dalian Shipyard were relatively higher than in the previous case. The average annual worker's income in 1992 was around 4700 yuan (around 400 yuan per month), due to profit-related pay. The determination of rewards was linked to the following factors (each month, on average):

1. *post* (70 yuan)
2. *technical skill* (160 yuan)
3. *plant efficiency* (8 yuan)
4. *years of service* (40 yuan)
5. *bonus*, plus extras (up to 800 yuan)

The old eight-grade system was discontinued in mid-1993. The highest salaries (managerial or production workers) were around 1000 yuan per month, although the average directors' pay was reported as in the region of 600 yuan. There was normally a six-day week – less in the warmer summer months.

7.2.5 Harbin Pharmaceuticals

The average wage in Harbin Pharmaceuticals was approximately 3800 yuan per annum, with directors getting up to three times as much. Some production workers could earn more than the latter, however, under the new incentive system (cf. very much lower rewards in Northeast General Pharmaceuticals in 1990 – see Thomas 1993, p.52). The eight-grade wage ladder had gone, and the new one was based on 'post-plus-skills', each carrying an equal weight, with years of service and bonus determining the final level of rewards.

7.2.6 Harbin Power Equipment

The wages system in Harbin Power Equipment was dependent on the 'post-plus-skills' system which was being introduced. Annual wages plus bonus were 3200 yuan a year. The 'post-plus-skills' factor had a 40 per cent loading, with individual productivity having 30 per cent, the residual relating to welfare benefits allocated. The bonus was based on the output of the workshop as a whole. Pensions were contributory, with the individual paying 5 per cent, with a similar sum from the enterprise and again from the Ministry. Employees could retire on 75–80 per cent of their original income. Social insurance was additional and the Bureau of Power Equipment dealt with this.

7.2.7 (Shenyang Area): Anshan Iron and Steel

The economic reforms have seen a closer relation between rewards and performance. Formerly, workers' incomes were set by the Ministry of Metallurgy; after 1988, they had to be related to the efficiency of the steel complex. Enterprises have the autonomy to increase Anshan employees' income by 0.8 per cent for each 1 per cent increase of profits.

Anshan Iron and Steel had adopted its own version of the 'post-plus-skill' rewards system. There were five elements: post, technical skill, enterprise efficiency, years of service and individual bonus. In 1992, the 'post' element ranged from four yuan per month to 40. Technical skills ranged from 47 to 346 yuan per month. An enterprise efficiency bonus ranged from 4 yuan per month for white-collar staff to 40 yuan for blue-collar ones. Years of service varied proportionately. Individual or 'competitive' bonuses were between 35 and 40 yuan per month. The average income per worker was approximately 4200 yuan per annum in 1992 (Interviews, Anshan Iron and Steel Company, August 1993).

7.2.8 Shenyang Gold Cup Auto

The rewards system at Gold Cup for production workers was determined by output and the number of hours worked. The range of wages went from 200 to 1000 RMB a month, with exceptional payments to those involved in 'dirty jobs', like paint-spraying. The average worker's annual income was 3800 yuan for 1992. The cadres were paid on the 'post-plus-skills' basis. There were five post grades (100–150 yuan per month), with 5 grades of skills (100–240 yuan per month) plus an individual bonus (50–100 yuan per month).

Managers' rewards were fixed by the Board of Directors, following the principle of basic salary plus increment. The average basic salary was approximately 800 yuan per month, plus 300 yuan for the General Director for each extra 1 per cent of production (and 280 yuan for the Deputy Director). Previously, these income-levels had been fixed by the State.

7.2.9 Shenyang Smelting Works

The average gross monthly wage in Shenyang Smelting in the first half of 1993 was in the region of 350 yuan including bonuses. In the second half, they were to be allowed to pay more (between 80–100 yuan) if profits rose. The annual average was set to rise to around 5000 yuan (in 1992, it was 3700 yuan). The level of wages was related to levels of efficiency and effort. If profits and tax grew by 1 per cent, wages grew by 0.87 per cent (before 1992). Under the new system, such increases were equally dependent on rises in efficiency, foreign exchange earnings and growth of output. In the metallurgy sector, Shenyang Smelting was only one of three firms with the above system. It had worked successfully since it was introduced, and in 1992 wages in aggregate grew by five million yuan.

Before the economic reforms, they had the old eight-grade system like other large state enterprises. Since 1992, they have had the new 'post-plus-skill' system. However, it also takes into account a further set of factors:

1. *post* – 22 grade-levels, ranging from the bottom at 25 yuan per month to the top at 200 yuan, according to the responsibilities of the job.
2. *technical skills* – 48 levels, the bottom being four yuan per month, the top 550 yuan.
3. *efficiency* – 12 levels, ranging from the bottom at 46 yuan per month to the top at 180 yuan; relates to the gross production level of the plant set by the General Manager and paid equally to everybody (75 yuan in 1992).
4. *years of employment* – paid at one yuan per month for each year of service.
5. *bonus* – 35–40 yuan for direct workers; 30–50 yuan for support staff.
6. *premium* – paid according to such considerations as the hazardous nature of the job, or for nightwork, and can vary.

If workers perform well, they can earn appropriate rewards. Each year, the heads of department select the best ten workers for promotion to a higher level of wages in their department.

Shenyang Smelting has a flexible system of rewards with a higher wage and a lower bonus. In the main workshop, for those under the contract system, the monthly bonus is 35–40 yuan for direct workers and 30–35 yuan for indirects (but only 25 yuan for non-contract workers). The bonus depends on production-levels, quality, costs, etc. If the worker has a second child, or an accident, the bonus is not paid. Workers who perform well, can earn up to 65 yuan. Administrative staff receive the lowest bonus, only seven yuan per month. The minimum of such staff are employed now, since the reforms gave the enterprise the right to slim-down the labour-force.

7.2.10   Shenyang Transformer Works

Wages were based on a ten-grade system for 'post' responsibilities in Shenyang Transformers, with a range of five yuan to 44 yuan, and an average of 20 yuan monthly for this factor in 1993. Cadres' salaries were allocated on eleven grades (actually twelve, but the lowest level was not used). The range of wages was broadly similar to that of salaries, except that the top (General Director) 'post' component of salary was higher. The average overall annual income per capita in the enterprise in 1992 was in the region of 4500 yuan. If profits increased by 1 per cent, workers' incomes could rise by 0.86 per cent. The average bonus in Shenyang Transformers was over 65 yuan per month, but could be as high as 200 yuan, which was higher than in the Smelting Works. The individual bonus depended on performance, such as completing work ahead of schedule.

7.3   SOCIAL INSURANCE REFORM

This section deals with the last element of the 'three systems' reform introduced since 1991. Since the scheme aspires to be national in its coverage, initially starting in the state-owned enterprise sector, we will briefly deal with its nature.

We have outlined earlier the broad characteristics of the social insurance reforms (*shehui baoxian xhidu gaige*) as sketched out by the Beijing, Dalian, Harbin and Shenyang local labour bureaux as applying to those areas. Basically, the national scheme sets out a *macro* framework to replace the *micro* one which previously existed under the iron rice-bowl arrangements in each enterprise and the earlier less comprehensive national scheme. (On the 1951 labour insurance scheme, see section 2.4.)

Between 1978 and 1992, the number of workers covered by a basic level of social insurance nationally rose from 87 to 204 million (involving just under 2 per cent to 5 per cent of national income). This scheme, dating from the 1950s, covered only accidents, illness and pensions. Around 70 million employees in over 430 000 state-owned work units were covered by unemployment insurance in 1993, however 140 million workers outside these are unprotected. Peasants (including 60 million city migrants) are also excluded (see Hussein, 1993).

Unemployment benefit is related to period of service and original wage of the worker. Currently, plans are being discussed to extend the scheme from the state-owned enterprise sector to workers in all factories, as noted earlier. Funds are also available for the unemployed to set up as self-employed or as small businesses. Unemployment insurance benefit was paid to 400 000 persons on a monthly basis in early 1993 (see *Chinese Trade Unions*, April 1993, p.6). This figure almost doubled by early 1994 (see *Beijing Review*, 21 February 1994, p.6).

The new national welfare scheme was outlined as follows:

> The new social security system will free enterprises, especially major
> state-owned ones, from the burden of taking charge of all employees'
> welfare, so that they will be able to participate fairly in market
> competition. The funds for social security will come from mutual
> assistance funds and will be distributed by relevant government
> departments. Mutual assistance funds will come from the state,
> enterprises and employees. An official of the Labour Ministry said that
> the pensions insurance system has already been instituted in the
> overwhelming majority of urban businesses. The nation's funds for old-
> age pensions shared by the state, employers and employees now total
> 30 billion yuan a year ... (*Beijing Review*, 21 February 1994, p.6)

Apart from the national scheme, there are local arrangements. For
example, Beijing initiated a new old-age pension scheme. It covers
workers in state-owned, collective and foreign-funded enterprises in the
city area. Workers there pay up to 2 per cent of their average monthly
wage of the previous year for welfare coverage. To compensate for this
cost, wages will be increased proportionally.

Trade unions in China have for a long time offered mutual-aid insurance,
as elsewhere. This started in the early fifties on a limited scale. More
recently, it covers areas like old age, medical care, childbearing, injuries,
funerals and so on. There were over 40 000 mutual-aid insurance organizations, run by trade unions, involving over 7.6 million people in 1994.

All SOEs in China had joined the new welfare scheme. It is not surprising
therefore that all the enterprises visited reported that they were involved in
the new social insurance system reforms.[12] They continued to pay welfare
benefits and to cover pensions for existing retirees. Contributions to the new
social and unemployment insurance schemes were now to be paid by the
individuals as well as by the enterprise and the state.

Most state-owned enterprises continued to pay welfare benefits as
before (and some examples follow) but on a supplementary basis to the
national arrangements. Pensions and unemployment insurance
contributions were paid, health care and housing were provided as before.
If workers had worked for more than eight years for the company, Capital
Iron and Steel paid all medical bills and invalidity benefit was set at
100 per cent of wages. As Capital Iron and Steel made more profit, it
provided better fringe-benefits than other companies.

There are over 100 000 retired employees dependent on Anshan Steel
(including cadres and workers) receiving benefits from the enterprise,

according to their years of service. Cadres retired at 60; workers at 55 (50 for women). There is a special pensions and welfare department. Part-time work is sometimes offered to retirees. Service companies have been set up to help them, such as 'The Old People's Bus Company', to provide additional income. Retirement in Shenyang Smelting also normally takes place at 60 for men and 55 for women (the state specifies 60 for both but there is a surplus of female employees). If jobs are hazardous, early retirement at 45 is permitted. Before the enterprise reforms, the company could not ask invalids to leave; now they can do so. It is likely that it will take some years before national comprehensive social insurance coverage becomes effective, although plans are in hand for one. (see *Financial Times*, 15 November 1994, p.6)

7.4   CONCLUDING REMARKS

The extent of the comprehensive labour reforms within the cities visited in the investigation, as a proportion of all state enterprises located there, is not as yet great in absolute numbers covered, but it is relatively important in terms of the total number of *large* state firms in the North-East. The pilot enterprises play a key role in the economies of the cities in question and constitute role-models for weaker economic entities. In that sense, the reforms were critical cases.

The main features of the sample of enterprises can be seen at a glance in Table 7.3. Although there was a *pre-selected* group of enterprises chosen by myself and those social scientists who collaborated with the research investigation via CASS, they also were well known locally as at the 'leading-edge' of the enterprise reforms.

The variation in *age* of the organizations was interesting. Four were founded pre-1914 by the Russians and then run by the Japanese in the North-East, two by the Japanese in the 1930s; and four after the Liberation, in the late 1940s or in the 1950s. They were all, therefore, well-established organizational entities, with the 'iron rice-bowl' well institutionalized.

All the enterprises investigated were *state-owned* and were previously either run directly by Ministries or Bureaux. Even today, one of them, Harbin Power Equipment was still formally under provincial-level Industrial Bureau direction. Dalian Port was run by the Ministry of Transportation and the city government. Otherwise the others were corporations or parts of similar groupings.

Although a high proportion of state enterprises made a loss – four out of every ten, it was claimed, in Shenyang – most of the sample made a profit.

Table 7.3   Summary of case studies

Case study No. Enterprise	1 Shougang, Beijing	2 Dalian Port	3 Dalian Locomotive & Rolling Stock	4 Dalian Shipyard	5 Harbin Pharmaceuticals	6 Harbin Power	7 Angang Anshan	8 Goldcup Auto	9 Shenyang Smelting	10 Shenyang Transformers
Product(s)	Iron & steel	Goods-handling	Rolling-stock	Tankers, etc.	Penicillin, etc.	Transformers, etc.	Iron & steel	Auto	Non-ferrous metals	Transformers
Sales (yuan) (1992)	12.6bn	60m tons	0.5bn	45m	0.5 bn	20m	20bn	3.6bn	1.2bn	0.5bn
Profits & Tax (yuan) (1992)	5.25bn	n.a.	60m	6m	38m	–	2bn	300m	100m	40m
Workforce (1992)	60 000*	25 000	12 000	17 000	5000	1300	220 000	39 000	7000	12 500
Av. yearly Employees income (yuan) (1992)	5000	3600	3800	4700	3800	3200	4200	3800	3700	4500
Labour contract system	10%	100%	10%	20%	100%	100%	10%	100%	100%	100%
Wage system	Post-skills 16 grades	Basic + hourly + bonus	Post-skills	Post-skills	Post-skills	Partial post-skills	Post-skills	Basic + hourly + bonus	Post-skills	16-grade
Soc. insurance system	new	new	new	new	new	new	new	new	new	new
Training	Highly dev.	Tech. school	Training dept	Highly dev.	Tech. school	Training dept.	Highly dev.	In-house + Japan	Tech. school	Training dept

*120 000 employees in city; 220 000 nationally.

The *average* sales turnover in 1992 was just over 9 billion yuan, and the *average* profits plus tax were just under 0.90 billion yuan, a ratio of 1:10 approximately.

The range of enterprises' *products* was also relatively wide, ranging from iron and steel to pharmaceuticals, but most were in the heavy industrial sector. Seven out of the ten were in the metallurgy-based sector. Only one was exceptional, namely Dalian Port, as it provided a service rather than a product, although very heavily capitalized.

The *variation in employee* numbers deserves noting, as the enterprises ranged from 1300 to 60 000 (and 220 000 if the entire Anshan Iron and Steel complex was taken into consideration). The *average* number of the nine was just under 20 000 (it would of course rise considerably if *Angang* was included.)

Workers' *average annual incomes* (for 1992) ranged from 3200 yuan to 5000 yuan (see Table 7.1), with an average of 4030 yuan over the ten organizations.[13] These were higher than the annual average of 3240 yuan cited for Dalian state-enterprise workers in 1993 but much less than the rather high estimates given locally, namely 6000 yuan for rural industry employees and 9600 yuan for those working in joint ventures in that area for 1993.[14] The national benchmark figure for wages and incomes of Chinese workers in all industrial sectors in 1992 was 2710 yuan per annum, up by 15.9 per cent over 1991 or 6.7 per cent if adjusted for inflation; it was 2878 yuan a year in SOEs. The national average wage in urban collectives was only 2109 yuan per annum, and for other categories, mostly private and foreign-funded firms, 3966 yuan per annum. These however were supplemented by bonuses averaging 564 yuan per year, see Table 7.2 (Interviews, August 1993).

Differentials between workers had increased as performance-related pay became more widespread: they varied from 5 : 1 to 2 : 1 depending on economic circumstances. The variance for each element in the rewards equation is indicated in the section for each enterprise. The gap between workers' and managers' pay had increased relatively, in most instances, but not excessively.

The data collected on the labour reforms are summarized in Table 7.3, showing the range of 'three-system' reforms and so on. Seven out of ten enterprises have all their employees on labour contracts (much higher than the national average: see Table 4.3) and six out of ten have fully adopted the 'post-plus-skills' wage system, for example. All had implemented the social-insurance reforms.

We now move on to Part Three to discuss the implications of the 'three systems' reforms for Chinese industry and the wider economy.

Part Three:
Beyond the Iron Rice-Bowl

If we do not uphold socialism, do not carry out reform and opening, do not develop the economy and do not try to improve the people's livelihood, then there will only be the road to ruin. This basic line should be valid for 100 years and not shaken.

(Deng Xiao-ping, speech on tour of Southern China, CPC Central Document No.2, early 1992)

8 Discussion

8.1 INTRODUCTION

In this chapter, we attempt to discuss fully the implications of the specific reforms in SOEs described and analysed in the preceding three (Chapters 5, 6 and 7), dealing with labour and personnel, wage systems and social insurance reforms, respectively.

It appears sensible to have tried to 'pilot' the 'three systems' reforms (*san xiang zhidu gaige*) in the North-East, as it was in the industrial heartland of China that the problems related to SOEs were most acute. Many enterprise reform experiments are taking place in that area involving a hundred or so industrial, commercial and high-tech firms (see *Beijing Review*, 28 March 1994, pp.4–5). It is also true that the North-Eastern cities, especially Harbin and Shenyang, needed a *direct* reform-stimulus as the influence of joint ventures and foreign-owned enterprises (with the exception of Dalian) was less marked compared with say, Guangzhou, Shanghai, or even Tianjin. (On the North-East's relative decline, see Yahuda, 1994.).

8.1.1 Enterprise Level

How representative the cases studied were of large state enterprises in general was hard to say. The field-work covered three out of the 12 experimental sites chosen to pilot the 'three-system' rewards in Shenyang, and two of a similar number in Dalian and Harbin. While most of the enterprises chosen turned out to be making profits in 1992, at that time about *four in ten* SOEs generally in those cities (in Harbin and Shenyang, if not Dalian) *were loss-making*.[1]

Most of the enterprises conveyed an impression of industrial backwardness, often with very old plant dating back to the 1950s or earlier. The Dalian Shipyard used rather old-style technology. Shenyang Smelting Works and Shenyang Transformers Factory recalled the earlier days of the PRC's industrialization. Some of the *Angang* Iron and Steel complex was modernized, however (even more of *Shougang* had been). The Harbin pharmaceutical site was also recently built. The industrial settings as well as the products belonged to 'first-wave' industrialization and to what in the West are called 'sunset' industries. The description of 'rust-belt' might be a little exaggerated but apart from a few case-studies (for example Cases 5 and 8, namely pharmaceuticals and commercial vehicles) many of the SOEs might be dubbed 'yesterday's' enterprises. The company settings and organizational culture also gave an impression of old-fashioned but worthy industriousness.

Management on the whole appeared a great deal more professional and technocratic, and above all rather young. If there was any one factor which was noticeable compared with industrial visits in China in the early 1980s, it was the age of the managers encountered at all levels, including middle and senior: far lower than a decade ago. Managers were also said to be freer to manage under the new reforms and this point was repeatedly made in interviews. Greater autonomy to hire, promote (and even fire) was supposed to be enhanced, although lip-service was usually paid to consultation with the representatives of the workforce, namely the trade union and Workers' Congress, as noted earlier.

Ji and Murray (1992, p.164) have however argued that the economic reforms have actually undermined participative management. Consultation, they claim, has declined with the introduction of both the 'direct responsibility system' and the 'management contracting system'! The unanticipated effect of these measures, they argue, has been to *centralize* management decision-making. They cite a survey of 386 managers of state-owned and collectively owned firms, of whom two-thirds opposed having to consult workers in decision-making (cf, Wang, 1989; 1994).

8.2   LABOUR AND PERSONNEL REFORMS

The extension of labour contracts to the whole of the workforce in many cases was the most noteworthy characteristic of the field-research. (For the average of 20 per cent of SOE employees see Table 4.3.) The significance of this development may be interpreted in a number of different ways. On the one hand, it represents a parity between new and existing (or long-serving) employees, and on the other, between workers and staff, and cadres. There was in any event a separate, distinct contract for cadres with a greater emphasis on values and attitudes.[2] According to Easterby-Smith et al. (1994) managerial selection in Chinese SOEs was based on four criteria: 'good moral practice' (*de*), 'adequate performance' (*neng*), 'working hard' (*qin*), and 'excellent performance' (*ji*) the first of these being seen as the most important, linked to 'political loyalty' and 'ability to get on with others' (1994, p.13). Article 4 of the 1986

Regulations on Labour Contracts laid down that workers should also be selected on the basis of virtue, health and knowledge. Virtue (*de*) has implications of political reliability and correct attitude, but such phrases were not apparent in the workers' contracts examined in 1993 in the field-work.

Labour contracts with workers were more matter of fact and were restricted to mutual obligations *vis-à-vis* a set of defined expectations. On the company side, a typical contract states that:

> With regard to production and job requirements, and after entry, the company will employ .... on the worker's side to make a labour contract. Both sides willing to obey the State Labour Contract System Regulations have made the following agreement ...
>
> (Sample contract, Shenyang Municipal Labour Bureau 1992)

The company then states how long it will employ the worker, including a probation period. Then follow clauses relating to management procedures, safe conditions for work and study, protection of worker benefits, bonuses and sanctions, and so on. On the worker's side, the clauses deal with benefits, discipline, safety and the economic targets. Targets, payments, safety-gear, labour insurance and welfare, and contract enforcement details are then listed (see Chapter 5, Figure 5.1). The company receives a copy of the contract, as does the worker. Provision is made for labour arbitration or, if settlement of disputes cannot be resolved there, to go to a local court. The copies have to be registered at the Contract Certification Office of the Municipal Labour Bureau. The labour contracts were then to be set out clearly in line with the Article 8 provisions of the 1986 Regulations stating that performance targets, contract-period, working conditions, wages, insurance and welfare, discipline, penalties and so on, were to be listed. In addition, the 'labour book', Soviet style, recording performance and discipline (different from the confidential personnel dossier accessible only to the enterprise and the bureau, and covered by Article 5 of the 1986 Regulations) did not feature in the contracts encountered in 1993 study.

To sum up, labour contracts represented a move away from an institutionalized Marxian world of *rights*, where the worker enjoyed lifetime employment as an extension of what were defined as 'civil rights' in the PRC and where the 'right to work' supplemented the 'right to vote', to an economy in greater part characterized by *market* and hence *contractual* arrangements according to one view (see Korzec, 1992, p.26). Labour contracts of limited duration directly signalled the end of 'iron rice-bowl' status for workers and 'iron-chair' tenure for state cadres, from the mid-1980s onwards, at least at the level of policy intentions.

According to a 1993 ACFTU survey (reported by the Xinhua News Agency) there was said to be general support for the overall direction of the economic reforms:

> The investigations consisted of interviews with 30,000 such people in 12 provinces, municipalities and autonomous regions, as well as questionnaires to another 50,000, federation officials told Xinhua today (19th October). The areas were the investigations were conducted included the country's best developed areas such as Beijing, Shanghai and Guangdong, as well as less developed Sichuan and Gansu in China's vast hinterland. In answer the question 'What do you think of the reforms?', more than 90 per cent of those covered by the investigations said these were 'excellent' or 'good'.
>
> When asked 'What if your personal interests are affected by reform measures adopted in the reforms?', some 43.2 per cent said that they would support the reforms so long as the country's overall economy was to benefit. The investigations also showed that 32.7 per cent were willing to support the reform measures 'if their aftermath is financially bearable'. (SWB, 21 October 1993)

It went on to say that the notion of competition was now acceptable to Chinese workers who formerly enjoyed the so-called 'iron-rice bowl' – with each having a secure job irrespective of his or her work performance, but with a minority in dire straits:

> The investigations revealed that 92.7 per cent of the interviewees favoured or basically agreed to the new concept of 'letting the superior win out through fair competition'. On 'how to handle the relationship of the country, the society, the collective and the individual', 28.9 per cent said that the interests of the country, the society and the collective should receive priority. Some 52.5 per cent said that the interests of the four aspects should be well coordinated. Only 1.9 per cent definitely said that their individual interests should be the foremost. According to the investigation report, with factors of inflation deducted, the average monthly income of the workers in 1992 was 2.89 times over 1979. However, the investigation also showed that the monthly living expenses averaged less than 50 yuan in five per cent of the workers' families. That means that 20m people – 7m wage earners and 13m

people they support – are living below the poverty line. (SWB, 21 October 1993)

As with similar ACFTU surveys, it is hard to vouch for the accuracy of such polling, and even harder to evaluate it. It is worth noting that only a third of those interviewed were supportive of the reforms if they did not suffer financially.

8.3   LABOUR MARKETS AND WAGE REFORMS

As described in earlier chapters in Part One, China embarked in the mid-1980s on an attempt to create factor-markets and the demand and supply of labour must be included in this consideration. China has a productive population of over 760 million (size of the labour-force being equal to the population in the productive age group, multiplied by the participation rate). Minami (1994, p.204) uses the international standard practice of those over 15 years old rather than the Chinese benchmark of 16). The PRC could not in past days have a 'labour market' (by definition) because in a socialist society labour could not be a 'commodity' and therefore not be bought or sold, as explained earlier (in Chapters 4 and 5). Labour was allocated and wages determined by state bodies until quite recently (see Takahara, 1992). When the wage system was reformed in the mid-1980s, progress was slow. By the early 1990s, however, several significant changes had occurred *vis-à-vis* matching rewards with skills and training, effort and productivity.

Now, even if fully-fledged labour markets on Western lines seem far away, many personnel policies have changed. New workers have fixed-term contracts; apprenticeships have been reformed; training has been expanded for both workers and managers in most SOEs. Even so, workers have been resistant to change and the seasoned observer will remain sceptical about reforming entrenched personnel practices in the short to medium term. Reward systems do now admittedly stress material benefits. As some firms did much better than others, a bonus tax was introduced to make sure personal incomes do not get out of line. Many enterprises have tended to pay equal (or almost equal) bonuses to all employees. Workers were said to have become increasingly calculative and that the 'red-eye disease', stemming from jealousy, had become widespread within the ranks of the lower-paid. To stress fair play, bonuses have now been rotated around different groups of workers each month. It is claimed that differentials were greater than in the past, but were much less than in Western firms in Child's (1990) investigation. Average pay varied with job level, and enterprise bonus levels, in the six firms studied. Age had been an important determining factor, which confirms the seniority principle mentioned elsewhere. But salaries were not yet fully related to technical expertise. Indeed:

> The profile which emerges of the bigger basic salary-earner in these Chinese state enterprises is an older man who has spent many years in the enterprise and worked his way up to a higher category of job. This sounds like a rather typical bureaucratic type of progression, an observation which is particularly strengthened by the fact that this profile characterized the staff (cadre) half of the sample rather than production workers. (Child, 1990, p.238)

The study found that much of the variation in basic salaries was predictable if age, job level and length of service in the enterprise were known (see Table 8.1). On the other hand, among production workers, only their age pointed to variations in basic salary (Child, 1990, p.238). It should be noted in any event that it is what an appraisal-system measures, rather than merely the presence of appraisal, which is crucial.

It can be seen from the earlier accounts of the 'three-systems reforms' (see Chapter 7) that the new personnel changes had enhanced promotion possibilities according to merit and performance, or so it was claimed. As the reforms had only recently been introduced and as no hard statistics were available to reveal significant shifts in practice, one must remain sceptical concerning the degree of progress here. It is, however, much likelier that the wages system has shifted even further towards performance-based criteria.

The reforms followed the earlier 'set-reform of wages' (*gongzi taogai*) by which the grades were systematized and streamlined into a uniform national scheme designed by the Ministry of Labour and Personnel (MoLP) in the mid-1980s.[3] This move occurred because the earlier 'structural wage reform' (linking wages to enterprise profits) had led to various kinds of problems, notwithstanding inter-unit *panbi* (or seeking higher wages without economic justification) often due to the lack of labour mobility as managers tried to maintain staff morale. Indeed, across-the-board wage increases followed to compensate for rising prices in the mid and late 1980s, often triggered off by protest by workers and staff (see Takahara, 1992, pp.157ff). As a result, new wage-scales for workers in SOEs were promulgated (see Table 8.2).

Table 8.1   Multiple regression of basic salary level on postulated predictors in Chinese enterprises (stepwise procedure, N = 143 job holders)

Postulated predictors	Beta coefficient	Cumulative multiple R^2
Age	0.88	0.60
Job level	−0.14[1]	0.63
Length of service in enterprise	−0.25[2]	0.65
Gender	−0.11[3]	0.66
Education level	0.08	0.67
Level of training	0.03	0.67

Notes: [1] Higher job level predicts higher basic salary
         [2] Shorter length of service predicts higher basic salary
         [3] Being male predicts higher basic salary

Source: Adapted from Child, 1990, p.238

It is therefore not the case that there was a linear move from 1978 onwards to smoothly implement greater material incentives. As Takahara points out:

> In reviewing the overall policy process of structural wages and 'set reform of wages', we find that the policy-elite compromised significantly with egalitarian demands and protests at the grass-roots level that had arisen from the conflicts in the implementation of previous wage reform measures. Some members of the policy-elite realised that the strict application of the principle of 'to each according to one's work' did not necessarily motivate staff and workers to work harder. In many cases it disrupted the unity among the workforce and demoralized those who considered that they were treated unfairly . . . To a large extent, it was a compromise of economic principles for the sake of political appeasement. (1992, p.176)

The post-1992 wage-system reforms, lately introduced in the ten 'pilot' SOEs studied in this field investigation, were more or less consistent with a new standard model, again imposed from the top by the reformers, namely the 'post-plus-skills' formula. However, only six out of the ten firms investigated adopted the full model. What was interesting was the

Table 8.2   Standard wage table in the mid-1980s for workers in large and medium-sized state enterprises (in yuan)

					Sets						
Grades	1	2	3	4	5	6	7	8	9	10	11
15	99	102	105	108	111	114	117	120	123	126	129
14	93	96	98	101	104	107	110	112	115	118	121
13	87	90	92	94	97	100	103	105	108	110	113
12	81	84	86	88	90	93	96	98	101	103	105
11	76	78	80	82	84	87	90	91	94	96	98
10	71	73	74	76	78	81	84	85	87	89	91
9	6	68	69	70	72	75	78	79	81	83	84
8	61	63	64	65	66	69	72	73	75	76	78
7	56	58	59	60	61	64	67	68	69	70	72
6	52	53	54	55	56	59	62	63	64	65	66
5	48	49	50	51	52	54	57	58	59	60	61
4	44	45	46	47	48	49	52	53	54	55	56
3	40	41	42	43	44	45	47	48	49	50	51
2	36	37	38	39	40	41	43	44	45	46	47
1	33	34	35	36	37	38	39	40	41	42	43

Note: Five out of these 11 sets of standard wages are used in each wage district, namely from 1–5 in the fifth wage district (the current lowest), to 7–11 in the eleventh wage district (the highest)

Source: Liu et al (1988) p.312
(See Takahara, 1992, p.172)

Table 8.3   Staff/workers' wages (% total wages)

	1978	1992
Total	100	100
Time wages	85.0	45.0
Piecework wages	0.8	8.9
Bonuses	2.3	20.0
Subsidies	6.5	23.8
Others	5.4	2.3

Source: SSB, 1993

Table 8.4   Real wages of staff/workers (percentage per annum increase)

	All staff/ workers	State industries	Urban collectives	Others
5th FYP (1976–80)	2.9	2.9	3.9	–
6th FYP (1981–85)	4.2	4.3	4.8	–
7th FYP (1986–90)	2.4	2.6	1.0	4.7

FYP = Five Year Plan

Source: SSB, 1993

variation between the firms, for as it was claimed there was greater managerial discretion. Enterprise directors could now modify the rewards system more closely to economic circumstances.[4]

A 1993 report noted that:

> In the past, all workers in state-owned factories (had) received similar wages and benefits, regardless of their productivity, according to a nationwide wage scale set by Beijing.
>
> [Under the new reforms] state enterprises were given authority to set their own wage scales with higher wages for better-performing employees. As a result, 52 million workers, over half of the workforce of state-owned factories, have their wage levels tied to their performance, skills or position. Only a few local governments have passed minimum wage laws. Among them is Zhuhai in southern China's Guangdong province, one of the country's most prosperous areas, where the minimum is set at 350 yuan (dlrs 60) per month. (*Associated Press*, 10 May 1993)

In the ten SOEs studied, it was clear that the 'post-plus-skills' element was proportionately balanced by the enterprise and individual bonus elements in most cases. For example in *Angang* the average monthly wage of approximately 350 yuan had combined bonuses amounting to 80 yuan; in Shenyang Smelting, with a wage of 300 yuan, it was 110 yuan; in Harbin Power Equipment, it was 280 yuan, and approximately 90 yuan, respectively.

These proportions for performance-linked bonuses (in the last three examples) exceed by far the proportion in the official statistics concerning wage composition in SOEs for the end of the 1980s, when 16.9 per cent was cited for bonuses (SSB, 1991) and had recently risen to 20 per cent (SSB, 1993) and even this had risen from an average of 2.3 per cent in 1978. Over the period, the percentage gained through the basic wage fell from 85 per cent to just under 50 per cent, representing the expansion of the 'floating wage' (see Takahara, 1992, pp.124ff). It is now below this figure (see Table 8.3). At the same time, the level of subsidies went up threefold in the 1980s (see Leung, 1993, pp.64–5). Real wages had risen less rapidly in the period of the Seventh Five-Year Plan covering 1986–90 (see Table 8.4).

None the less, the view that the wage-system suffers from incoherence and arbitrariness as opposed to over-systematic management (Korzec, 1992, pp.54–74) has a plausible ring to it and has been endorsed by other observers who have carried recent field-work in the PRC (for example see Leung, 1993, p.66). Inter-group conflicts were increasingly noticeable (see Figure 8.1). The upshot of such a shift in the structure of rewards has been to increase the inequality of income distribution which has reportedly led to greater worker resentment and even industrial action (see Chan, 1993, pp.39ff). The losers were said to be 'the old, the physically weak and women, deprived of the welfare to which they had previous access ...' (Takahara, 1992, p.151; Stockman, 1994, pp.772–5). The workers in SOEs were generally no exception in such feelings of discontent, even though they were relatively better off than their counterparts in TVEs:

> Though their incomes and welfare benefits are better than those of the peasant workers, they are also considerably better educated and better informed, and hold feelings of 'relative deprivation' under the reforms, which continue to threaten their job and welfare provisions. (Chan, 1993, p.43)

8.4   CREATING A 'LABOUR-SERVICE MARKET'

Debates about the 'labour market' certainly continued long after the 1986 reforms and even after its 1992 extension. Whilst the term was extensively used in everyday usage amongst experts, managers and officials, there was still some caution at the ideological level. The euphemistic concept of a 'labour-force market' was first advanced in the Decision of the CPC Central Committee on 'Some Issues Concerning the Establishment of a Socialist Market Economic Structure' published in November 1993 (See *Beijing Review*, 3 January 1994, p.14).

Figure 8.1   Intergroup conflicts in Chinese industrial enterprise

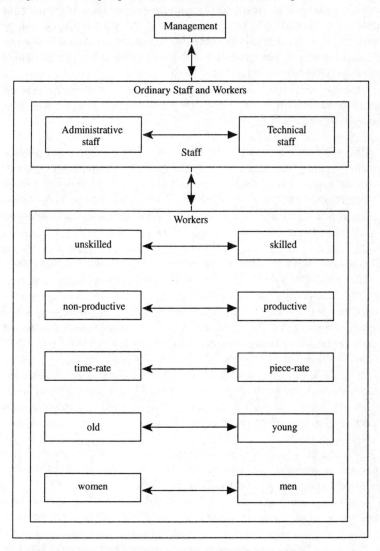

Sources: Adapted from Takahara, 1992, p.178

A Chinese academic, Gao Shangquan, has set out the official formulation of this concept from a theoretical point of view which is interesting and relevant for the present discussion. It is therefore worth discussing and citing at length (see Gao, 1994). He notes that economists have used the terms 'labour-service market', 'labour-employment market' and even plain 'labour market'. As part of the Party's 1992 reform programme, he believes 'we should clearly advance the "labour-service market" concept ... [because it] will help us accelerate the construction of a socialist market economic structure' (1994, p.14).

First, he argues, the 'labour-force market' distinguishes the 'labour force' from 'labourer' and 'labour employment', the first of these three being a commodity:

> Under socialist conditions, the labor force is by nature a commodity, which means labor force has the dual nature of use value and intrinsic value. Equally, the value of labor force can only be realized through exchanges, hence, the formation of a labor force market. Labor force, laborers and labor employment are three concepts which, although differentiated are mutually related. (1994, p.14)

The physical site where exchange takes place is the 'labour-force market'. The concept of 'labour' differs from that of the 'labour force', hence:

> Labor employment is the course of employment itself, and not a production factor. In fact, the course of employment cannot be exchanged. The concept of labor differs from that of labor force. Labor means the use of labor force, and is the entity and an innate yardstick of value. Labor cannot be exchanged as a commodity on the market, and can only be used by the production sector. Only the labor force is priced on the market. Therefore the term of labor force market cannot be replaced by that of the labor market. (ibid.)

Clearly, the ideologists find it important to make these distinctions, but in practice the general term 'labour-market' has proved sufficient to cover pragmatic concerns in the world of work.

Gao goes on to say that in the West, the labour-market has long been seen as the most important factor market and even cites a common belief among some economists that it may determine 'the balance of all markets' (1994, p.14) by the comparison of marginal costs and returns of workers. He therefore argues that a 'labour-force market' is part and parcel of establishing a socialist market and that in any case it already exists as an 'objective reality of economic life'. (1994, p.15). Using the 1992 official statistics, he notes that 109 million people worked in the SOEs (SSB 1993) which was 43 per cent of all those outside agriculture. Employees in non-SOEs were 145 million (including public and private services) or 57 per cent of this total. In the above, around half, he claims, were allocated by the market, as were 56 per cent of the industrial labour force and as high as 77 per cent in construction. This conjecture, we may note, seems somewhat on the excessive side.

From this, the analysis goes to argue, however, that:

> If surplus agricultural labor force resources are considered, the proportion of labor force resources allocated by the market would be even greater. In front of the enormous labor force resources that have entered the market, we should place the cultivation and development of the labor force market on the agenda for future efforts to deepen reform. (Gao, 1994, p.15)

Given the total surplus manpower in the economy, including agriculture, plus displacement due to reforms, he argues that by the turn of the century 320 million new jobs will be needed. The implication is that only deregulated factor-markets are the answer.

According to the late David Granick (1987, p.103) writing in the World Bank study of Chinese SOEs, the labour-market was previously weak in China compared with the Soviet Union in the mid-1980s, although planning generally was much less detailed than in CMEA countries. He made the perceptive observation that:

> So long as social considerations in China keep the dismissal rate exceedingly low by international standards (this is a phenomenon found in all European CMEA countries and in Yugoslavia), an active labour market in the state sector will not be possible. (Granick, 1987, p.14)

Relative wages too were inflexible except perhaps for scarce top managers, and generally seniority determined the level of rewards for workers.

Against this view, Gao argues that only a 'labour-service market' will enable the labour surplus to be absorbed:

> Judging from the market competition, the labor personnel system in state-owned sectors has not yet been thoroughly reformed, hampering the formation of the market. Although the main body of the market has basically taken shape in non-state-owned sectors, the rights and interests of the market are not fully guaranteed. In terms of the operational mechanism of the market, there is not a unified standard for

the prices of the labor force and, in a considerably wide scope, the payment fails to reflect both the true cost of labor and its supply and demand, making it unable to play its role in regulating the market operation. (Gao, 1994, p.16)

Last, he goes on to square the ideological circle by arguing that the reforms will help workers to remain 'masters of the country' as a class:

Recognition of the labor force market means to recognize the nature of labor force as a commodity. However, laborers have the right to exchange and retain their labor skills, and have the freedom to choose jobs. This shows that laborers are masters of their own labor ability, thus making it possible for us to realize the equality in job selection and provide equal employment opportunities.... Undoubtedly, these actions will further strengthen and consolidate the position of the working class as masters of the country. (ibid.)

By a dialectical sleight of hand, by postulating workers becoming 'masters of their labour ability', that is, being free 'to choose jobs', he argues, the position of the working class is actually 'strengthened and consolidated'.[5] As an 'official' interpretation of the problem in that it appears in that publication, it is noteworthy for its lack of discussion of employment protection rights of any kind.

8.5   BUILDING A SAFETY-NET

Turning now to social insurance issues: comprehensive social welfare coverage has to date been the privilege of SOE employees in the urban sector (Minami, 1994, p.217). Total work-related insurance and other welfare costs amounted to as much as 500+ yuan per worker per year, even excluding low-cost housing. Rents have been very low, absorbing just under one and a half per cent of the average family income. A state employee in a 50 square-metre flat might have benefited to the tune of nearly 100 yuan per annum for administrative and maintenance costs (Minami 1994, p.217). Up to recent times, the SOE has run the social welfare set-up on behalf of its own employees, but a transfer of such expenditure to the individual worker is now under way on a limited scale, as we have seen.

For example, medical care is no longer a 'free good':

> Nationwide, the bulk of medical costs for most urban workers is still covered by their employers. In a change from the past practice, however, workers now have to cover a portion of their medical costs – ranging from 5 to 20 per cent.
>
> In the new social security system, medical insurance costs are set to be shared by the state, work units and employees, said the official. With the implementation of the wage reform and the increase in wages, the ratio of medical costs to be covered by individuals is expected to rise gradually. (*Beijing Review*, 21 February 1994, p.6)

The introduction of unemployment insurance was a wholly new and crucial part of the 1986 labour contract regulations, 'without precedent in the history of labour relations in state socialist countries' (Korzec, 1992, p.43). It affected workers made redundant in SOEs reorganizing to avoid being closed down, or becoming bankrupt, or where their labour contract had expired or who had been sacked. The unemployment insurance fund was to constitute 1 per cent of the total standard wages in the enterprise as relating to workers and staff, but excluding temporary employees. The standard wage represented about 60 per cent of earnings of workers and staff in the middle 1980s. If unemployed, workers (of five years' standing) would receive between 60 and 75 per cent of the standard wage for the first year and then 50 per cent for the remaining period up to the end of the second year. If workers had their contracts ended, they would officially be entitled to one month's standard wage for each year worked up to 12 months' share, but this would be deducted from their dole. In reality, 140 million workers outside SOEs have no unemployment protection.

The unemployment insurance fund was also to cover welfare benefits and pensions for those whose SOE had to close (a limited number, however). As well as this, retraining expenses for displaced workers had to be met out of the fund to support those 'waiting for work' and to help reintegrate them into the working population. About a quarter of the fund's budget will be spent in 1995 for training (BBC World Service News, 27 November 1994). Many SOEs had no funds to pay pensions or welfare benefits: perhaps one in three and were laying off workers (see *Chinese Labour Bulletin*, March 1994, p.8; September 1994, p.5). Creating such an unemployment insurance machinery clearly recognized that 'full-employment' was now off the agenda in urban China and that a 'labour market' was most certainly on it.

8.6   CONCLUDING REMARKS

Chinese SOEs had in the past not only hoarded labour, but also complied with government requests to absorb surplus urban labour. To do this, they often set up secondary work-units unrelated to their main field of activity, such as hotels, restaurants or shops. Frequently, more than one person shared the same job, hence depressing the level of productivity. Up to the early 1970s, state-run People's Communes performed a similar role in rural areas. Later, the encouragement of TVEs helped to absorb the growing labour surpluses. Minami (1994, p.206) believes that economic rigour must prevail and unproductive labour be released from SOEs: 'in other words there must be a trade-off between modernization and full employment.' Such a formulation of the problem reveals the dilemma for the policy-makers in Beijing. If 'economics is now in command', the political fall-out could be considerable, if urban discontent were to grow at the same time as the monetary controls were tightened to alleviate 'overheating' at the macro-economic level and the standard of living was undermined by rising prices and growing joblessness.[6]

The problem of loss-making enterprises continues to haunt those concerned with Chinese economic policy. Wood (1994, p.37) for example believes that even apart from the political and social consequences it would not make economic sense to close down all the loss-making firms. It would be wiser to see which enterprises could be rescued and turned round. If state resources are involved, it should not be to keep the corporate losers afloat but to help their employees and localities adapt to new opportunities. It would be preferable to withdraw the state from small business altogether, in this view (1994, p.37). Such firms should be collectively or family-owned, although one worry is that some TVEs have similar characteristics to SOEs and some of their problems. Privatization may not be the answer either as there are 'too few potential private purchasers and owners, either foreign or domestic'. (1994, p.38). One way out may be to diversify the ownership of SOEs (see *Beijing Review*, 17 October 1994, pp.5–6), with a mixture of private and public ownership. New large companies then could coexist with the reconverted former state firms.[7]

Given that the 'three-systems' reforms are further implemented, will this help to make the SOEs more effectively managed, particularly *vis-à-vis* human resource deployment? In the next chapter, we move on to examine whether Chinese practice in this domain can be compared with HRM management in other countries.

9 Human Resource Management 'With Chinese Characteristics'?

9.1 INTRODUCTION

Can we now speak of 'Human Resource Management' (HRM) in the Chinese context in any strict sense, given that the 'Open Door' and the 'Four Modernizations' policies have now been in place for a decade and a half? Has Chinese practice moved closer to that of the West – or Japan, for that matter – with the introduction of the economic reforms of the 1980s? Is the problem of 'Managing Human Resources in China' (see Warner, 1986; 1993) meaningful in terms of HRM, defined as seeing employees as valuable resources to be effectively developed?

Few would doubt that China today is a very different place from what it was in the days of Mao Zedong. Chinese industry, for example, is decidedly more managerialist than Maoist; Deng Xiaoping's reforms have been far-reaching in their implications since the late 1980s, both in general and in particular. Managing people more effectively has become a priority, but the use of Western-based innovations and techniques in the human resources field may probably still be in its early days, as we shall shortly see.

Applying Western concepts to analyse what has been going on in China across a wide range of structural and behavioural patterns therefore presents a number of difficulties. HRM, for example, is seen by some as an essentially American concept, finding its fullest exemplification in non-unionized multinational firms (see Guest, 1992, p.12) and overlapping with practice found elsewhere in enterprises in many capitalist economies. It could be said to be an image 'in pursuit of excellence', to coin a phrase. We might even say that it cannot be comprehensively applied, let alone understood outside its cultural context and the setting in which it developed (that is, the United States), and if diffused outside this, cannot be analysed without conceding limited managerial/knowledge/software transfer. Even where transmitted across the Atlantic to a cousin-economy like the British, its applicability may still be seen as controversial (see Storey, 1989, p.3).

145

While the degree to which HRM has developed has mainly been seen in Western settings (see Mahoney and Deckop, 1989, pp.229 ff) the average Chinese state-owned industrial enterprise on the other hand (see Tidrick and Chen, 1987) has developed its own human resources profile. In broad brush-strokes, it emerges as follows:

1. Employment planning within enterprises in the PRC has tended to be fairly basic and bedevilled by both the shortage of sufficiently trained personnel, and the use of 'political' criteria of one sort or another (see Easterby-Smith et al., 1994). Aggregate personnel planning was carried out at a higher level than the enterprise, by provincial and municipal bureaux (see Warner, 1992). The national government decided the total net addition to permanent state employment; each enterprise was given a hiring quota. On leaving university, for example, graduates were in the past 'allocated' jobs in enterprises by the bureaucratic machinery at provincial or municipal level and often mismatches were made, causing low morale amongst those professionally qualified, and almost zero labour-mobility for many over the years (Granick, 1991, p.272).

2. The system of labour-management relations being what it is in the PRC, meaningful collective agreements were rare and not too sophisticated, although use of participative mechanisms both in the form of Workers' Congresses (see Wang, 1989) and long-standing practices of group-based work organization was well institutionalized (see Laaksonen, 1988, pp.261 ff).

3. 'Morale' was also an ongoing concern for many years, as ideology was preferred to material rewards (Barnowe, 1990).

4. Selection, appraisal and so on were only recently 'professionalized' rather than managers relying on group norms (see Warner, 1992).

5. A concern with tightening labour discipline by the attempted removal of the job security practices known as the iron rice-bowl policy has only relatively recently been a priority (Tung, 1991).

6. Training has been mostly defined rather narrowly, in contrast to the Western HRM notion of planning for long-term staff development. However, all top managers have to undergo training and certification, extending an earlier scheme which had narrower coverage (*Times Higher Educational Supplement*, 7 February 1992, p.6). This new mandatory policy builds on previous management training policies introduced in the early 1980s (see Warner, 1992).

I hope to amplify and illustrate most of these points later in the chapter and ask how far HRM 'with Chinese characteristics' is a meaningful term. This question is an important one because in the early 1990s some academic papers on Chinese personnel and employment practices began to use the Western-style HRM terms, often uncritically, and job-titles even appeared in joint ventures using similar descriptions.[1] The former were often trying to be topical in their usage, even intellectually fashionable. The latter instances were mostly copying the latest managerial mode. If the term 'HRM manager' was found extensively in foreign trade corporations (see Brown and Branine, 1994, for example), it was virtually unknown in the large SOEs studied by the present writer (see Chapter 7) in mid-1993. These authors take issue with my own views on training, which they see less narrowly defined, and more in line with, for example, longer-term staff development as in Western HRM practice, although agreeing with the lack of comparison between Western collective bargaining and the Chinese model of labour management. As they were largely interfacing with Western enterprises outside China, these foreign trade corporations may be seen as atypical, although it is certainly the case that personnel management practices in Chinese firms are changing because of the economic reforms, as we have already see in Part Two.

9.2   POINTS OF POSSIBLE CONTRAST

A major conceptual problem we must first confront in applying HRM (in the above context) is that it is basically premised upon individualistic assumptions (see Guest, 1992) although this may not always be the case. This hurdle presents initial difficulties as many non-Western societies are non-individualistic (see Hofstede, 1980; 1991; Whitley, 1990). Whether we are speaking of Chinese values before or after Mao, we are dealing with some degree of Chinese traditional values (see Laaksonen, 1988; Pye, 1991). Confucianism and later the Chinese version of Marxist-Leninism both played down the role of the individual *vis-à-vis* the state and society. Pye used the term 'Confucian-Leninism' (1991, p.455). The individual was subordinated to the group or larger collectivity: in urban areas to the work-unit, and in rural areas to the production brigade (1991, p.455). His or her role was of course relatively defined and in recent years, the young especially have shown themselves keener to march to an individualistic drum than their elders, hence the balance may eventually shift over time. Clan, family and work-group, however, still governed allegiances (see Bond, 1986). Connections – the term '*guanxi*' is used in Mandarin – were and still are very important in 'getting on' in Chinese society, even if technocratic qualifications have become more necessary. 'Who you know' is still very useful in one's working life and career. 'Networking' is clearly *de rigueur* for Chinese aspirants to higher status, whether administrators, managers or entrepreneurs (see Lockett, 1988; Child, 1994).

In spite of modernization, China is still very much an 'ascriptive' society, so the problem is more acute than it would be in the West where managers' informal links are of course a factor, but are perhaps more in the background. HRM, it may be argued, is predicated upon Weberian bureaucratic values, but the latter are perhaps less to the fore in China than is imagined. The Western large-scale enterprise, the 'mega-corporation' like General Motors, IBM and the like, has a highly specialized personnel structure managed by so-called professionals. It is unencumbered by explicitly 'political' intermediaries in its appointments, and arguably uses 'scientific' selection, appraisal and promotion procedures as standard practice. In the PRC, personnel cadres have, in the past, been 'red' rather than 'expert', with the 'correct' class and often army background (Meaney, 1988, p.130).

In sum, Western (largely US-based) theories of motivation (see Cascio, 1986; Hollway, 1991; Miner 1993) may not apply to East Asian societies. Even if Maoist ideology has been displaced by a more pragmatic, diffuse Dengism, cultural differences remain strong. Nevis (1983) for example tried to apply Maslow's theory of the needs-hierarchy to the PRC and found social needs to be the most important. Whether the result would be the same if the study was replicated ten years later is hard to know, but it is possible that material needs might be as prominent.

One study, Bond and Hwang (1986, p.229) has argued that 'American culture differs from Chinese culture most strongly on precisely those dimensions where the Chinese cultures cluster, namely individualism/ collectivism and power distance'. Even so, Hofstede (1991) reported that the PRC scored highest on what he called 'Confucian dynamism' (referring to those values he sees as conducive to economic activity) in a study of East Asian countries, indeed 'the mainland Chinese seem to have the mental software to turn their country into a sixth and giant Dragon' (1991, p.170).

Shenkar and Ronen (1987; 1993) found that promotion was not pursued too strongly in their Chinese sample, as it meant greater risk *vis-à-vis* the possible reward. Takahara (1992) in his study of wages policy in the PRC notes the inter-unit, inter-strata and inter-personal conflicts *vis-à-vis* material incentives as rewards led to gainers and losers (1992, p.152) as we have seen earlier (in Chapter 8). Shenkar and Ronen point out elsewhere that:

The stability of interpersonal norms suggests their probable perseverance in the PRC, despite the influence of Mao Zedong. Maoist ideology has challenged only some of these norms, while frequently using the very practice of kinship allegiance it officially opposes, ... thus leaving intact a major basis of traditional interpersonal relations. Furthermore, the volatility associated with applying Maoist ideology and subsequently withdrawing it seems to have strengthened the position of traditional Chinese values and norms as a 'stable anchor'. (1993, p.192)

Thus, whilst there are many similarities in work-values between East and West, national differences based on deeper cultural roots may well be factors to be reckoned with when coming to grips with that particular country's environment. It can therefore be expected that such values will act as 'filters' when technology-transfer, whether involving hardware and/or 'software', occurs.[2]

A second point of difficulty is that HRM is characterized by a historical evolution of management practices over time, that is, a shift from industrial relations to employee relations, from personnel management to human resource management, as exemplified in Mahoney and Deckop's (1986, pp.229ff) schema. Chinese firms, it may be argued, have not yet embarked on this route, and their point of departure was indeed very different from the start. Take industrial relations: we find here that there is little comparison between Western collective bargaining and the Chinese model of labour-management, as in the latter the trade unions have a clearly subordinate role in the enterprise. If there are industrial rather than employee relations, the analogy remains limited. As for personnel management as a 'professional' activity in China, it is still only in nascent form, let alone any evolution further along the spectrum. 'Free' collective bargaining is thin on the ground, so we do not find anything approximating to a Western model of industrial relations as we know it (see Warner, 1991, pp.210–13).

Another problem is the degree of management decentralization or divisionalization needed to set up strategic business units. China's economic reforms have led to a departure from the past central planning mechanisms of the Maoist past, slimmer though these were *vis-à-vis* the Soviet Union. In many ways, greater enterprise autonomy has evolved since 1979, and has certainly grown in the collective (non-state) sector. Child (1994) showed how far this had gone in the six Chinese state enterprises in his sample. Yet although the degree of autonomy varied, the managers he studied did not have control over the numerical flexibility of their workforce, nor did they have much leeway on salaries of cadres or workers. They may have won some autonomy in areas like internal work-organization and marketing, but strategic decisions were still out of their hands, as in the case of investment for example. A modicum of decentralization does not therefore necessarily mean HRM is imminent. Indeed, a greater degree of centralization in enterprises may be an advantage for the introduction of HRM.

According to Laaksonen's major study those managers beneath the level of:

> top management in all decision types have less influence in China than in Europe and Japan. The phenomenon that in China top management seems to keep nearly all the decision-making strings in its hands comes out clearly ... Most of the differences are greater in China, thus reflecting the greater centralization of power in the hands of top management of enterprises. This phenomenon is illustrated where the great power distance between top and middle management in China comes out clearly. The hierarchical pyramid looks much the same in Europe as in Japan, although in Japan the power distance between top and middle management is somewhat smaller and between foremen and middle management somewhat larger. (1988, p.300)

This investigation had replicated previous research on worker involvement originally carried out in 12 Western European countries (IDE, 1981; see also IDE, 1993) in Chinese enterprises, with additional data collected from Japanese firms. The data underscore the higher level personnel decisions which have in the past been made in the PRC, scored out of a total of 16 decisions on a five-point scale:

> If we pick out those individual decisions ... where the means of Chinese top managers are higher than those of European and Japanese managers, we see ... that the decisions concern either (a) personnel matters directly, eg 'appointment of new department head' (2), 'permanent transfer of workers' (5), or (b) organization of work of the whole enterprise, eg 'reorganization' (11), and 'work study' (14). We earlier noted that an area which top management likes to control strictly is the recruitment, development and organization of personnel resources. This seems to hold true both in Europe and in the East. The only exception in the decisions of this area is 'Establishment of criteria and procedures for hiring and selection of new employees' (no. 3). Here the mean for European firms is 4.0 and for both Chinese and Japanese 3.5. However,

... we see that this decision is not underestimated in the last-mentioned countries; on the contrary these decisions are considered so important there that they are concentrated at the higher hierarchical level, ie the level above the plant. The corresponding means are for China 4.3, for Japan still higher 4.6, but for Europe only 2.2. These differences also reflect of course differences in organizational structures in the countries, but in any case they show the key position of personnel matters in decision-making in enterprises (Laaksonen, 1988, p.304).

Other areas of practice produce fewer problems *vis-à-vis* the debate as to how far China has moved closer to modern management. These are at least demonstrable in 'key' or 'showpiece' enterprises, and especially in joint ventures. Yet further patterns of behaviour may have points of affinity or similarity with what looks like HRM, which are not new features of the Chinese enterprise (see Wang, 1989; Wang and Heller, 1993)

9.3 POINTS OF POSSIBLE COMPARISON

We can see here some aspects of Western-style HRM, as well as some features of Japanese employment practice (which does not always mean the same thing). In the former, we can see that the 'unitary' framework as opposed to the 'pluralistic' one (see Legge, 1989, p.22) might be a major point of convergence (see Figure 9.1). It may also apply to the Japanese case.[3] 'Corporate culture' might be highlighted as an HRM type feature and some writers claim it has been a feature of Chinese firms (Barnowe, 1990). The building-blocks of 'organizational culture', however, it could be argued, resemble HRM of a sort, with 'Chinese characteristics' providing a framework for an evolving set of approved goals (see Figure 9.1). However, as Barnowe notes:

it may be more realistic to see such statements as oblique reinforcement of the government and Party's *Four Basic Principles* of: (1) adherence to the socialist road; (2) the people's democratic dictatorship; (3) leadership by the Chinese Communist Party: and (4) Marxism-Leninism and Mao Zedong thought. It is indisputable that many reforms are taking place, but they are occurring in a measured, rather than in a radical, way. (1990, p.334)

These values, he argues, may be contradictory and they may not be a real guide to what managers actually do.

Figure 9.1   Fundamental values implicit in PRC official goals

Official goals	Value
Four modernizations	Productivity
	Hard work
Workplace democracy	Job involvement
	Cooperation
Socialist spiritual civilization	Morality
	High ideals
	Rules of conduct
	Equality
	Solidarity
	Friendship
	Mutual assistance
	Honesty, etc
Quality	Improved product quality
	Improved quality of services
Rationalism	Scientific approach
	Learning from experience
Individualism	Individualism acknowledging needs of society
	Pride in work
	Initiative

Source: Adapted and abbreviated from Barnowe, 1990, p.334

Some family resemblances with Japanese practice may also be suggested: we might, for example, mention here 'life-time employment', 'promotion by seniority' and 'enterprise-based unions' as key Japanese traits (see Whitehill, 1991). The first practice has certainly been general in China; employment from apprenticeship to retirement in one firm was for the last four decades or so the norm in the PRC (see Figure 9.1); however, job security is now relatively less firm, as has been discussed earlier (in Chapter 7). It is true, on the other hand, that dismissals are still relatively difficult to implement and the proportion of workers sacked statistically very small. Reductions of the labour-force in some SOEs have taken place, but relatively few bankruptcies have resulted in plant closures in that sector. In total, there were 675 bankruptcies in 1992 (see *Beijing Review*, 7 February 1994, p.21), probably in the state sector alone. This number (see Chapter 4) is, however, small *vis-à-vis* the one million or so enterprises to be found, and probably represents hardly any *large*-sized SOEs, of which there are approximately 8000.

The second feature, job security, was commonly *de facto* in many Chinese firms as implied by the above observations but this system is now changing (see *Financial Times Survey: China*, 7 November 1994, p.iv). The parameters may have been set nationally at the highest level, but who moves up the wage-grade ladder and how quickly may be left to decision-makers on site, with of course scope for favouritism and frustration. HRM, on the other hand, hinges on consistency of reward systems. Child (1990) notes similarities with the Japanese *nenko* system (see also Sano, 1977; Ballon, 1992) when examining pay and seniority in the six Chinese state enterprises studied. It is clearly not seen as dysfunctional in Japan, he argues (Child, 1990, p.242). However, the Japanese economist Aoki (1988, p.9) does not see lifetime employment as highly correlated with workers' diligence.

The third possible common trait may have validity in that with the union's subordinate role in the Chinese workplace, they may be said to behave as if they were enterprise-centred, enforcing discipline and production targets. It is largely true that the work-unit – the *danwei* – is encouraged to be the central focus of Chinese workers' lives and where they spend most of their time, as in Japan or South Korea, but in the latter two it is said to be even more production-oriented (see Whitley, 1990).

9.4   FURTHER POSSIBLE SIMILARITIES

While we have seen that Western and Chinese enterprises may differ enough to make the application of HRM problematic to the latter, a recent comparison of a sample of large companies in China and Britain has concluded that there are more similarities in *manpower planning* systems between Chinese firms and *some* of the UK ones in their sample than there are between *all* the UK ones (Easterby-Smith et al., 1994). The Chinese sample consisted of four SOEs matched by size, technology and industry with four UK private firms.

The main criteria for promotion reported by the researchers are set out in Figure 9.2. The main difference is that the UK firms veer to using 'hard' performance criteria, whereas the PRC companies tend to underline 'soft' criteria such as loyalty and relationships (Easterby-Smith et al., 1994, p.16). The Chinese system, it should also be noted, was a *dual-track* system, with the Party having a say in personnel matters for managers who were members where appropriate.[4]

Figure 9.2   Promotion criteria in PRC and UK firms

UK	Both	PRC
'Bottom-line' delivery potential	Sound functional experience	Party-loyalty
Greater than one business area	Excellent track-record	Good personal relationships
Wider experience than one country	–	'Hard-work' ability
–	–	Sound 'moral' practice

Source: Adapted from Easterby-Smith et al., 1994, p.16

The researchers sum up as follows:

> The main differences in HRM between the two countries ... appear in the 'softer' areas where relationships are important: appraisal, reward systems, the process of assessing potential, and the basic stance of unions towards management. These differences can be linked to known cultural factors such as the greater concern for relationships, for harmony, and the preservation of 'face' in China. (Easterby-Smith et al., 1994, p.32)

The above authors, it should be noted, have *in effect* used the term HRM as synonymous with personnel administration.

9.5   CONCLUDING REMARKS

To sum up, whilst we can conclude that HRM has probably not yet taken deep roots in Chinese enterprises, there are possibly some *limited* family resemblances (see Figure 9.3 for a comparative presentation of likes and unlikes). The optimists may well see Chinese management as set on a course of 'convergence' with Western HRM. There are strong historical and structural constraints which must be placed on such optimism. The gap between intention and practice is always problematic in the Chinese context. Organizational and behavioural inertia are not going to be overcome overnight. Changes towards a more Westernized system of labour management relations may take at least a decade to take root and

Figure 9.3 Summary of family resemblances in HRM characteristics in different countries' models, *vis-à-vis* Chinese enterprises

Model's characteristics	Western traditional IR model[1]	Western HRM model[2]	Japanese model[3]	Chinese model[4]
1. Values	Collective	Individual	Neo-Confucian	Confucian-Leninist
2. Economic system	Market	Market	Market	Market socialism
3. Political system	Pluralistic	Unitaristic	One-party in effect	One-party Marxism
4. Frame of reference	Pluralistic	Unitary	Unitary	Unitary
5. Management hierarchy	Tall	Broad	Well-defined	Little accountability
6. Corporate culture	Conflictual	Non-conflictual	Non-conflictual	Non-conflictual
7. Employment policy	Short-term	Long-term	Long-term	Long-term
8. Labour market	External	Dual	Moderately dual	Marginally dual
9. Lifetime employment	Not formal	Sometimes, in effect	Mostly normal	Normal
10. Turnover	High	Low	Low	Almost zero
11. Unionization	High	Low	Medium	High
12. Form of worker participation	Bargaining organizations	Consultative bodies	Consultative bodies	Workers' Congresses
13. Collective bargaining	Normal	Mixed	Normal	Recent
14. Human resource planning	Weak	Strong	Strong	Weak
15. Training & development	Limited	Extensive	Extensive	Limited
16. Careers	Unplanned	Planned	Planned	Less planned

[1] Wide range of large firms and SMEs in Western economies (see Guest, 1991)
[2] Large multinational companies, often US-owned (see Storey, 1989)
[3] Large industrial corporations in Japan (see Ballon, 1992)
[4] Large state industrial enterprises in the PRC (see Tung, 1991)

even then may not cover the whole economy. In time, that might occur for the enterprises at the 'leading edge', especially those involved in joint venture activities, but one must be cautious in assessing progress here. The realists, let alone the pessimists, might think more than twice, given the present status quo in China (as seen in Part Two), in imagining shadows on the wall of the cave as far as recognizably HRM practices are concerned.

We now move on to the final chapter, in which we attempt to sum up the arguments used in the book, summarize the findings, and try to formulate some conclusions.

10 Conclusions: Summing Up

10.1 INTRODUCTION

By 1996, it will be 20 years since Mao Zedong and Zhou Enlai died. Almost two decades of reform will have passed and China will have moved even further centre-stage as an economic superpower. The People's Republic is already a very different place from what it was when the Open Door policy was first launched and the Four Modernizations were conceived. If, in the 1980s, the ground was prepared for a socialist market economy, by the early 1990s China had developed a 'halfway house' economic model, neither capitalism nor socialism, and had survived the trauma of June 1989. As Nolan puts it: 'neither the momentum of reform nor the economic reform was halted' (1994a, p.1).

By 1992, the socialist market economy was formally legitimized. Plan and market were supposed to coexist side by side, although the latter expanded its environmental domain as the former receded. The organizational parameters in turn began to change. Enterprises became more loosely-coupled systems, their resource dependence less closely tied to state organs, in organization theory terms. In the new market environment, managers and workers would now increasingly face greater competition in their respective niches in the economy, even if they were not fully aware of the pressures to come in those terms. As a major consequence of such broad changes, the work-unit (*danwei*) was set to be redefined from a 'total institution' to a less inclusive organization with more open boundaries, with relations defined in economic rather than political and social terms. That at least was the implication, if not the stated goal, as a result of 'marketization'.[1] Even the term 'corporatization' raised its head, although less prominently than in the former socialist economies of Eastern Europe. 'Property rights' already pragmatically evolving in agriculture, and the 'collectively-owned' rural industries were becoming increasingly blurred in the state-owned industrial sector, split between government agencies, banks and the enterprises themselves (World Bank, 1990; 1993).

If a 'second-best' solution was implied in the transition from plan to market, then this may be as true at the micro-level. Whatever may be envisaged *vis-à-vis* organizational change, it is clear that experimentalism and incrementalism (see Warner, 1983) may be advised there, parallel to

157

pragmatism at the macro-level. The broad strategy of reform at both the macro- and the micro-level implies a new role for the organizations most closely dependent on the state: how their inputs are allocated and their outputs distributed. Land, capital and labour as factors of production would now be considered in a new light.

10.2   AN OVERVIEW

In this book, we have therefore set out to examine the *management of human resources* in Chinese industry in general in the above context, and looked at the problems of state-owned enterprises (SOEs) in particular. The examination of this theme comprised three parts. First, the *origins* of the iron rice-bowl employment system. Second, attempts to *dislodge* or *overturn* this system. Third, to see what might be *beyond* the iron-rice bowl. The very selection of this focus, it should be noted, has biased this study towards urban workers, as opposed to those in townships and villages (see Weitzman and Lu, 1992), and towards the industrial rather than rural sectors of the Chinese economy, and by doing so excluded around four-fifths of the total labour force.

In the *first* chapter we looked at the reasons for focusing on this particular variable, human resources and why managing it more effectively was important in the context of China's drive for development and modernization since 1949. State-owned enterprises ('owned by the whole people', in the official jargon) had long been the work-horse of Chinese industry and found in the major industrial cities. Since the late 1980s, it was increasingly believed that the volume of state subsidies they enjoyed had become not only a drain on resources that could best be used elsewhere, but also anomalous in an emergent, if still regulated, market economy 'with Chinese characteristics'. Overmanning was (and still is) a major problem in such enterprises. For four decades this sector had not been appreciably open to market forces, and even in recent years it had been relatively insulated compared with the burgeoning sets of firms outside the state-owned sector, such as many TVEs, privately owned firms, joint ventures and the like. Since SOEs employed over a hundred million people, how they managed their human resources was a matter of primary economic importance.

In the *second* chapter, we outlined the early origins of the iron rice-bowl employment system in the early 1950s and highlighted its roots in Soviet practices as well as noting the less well-known influence of Japanese personnel policies in North-East enterprises in the decades previously. It was originally intended to protect skilled workers, but eventually spread to cover the majority of urban workers. Although in some respects it exemplified a 'Lifetime Employment System', comparisons with Japanese enterprises not always be appropriate, as the two countries' contexts markedly differed.

In the *third* chapter, we dealt with the way in which the Chinese system of labour-management relations evolved and how the trade unions institutionalized the goal of the workers as 'masters of the country'. The early development of Chinese unions was explored, culminating in the setting-up of the All-China Federation of Trade Unions (ACFTU) in the early 1920s, its role in the Liberated areas, and its role as a Leninist 'transmission-belt' after 1949. The role of trade unions and Workers' Congresses in the *danwei* in the period of economic reforms was also discussed, and their largely reactive role *vis-à-vis* shifts of official policy.

In the *fourth* chapter, we set out the ways by which the economic reforms since 1978 have led to the introduction of 'labour-market' solutions, the closer linking of wages to productivity and the eventual introduction of labour contracts. In the late 1980s, economists had begun discussing proposals to create a 'labour market', although they had difficulties accepting that labour was a 'commodity' under socialism. Euphemisms like 'labour-service market', or 'labour-force market' were employed to get round these difficulties. As a result of such thinking, material incentives were introduced. Bonuses became more important as a method of rewarding effort and productivity. Whilst such new practices, as set out in the chapter, were welcomed by workers who stood to benefit, potential losers were resentful. The reforms, we saw, began a move away from the old Soviet-style grading system and to build-in greater rewards for flexibility, edging towards a more market-based model, albeit very much adapted to Chinese circumstances.

In the *fifth* chapter we focused specifically on the attempts to introduce a further wave of labour reforms in the early 1990s, in the 'rust-belt' industries of the North-East, as it is in this region that so many loss-making SOEs are concentrated. In 1992, the State Council selected a set of 'pilot' enterprises, which we described in detail (see Table 5.1), many of them located in the North-East (in Dalian, Harbin and Shenyang) and it was from these that a subset was selected for field investigation. The chapter also discussed the rationale of the reforms and the emergent labour-markets in each of the three cities, as well as in Beijing.

In the *sixth* chapter, the characteristics of the ten SOEs chosen for study in depth were set out. They covered both heavy and light industrial development. The range of enterprises' products was also relatively wide, ranging from iron and steel to pharmaceuticals, but most were in the heavy industrial category. Seven out of the ten were in the metallurgy-based sector. Only one was exceptional, namely Dalian Port, in that it provided a service rather than a product. All the enterprises investigated, we saw, were state-owned and were previously run directly either by Ministries or Bureaux. One of them was still formally under provincial-level Industrial Bureau direction: Harbin Power Equipment. Dalian Port was run by the Ministry of Transportation and the City Government. Otherwise, the others were corporations or parts of similar groupings. The variation in employee-numbers also deserved noting, as the enterprises ranged from 1300 to 60 000 (and 220 000 if the entire Anshan Iron and Steel complex was taken into account). Although a high proportion of state enterprises operated at a loss (it was claimed for example that four out of every ten enterprises in Shenyang were 'in the red') most of the sample made a profit.

The *seventh* chapter discussed each of the 'three-systems' reforms (*san xiang zhidu gaige*) in turn, namely dealing with labour and personnel, wages and salaries, and lastly social insurance, examining the implementation of the new policies in each of the ten enterprises in detail. The data on the labour reforms collected is summarized in Table 7.3, showing the range of 'three-system' reforms and so on. We found that six out of the ten enterprises had all their employees on labour contracts and six out of the ten had fully adopted the 'post-plus-skills' wage system, for example. All the firms had implemented the national-level social insurance reforms. If those at the leading-edge of reform conformed to the experimental initiative encouraged from above, the recalcitrants were, on the other hand, most likely to have had the political clout to resist such pressures (see Chan, 1993). It was probably in industrial concentrations where political 'conservatives' (in Chinese terms) were strong and where enterprise-party/union factions were resilient. One may also surmise that it was in the older enterprises and industries that such tendencies would have been strongest, such as iron and steel and so on. Yet it is puzzling that if this reform (that is, labour contracts) was not implemented, others in the same SOE were, particularly the other two out of three system reforms, such as those dealing with wages and social insurance. Moreover, it was true to say that all newcomers in the recalcitrant SOEs had been put on labour contracts since the mid-1980s.

The *eighth* chapter discussed the implications of the preceding empirical chapters in further depth, taking each of the reform areas in turn. First, the labour contracts system was analysed; then the new rewards systems; the moves to a 'labour-force market'; and last, creating a 'safety-net' for those made redundant by the new policies. The reforms themselves, we must note, however, have dangers built into them, as the consequence of moving to a more market-geared economy threatens social effects which could present a challenge to the hegemony of the Party on the lines of the events of early summer 1989, should urban unemployment and uncurbed inflation rise above a critical level.

The *ninth* chapter sets out to ask if we can better understand the labour reforms in terms of Human Resource Management (HRM) as practised in Western enterprises. It first sets out the 'family resemblances' of Chinese personnel policies to HRM ones, but also, more importantly, notes the differences, concluding that it would be misleading to interpret the comprehensive reforms in the former as pointing to 'convergence' with Western practice. The discussion concludes that it would be premature to talk about HRM 'with Chinese characteristics', although a *hybrid* form of labour-management relations in Chinese enterprises has probably evolved in many cases.[2]

10.3 CONCLUDING REMARKS

To sum up, although enterprise reforms were successively introduced throughout the 1980s, the iron rice-bowl has proved to be rather resilient and still characterized the SOEs by the early 1990s. If a 'socialist market economy' was slowly emerging, there was none the less only limited progress towards what is now called a 'labour-force market'. By the mid-1980s, for example, jobs for life were still *de rigueur* in the typically large state firms, and seniority-based promotion systems very common. In other words, it was only after that time that attempts to introduce labour contracts and efficiency wages were seriously placed on the economic agenda.

Even after state regulations were implemented to achieve employment and wage reforms in the mid-1980s (see Korzec, 1992, pp.26–50) such reforms could be described by a leading Western writer on Chinese economics as 'ineffectual' (Howe, foreword to Korzec 1992, p.ix). Indeed, this source concluded that, in spite of the reforms of the last decade, no significant dismissals had in fact taken place, and that the new regulations would only allow a worker to be sacked in terms of severe infringements of discipline or imminent bankruptcy. Indeed, dismissals to cut costs continued to be illegal in the period in question. On the worker's side, the reforms had not given him or her the right to leave their job or take a better post elsewhere. 'Thus neither employer nor employee is in a position to strike a market-style wage-employment bargain' (1992, p.ix).

Even after the 1992 reforms, it was evident that only partial headway had been made. In the ten SOEs investigated (see Table 7.3) labour contracts for all employees were restricted to seven out of the ten sites. Wage-reform was fairly generally implemented and social insurance was comprehensively introduced. The upshot is that 'Western-style' practices in the areas of personnel, rewards and social insurance may be grafted on to status-quo characteristics, producing the 'hybrid' form of labour-management relations noted earlier (see Warner 1993). It is clear then that there is frequently a gap between intent and practice in China. The (mainly) North-Eastern state-owned enterprises, although 'pilot' sites for the 'three systems reforms' experiments, still provided evidence of organizational inertia.

In this context, with the transition to the 'socialist market economy', officially proclaimed in October 1992, different ownership bases may coexist and hybrid organizational forms may result. Old and new managerial characteristics may combine in the key sectors of the economy, whether involving SOEs, TVEs, joint ventures or private firms. Residual elements of the plan may blend with the market: hence, reforms will frequently be incomplete. As in previous phases of economic and organizational development, the position is far from neat and systematic. The policies eventually adopted, as is often the case, are blurred at the edges, fuzzy in their applications and fudged in their political impact (see Link, 1994).

In order to keep the 'social peace', for example, the state may try to keep many of the large SOEs afloat, and run them partly according to the old rules, by maintaining the level of subsidies if trouble looms, exacerbating the budget deficit and inflation. It does this to avoid too many workers being made redundant at the same time. Yet the level of rural migration to the cities continues apace. The labour surplus is being geographically transferred from the countryside to the conurbations where there are not enough jobs available. A new urban proletariat is in the making, with higher consumer-expectations than ever before (see Sklair, 1991, pp.195–202). Such ambitions are likely to be only relatively satisfied if the growth-rate holds, and not at all for many if it falters.[3]

Conversely, some of those excluded from the iron rice-bowl sector may find better things, but even so, many will not. Deprived of a social buffer in many cases, with reduced real incomes afflicted by inflation, aggrieved by widespread corruption,[4] and competition in the 'labour-service market' from the new urban proletariat, those losing their iron rice-bowls will experience acute relative deprivation and may be politically volatile rather than passive. Strikes, demonstrations and riots on a limited scale are beginning to be reported on an almost weekly basis in both urban and rural contexts. Official figures put industrial actions at over 10 000 in 1993 alone.[5] An ACFTU survey notes an increase of 30 per cent over this figure in 1994.[6] Fear of disorder (*luan*) has always been a prime preoccupation of China's rulers (see Fairbank, 1987).

If the 'comprehensive' or 'three systems' reforms can be incrementally implemented *beyond* the 'pilot' enterprises spoken of earlier, then there is a reasonable chance that enterprise reform can succeed. In this sense therefore, the initial hypothesis raised at the beginning of Chapter 1, that the iron rice-bowl will diminish as the SOE sector both reforms itself and attenuates, begins to make sense. As the economists always put up the caveat, other things being equal, there are risks, particularly where they are *not* equal. To keep the economy growing at a rate to absorb the labour surplus referred to above, there are clearly dangers of 'overheating' and if the brakes are applied to mitigate this and avoid rampant inflation, the subsidies for the SOEs will continue to be reduced. Discontented workers then cannot be bought off with wage increases beyond the growth in productivity levels. It is a 'vicious circle' indeed. If the labour-force in the SOEs cannot be slimmed down for political reasons, the subsidies cannot be trimmed back. In this case, the costs of sustaining the enterprises' social infrastructure of schools, hospitals and so on will remain steep and prevent the SOEs being further 'marketized' via the stock exchange whether internally and/or externally. Pragmatic, incremental change remains fundamentally the only realistic option open to the policy-makers.

Appendixes

Appendix 1

TRADE UNION LAW
OF THE PEOPLE'S REPUBLIC OF CHINA

Adopted at the Fifth Session of the Seventh National Peoples' Congress
on April 3, 1992, promulgated by Order No. 57 of the President
of the People's Republic of China on April 3, 1992,
and effective as of the same date

[The text of the law is divided into six sections as follows]

Contents

[The initial chapters cover general matters, such as their status, eligibility for membership and so on in the broadest possible terms only. Some observations are presented in passing by the present writer. A detailed critique is provided in Chapter 3]

Chapter I
General Provisions

Article 1 This Law is formulated in accordance with the Constitution of the People's Republic of China with a view to ensuring the status of trade unions in the political, economic and social life of the state, defining their rights and obligations and bringing into play their role in the cause of socialist modernization.

Article 2 Trade unions are mass organizations of the working class formed by the workers and staff members on a voluntary basis.

Article 3 All manual or mental workers in enterprises, institutions or state organs within the territory of China who rely on wages or salaries as their main source of income, irrespective of their nationality, race, sex, occupation, religious belief or educational background, have the right to organize and join trade unions according to law.

167

Article 4   Trade unions shall observe and safeguard the Constitution, take it as the fundamental criterion for their activities and conduct their work in an independent and autonomous way in accordance with the Constitution of Trade Unions of the People's Republic of China.

The National Congress of Trade Unions formulates or amends the Constitution of Trade Unions of the People's Republic of China which shall not contravene the Constitution and other laws.

The State protects the legitimate rights and interests of trade unions from violation.

[The next four articles deal with union members' rights but only in general terms]

Article 5   Trade Unions shall organize and educate the workers and staff members to exercise their democratic rights in accordance with the provisions of the Constitution and other laws, to give play to their role as masters of the country and to participate in various ways and forms in the administration of state affairs, management of economic and cultural undertakings and handling of social affairs; trade unions shall assist the people's governments in their work and safeguard the socialist state power of the people's democratic dictatorship led by the working class and based on the alliance of workers and peasants.

Article 6   While protecting the overall interests of the entire Chinese people, trade unions shall safeguard the legitimate rights and interests of the workers and staff members.

Trade unions must maintain close ties with the workers and staff members, solicit and voice their opinions and demands, show concern for their life, help them solve difficulties and serve them wholeheartedly.

[The remaining articles deal with 'participation', 'mobilization' and relevant values in Chinese society, such as 'patriotism', 'collectivism' and so on]

Article 7   Trade unions in enterprises and institutions owned by the whole people or the collective shall organize the workers and staff members to participate in the democratic management of and democratic supervision over their own work units according to provisions of the law.

Article 8   Trade unions shall mobilize and educate the workers and staff members to approach their work with the attitude of masters of the country, to safeguard the property of the state and the enterprise and to observe labour discipline; they shall call on and organize the workers and staff members to strive to fulfil their production targets and work.

Trade unions shall organize the workers and staff members in launching socialist labour emulation drives, encouraging mass rationalization proposals, and promoting technological innovations and technical cooperation, so as to raise labour productivity and economic returns and develop social productive forces.

Article 9   Trade unions shall educate the workers and staff members in patriotism, collectivism and socialism, in democracy, legal system and labour discipline, and in science, culture and technology and raise their qualities in all aspects: ideological and ethical as well as scientific, cultural, technical and professional, so as to turn them into well-educated and self-disciplined labourers with lofty ideals and moral integrity.

Article 10 The All-China Federation of Trade Unions shall strengthen friendly and cooperative relations with trade union organizations of other countries on the basis of the principle of independence, equality, mutual respect and non-interference in each other's internal affairs.

[The next section deals with principles of organization, and how basic-level units are linked to national and industrial organizations and so on. This part does not represent much of a change from the earlier *status quo*]

Chapter II
Trade Union Organizations

Article 11 Trade union organizations at various levels shall be established according to the principle of democratic centralism.

Trade union committees at various levels shall be democratically elected at members' assemblies or members' congresses.

Trade union committees at various levels shall be responsible, and report their work, to the members' assemblies or members' congresses at their respective levels and be subjected to their supervision as well.

Trade union members' assemblies or congresses have the right to remove or recall the representatives or members of trade union committees they elected.

A trade union organization at a higher level shall exercise leadership over a trade union organization at a lower level.

Article 12 A basic-level trade union committee may be set up in an enterprise, an institution or a state organ with a membership of twenty-five or more. Where the membership is less than twenty-five, an organizer may be elected to organize the members in various activities.

Trade union federations shall be established at or above the county level.

Industrial trade unions may be formed, when needed, at national or local levels for a single industry or several industries of a similar nature.

The All-China Federation of Trade Unions shall be established as the unified national organization.

Article 13 The establishment of basic-level trade union organizations, local trade union federations, and national or local industrial trade union organizations shall be submitted to a higher-level trade union organization for approval.

A basic-level trade union organization shall be dissolved accordingly when the enterprise or institution or state organ to which it belongs terminates or is dissolved.

Article 14   The All-China Federation of Trade Unions, a local trade union federation or an industrial trade union enjoys the status of a legal person in the capacity of a social organization.

A basic-level trade union organization, which has acquired the qualifications of a legal person as prescribed in the General Principles of the Civil Law, shall be granted according to law the status of a legal person as a social organization.

Article 15   A trade union chairman or vice chairman shall not be arbitrarily transferred to another unit before the expiration of his tenure of office. When such a transfer is prompted by work necessity, approval shall be sought from the trade union committee at the corresponding level and the trade union at a higher level.

[The next section concerns rights and obligations of trade unions, including workers' rights *vis-à-vis* labour discipline, collective contracts, and so on]

Chapter III
Rights and Obligations of Trade Unions

Article 16   If an enterprise or institution owned by the whole people or the collective acts in contravention to the system of the congress of workers and staff members or other systems of democratic management, the trade union has the right to advance its opinions so as to ensure the workers and staff members the exercise of their right in democratic management as prescribed by law.

Trade unions may send representatives to investigate into any infringement of the lawful rights and interests of the workers and staff members by enterprises, institutions or state organs to which their affiliated trade union organizations belong, and the relevant units shall render them necessary assistance.

Article 17   If an enterprise or institution violates labour laws or regulations and encroaches upon the lawful rights and interests of the workers and staff members, the trade union has the right to demand that the management or the relevant department seriously handle the case.

If an enterprise or institution violates the state provisions concerning labour (work) hours, the trade union has the right to demand a rectification by the management of the enterprise or institution.

If an enterprise or institution violates laws or regulations concerning the protection of the special rights and interests of female workers and staff members, the trade union and its female workers' organization have the right to demand a rectification by the management.

[The mention of labour contracts subsequently is a novel feature of the amended law]

Article 18   Trade unions shall help and guide the workers and staff members to sign labour contracts with the management of enterprises or institutions.

Trade unions may, on behalf of the workers and staff members, sign collective contracts with the management of enterprises or institutions. The draft collective contracts shall be submitted to the congresses of workers and staff members or all the workers and staff members for deliberation and approval.

[The phrase below, 'the right to advance an opinion' (only), should be noted]

Article 19   If an enterprise dismisses or punishes a worker or staff member in a manner that the trade union considers improper, the trade union has the right to advance its opinion.

An enterprise owned by the whole people or the collective shall, when deciding to expel a worker or staff member or remove his name from the rolls, inform in advance the trade union of the reason for its decision; and, if the management of an enterprise violates laws, regulations or relevant contracts, the trade union has the right to demand a reconsideration of the decision.

If the worker or staff member in question does not accept the decision of the enterprise management to dismiss or expel him or remove his name from the rolls, he may request that his case be dealt with according to state provision on handling labour disputes.

[The following sets out the unions' role in labour disputes, legal advice, health and safety and so on]

Article 20   Trade unions shall participate in the conciliation of labour disputes in enterprises. Local labour dispute arbitration bodies shall include representatives of trade unions at the same levels.

Article 21   Trade unions may advance their opinions for the conciliation and settlement of labour disputes arising out of infringement of the rights and interests of the workers and staff members by enterprises. Trade unions shall give support and assistance where the workers and staff members bring a case before a People's Court.

Article 22   Trade union federations at or above the county level may provide legal advice for their affiliated trade unions and the workers and staff members.

Article 23   Trade unions have the right to advance their opinions on the working conditions and safety and health facilities in newly-built or extended enterprises and in technological transformation projects, in accordance with state provisions. The enterprises or the departments in charge shall treat these opinions seriously.

Article 24   Where the management of an enterprise gives a command contrary to the established rules and compels workers to operate under unsafe conditions, or, major hidden dangers and occupational hazards are found in the course of production, the trade union has the right to put forward proposals for a solution; where the very life of the workers and staff members is in danger, the trade union has the right to make a proposal to the management that a withdrawal of the workers and staff members from the dangerous site be organized, and the management must make a decision without delay.

Trade unions have the right to participate in investigations into accidents causing death or injury and other matters seriously endangering the health of the workers and staff members, and to make proposals on solutions to the departments concerned, and they also have the right to demand that the administrative leaders directly responsible and other persons held responsible be investigated for their responsibilities.

Article 25   In case of work-stoppage or slow-down strike in an enterprise, the trade union shall, together with the management or the parties concerned, strive for a settlement through consultation on any demands made by the workers and staff members and that are rational and can be met, so as to restore the normal order of production as soon as possible.

[The remaining articles, dealing with welfare, labour insurance, economic and social planning and so on appear to be at best mildly consultative]

Article 26   Trade unions shall assist the management of enterprises, institutions and state organs in providing adequate collective welfare services for the workers and staff members and in properly dealing with matters concerning wages, labour protection and labour insurance.

Article 27   Trade unions shall join the management in organizing the workers and staff members in sparetime cultural and technical studies and vocational training so as to improve their educational level and professional qualifications, and also in organizing them in recreational and sports activities.

Article 28   When the people's governments at or above the county level work out plans for national economic and social development, and when the people's governments of cities where the people's governments of provinces or autonomous regions are located as well as the People's governments at or above the level of big cities, as approved by the State Council, study and draft laws, regulations or rules, the opinions of the trade unions at the same levels on major problems concerning the interests of the workers and staff members, shall be listened to.

When the People's governments and their relevant departments at or above the county level study and formulate important policies and measures on wages, prices, safety in production, as well as labour protection and labour insurance, the trade unions at the same levels shall be invited to take part in the study and their opinions be listened to.

Article 29   The People's governments at or above the county level may adopt appropriate forms to inform trade unions at the same levels of their important work programmes and administrative measures related to trade union work, and study and settle the problems as reflected in the opinions and aspirations of the masses of workers and staff members conveyed by the trade unions.

[The subsequent chapter mostly deals with basic-level trade unions, workers' congresses and, union committees, and apart from references to joint ventures and foreign-funded firms, does not contain many surprises]

Chapter IV
Basic-Level Trade Union Organizations

Article 30　In an enterprise owned by the whole people, the congress of workers and staff members shall, as the basic form of democratic management of the enterprise and the organ by which the workers and staff members exercise their right to democratic management, discharge its functions and powers in accordance with the stipulations of the Law of the People's Republic of China on Industrial Enterprises Owned by the Whole People.

The trade union committee of an enterprise owned by the whole people shall, as the working body of the congress of workers and staff members, take care of its day-to-day work and check and supervise the implementation of its decisions.

Article 31　The trade union committee of a collectively-owned enterprise shall support and organize the participation of the workers and staff members in democratic management and democratic supervision, and defend their rights in electing and removing managerial personnel and in deciding on major problems concerning operation and management.

Article 32　The trade union in an enterprise owned by the whole people shall be represented in the administrative committee of the enterprise.

The trade union in an enterprise owned by the whole people shall have its representative(s) attending any meetings held by the enterprise to discuss matters on wages, welfare, safety in production, labour protection and labour insurance and other problems related to the vital interests of the workers and staff members.

The director (manager) of an enterprise owned by the whole people shall support the trade union committee in carrying out its activities according to law, and the trade union committee shall support the director (manager) in exercising his functions and powers in accordance with the law.

[The following articles on foreign-funded enterprises are another novel feature of the amended law]

Article 33　Chinese–foreign equity joint ventures and Chinese–foreign contractual joint ventures, while making studies and decisions on issues of wages, welfare, safety in production, labour protection and labour insurance which affect the vital interests of the workers and staff members, shall listen to opinions of the trade unions.

The trade unions in foreign-capital enterprises may advance suggestions on problems affecting the workers' wages, welfare, safety in production, labour protection and labour insurance, and settle such problems with the management through consultation.

Article 34　Basic-level trade union committees shall hold meetings or organize activities for the workers and staff members outside production- or work-hours; they shall seek prior consent from the management, where such meetings or activities are to take up production- or work-hours.

Trade union committee members in enterprises owned by the whole people or the collective, who are not released from production or regular work, shall receive their normal wages if their meetings or activities organized by trade unions take up production- or work-hours, and their other treatments shall also remain unaffected.

Article 35   Full-time functionaries of trade union committees in enterprises and institutions owned by the whole people or the collective and those in state organs shall have their wages, bonuses and subsidies paid by the management of their units. They enjoy the same treatment as other workers and staff members of their units as to labour insurance and other welfare.

[The penultimate and largely uncontroversial chapter deals with trade union funds and property, membership dues, auditing commissions, etc.]

Chapter V
Trade Union Fund and Property

Article 36   The sources of trade union funds are as follows:
(1)   membership dues paid by union members;
(2)   a contribution equivalent to two per cent of workers' monthly payroll paid by the enterprise or institution owned by the whole people or the collective or paid by the state organ where the trade union is established;
(3)   incomes derived from enterprises and undertakings run by trade unions;
(4)   subsidies provided by the people's governments; and
(5)   other incomes.

Chinese–foreign equity joint ventures, Chinese–foreign contractual joint ventures and foreign-capital enterprises where trade unions have been set up shall make contributions to the funds of the trade unions in accordance with the state provisions.
   Trade union funds are used mainly to finance education and other activities for the workers and staff members at the grass-roots level sponsored by trade unions. Measures for the use of trade union funds shall be drawn up by the All-China Federation of Trade Unions.

Article 37   Trade unions shall establish budgets, final accounts and auditing and supervisory systems based on the principle of financial autonomy.
For trade unions at various levels, auditing commissions shall be set up.
Trade unions at various levels shall subject their incomes and expenditures to the examination by the auditing commissions at the corresponding levels, report them regularly to the members' assemblies or congresses and receive their supervision. The trade union members' assemblies or congresses have the right to express their opinions on the use of funds.

Article 38   The People's governments at various levels and the enterprises, institutions and state organs shall make available such necessary material means as facilities and places for trade unions to function and develop their activities.

Article 39   Trade unions' property, funds and immovable property allocated by the state may not be encroached upon, diverted to other uses or arbitrarily disposed of, by any organization or individual.

Article 40   Enterprises and institutions run by trade unions to serve the workers and staff members may not have their affiliation changed arbitrarily.

Article 41   Retired trade union functionaries at or above the county level enjoy the same treatment as retired functionaries of state organs.

Chapter VI
Supplementary Provisions

Article 42   This Law shall come into force as of the date of promulgation. The Trade Union Law of the People's Republic of China, promulgated by the Central People's Government on June 29, 1950, shall be nullified on the same date.

[The 42 Articles constitute the complete text of the Trade Union Law and stand as the formal guide-lines for Industrial Relations practices in contemporary China. Brief comments have been provided by the present writer to highlight the basically bland nature of most of the amended law]

Appendix 2

LABOUR LAW OF THE PEOPLE'S REPUBLIC OF CHINA

The National People's Congress passed a new Labour Law on 5 July 1994 (to come into effect on 1 January 1995). The text was published in the *Renmin Ribao* (People's Daily) and consists of 13 parts. The main points setting out the new legal framework are as follows:

- *workers have the rights to choose jobs, to be paid, to have rest and holidays, to have protection in the workplace and to receive training to improve their skills.*
- *no employment permitted of children below the age of 16.*
- *no discrimination on the basis of race, nationality, sex or religion.*
- *women to enjoy same rights as men.*
- *minimum wage-levels to be set by local governments and reported to the State Council.*
- *contracts must be customary between employers and workers, setting out pay, conditions, tasks to be performed and terms when contracts can be terminated.*
- *enterprises on brink of bankruptcy or in grave difficulties may reduce working staff, provided that the decision is agreed upon by the trade union organization in the enterprise or after consultation with all staff members.*
- *average working week not to exceed 44 hours, with one day off per week.*
- *working day to be limited to eight hours.*
- *women not to work in mines, in conditions of extreme temperatures and after seventh month of pregnancy. After birth, at least 90 days of leave should be given.*
- *dispute committees to be set up in work places and to include both employers and workers.*

Li Boyong, the Minister of Labour, had set out the draft on 2 March 1994 to the legislators at the sixth session of the Standing Committee of the Eighth National People's Congress (NPC) stating that: 'The rights of enterprises to dismiss employees for reasons other than employees' faults will guarantee the legal rights of employers to run businesses independently and will give enterprises a certain edge in market competition.' However, he continued, the limits set for job reductions are 'necessary for China's social stability.' Because China has far more workers than required and such a disparity cannot be changed in a short time; massive job reductions would, he argued, lead to social chaos.

The session had conducted a preliminary review of the draft law. It ruled that the contract system would be the fundamental form in shaping China's labour relations between employers and employees, in both private and publicly owned enterprises. 'This is based on China's experiments in implementing the systems and experiences of other market economies,' he noted.

The draft also accepted in principle the form of 'collective contract' reached by the trade union organization and the enterprise on matters of payment, working conditions and welfare. This system would be mainly implemented in private enterprises. Publicly owned ones would follow after property rights were cleared and operations improved (Xinhua News Agency/SWB, 2 March 1994).

Li Peng, China's Prime Minister, set out the rationale of the new law as follows:

> To meet the requirements of established a socialist market economic structure; promote reform of the labour system; protect labourers' legitimate rights and interests; establish, safeguard and develop a stable and harmonious labour relationship between employers and labourers; and promote economic development and social progress, the Ministry of Labour and departments concerned have drawn up a draft Labour Law. The draft has been discussed and adopted by the State Council's executive meeting. (SWB, 5 March 1994)

The draft had clearly not had an easy path through the political decision-making process, as it had been revised over 30 times over the past ten years.

The degree to which the Labour Law is enforceable and the degree to which it *will* be strictly applied is, of course, moot. The initiative is probably aimed partly to meet the needs of a modernizing economy and partly to answer international criticism of Chinese labour practices. It sets out, like previous legislation in this field, no doubt worthy principles and detailed potential ways of implementing them, but the actual degree of compliance has yet to be tested.

Sources: Xinhua News Agency/SWB 2 March 1994; SWB, 5 March 1994; *Renmin Ribao* (People's Daily) 7 July 1994, p.2; Reuters News Agency Report, 6 July 1994; *Financial Times*, 7 July 1994, p.6.

The text of the Labour Law is reproduced below in full, with brief notes added in brackets. It is an *unofficial* translation into English of the original document published in the *Renmin Ribao*, as noted above. I am most grateful to Yang Weibin for his kind assistance in the matter: see Acknowledgements.

[TEXT OF LABOUR LAW]
Contents

[The document is divided into 13 chapters, each with many sub-sections numbered consecutively throughout, from Item 1 to 107]

Chapter 1: Principles

1. This law is enacted in order to protect the legal interests of labour, regulate labour relations, establish and maintain a labour system compatible with a social market economy, and promote economic development and social progress based on the Constitution.
2. This labour law is applicable to all enterprises, individual economic organizations (named employment units hereafter) and workers involved in labour relations.

   State organizations, institutions, social organizations and workers in labour-contract relations, are all covered by this law.
3. Workers shall have rights of equal employment and choice of job, remuneration for work, rest and holidays, labour safety and hygiene protection, vocational training, social security and welfare and also the rights to seek labour arbitration and other legally regulated labour rights.

   Workers shall complete their given tasks, enhance vocational skills, abide by labour safety and hygiene regulations, as well as labour discipline and professional responsibilities.
4. Employing units shall establish and perfect regulations in systems according to the law, to ensure workers can enjoy their labour rights and also carry out their work duties.
5. The State shall, by all possible means, promote employment opportunities, develop vocational education, establish labour standards, regulate income levels in society, perfect social security, coordinate labour relations, and incrementally enhance living standards of workers.
6. The State shall encourage workers to take part in voluntary work for social ends, promote labour competition and offer constructive suggestions regarding work-improvements, encourage and protect workers in carrying out scientific research and technical innovation, as well as praise and reward workers and professionals.
7. Workers have the right to take part in and organize trade unions according to the law.

   Union representatives shall protect the legal rights and interests of workers independently and autonomously and develop their activities according to the law.
8. Workers shall take part in democratic management, and equal consultation with employment units on the protection of legal interests and interests of workers through workers' conferences, workers' representative congresses and other similar forms within the framework of legal regulation.
9. The Labour Administrative Department of the State Council shall be in charge of labour affairs for the whole country.

Appendix 2

Labour Administrative Departments of local People's Governments at and above county level shall be in charge of labour affairs within their administrative districts.

Chapter 2: Employment and Promotion

10. The State shall create and expand employment opportunities through the promotion of economic and social development.
    The State shall support employing units to set up employment opportunities or to be voluntarily involved in individual businesses.
11. The People's Government at all levels shall, by all means possible, develop multiple types of vocational job-centres to provide employment services.
12. Workers shall not be discriminated against for differences of nationality, race, gender or religious beliefs when seeking employment.
13. Women shall enjoy equal rights with men in employment, when workers are recruited, women shall not be refused work because of their gender or other recruitment criteria, shall not be treated differently because of their gender, except for categories of work and in conditions specified by the State as unsuitable for women.
14. The employment of the disabled, minorities, and ex-military-service personnel as has been specifically regulated by law and other rules previously, shall be continued to be regulated accordingly.
15. Employing units shall not recruit or employ juveniles below the age of 16.
    Arts, sports and other specific units when recruiting juveniles below 16 must abide by the related regulations of the State, go through the procedures for permission and guarantee that such workers have the rights of education.

[After the first two chapters setting out the framework of the law, the next three chapters on labour contracts, wages and work hours are particularly noteworthy and substantive concerning the new directions in enterprise reforms]

Chapter 3: Labour Contracts and Collective Contracts

16. A labour contract is an agreement which defines the employment relations between the employing unit and its workers and clarifies the rights and obligations of both parties.
17. When making or altering a labour contract the principles of equality, voluntariness and agreement through consultation shall be followed; legal and administrative regulations shall not be violated.
    Labour contracts are legally binding when signed according to the law and the parties must fulfil their duties regulated by the contract.

18. Labour contracts are invalid when they are:

    (i)   violating legal and administrative regulations;
    (ii) made by means of cheating, threatening, etc.

    Invalid labour contracts are legally non-binding from the beginning. When partially invalid, the rest of the contract can still be valid if unaffected.

    The invalidity of a contract is to be confirmed by the Labour Dispute Arbitration Committee or the People's Court.

19. A labour contract shall be made in written form and have the following items:

    (i)   period of validity of the contract;
    (ii)   work content;
    (iii) labour protection and conditions;
    (iv)   labour remuneration;
    (v)   labour discipline;
    (vi)   conditions for the termination of the contract;
    (vii) obligations for violating the contract.

    Besides the above indispensable items, other contents can be put into the contract through consultation between the parties.

20. The period of validity of a labour contract can be fixed, unfixed or terminated at the completion of a certain task.

    When a worker has worked in the same employment unit continuously for over ten years and both the worker and the unit agree to renew the contract, indefinite contracts shall be made if demanded by the worker.

21. Trial periods can be regulated in the contract, which cannot exceed six months at the longest.

22. Items concerning the keeping of the business secrets of the employing unit can be regulated by the parties in the labour contract.

23. When the labour contract expires or conditions of termination as agreed by the parties appear, the contract shall be terminated.

24. Labour contracts can be terminated if agreed by the parties after consultation.

25. An employing unit can terminate the labour contract if the worker:

    (i)   is proved to be unqualified during the trial period;
    (ii)   has seriously violated labour discipline or the regulations and systems of the employing unit;
    (iii) has seriously neglected his (or her) duties, or engaged in malpractices for selfish ends so that seriously harmful consequences are caused to the employing unit;
    (iv)   has been charged with criminal offences according to the law.

26. An employing unit can terminate the labour contract, with 30 days' notice in written form directly to the worker, when:

    (i)   a worker has been ill or injured in non-work situations and cannot go on with the original work nor can be assigned other types of work after the period of treatment;

    (ii)   a worker is not qualified for the job and still unqualified after training or changed to another job;

    (iii) the conditions under which the labour contract was made have changed greatly so that it became impossible to carry it out and the parties cannot reach agreement in altering the contract after consultations.

27. When it is necessary to reduce the number of personnel during the period when an employing unit is facing bankruptcy and going through reorganization according to the law or when the state of production or business has serious problems, the trade union or the whole staff shall be notified 30 days in advance and their opinions should be listened to. After a report to the Labour Administration Department, personnel can be made redundant.

When the employing unit which has reduced its personnel numbers according to these regulations is recruiting new staff within the following six months, priority should be given to those who have been made redundant.

28. When an employing unit terminates a labour contract according to Items 24, 26, or 27, financial compensation shall be given according related regulations of the State.

29. An employing unit cannot terminate a labour contract according to Items 26 or 27 of this law when:

    (i)   a worker is suffering from occupational disease or injured at work and has been confirmed to have lost or partially lost his (or her) working capabilities;

    (ii) a worker is in the regulated period of treatment of illness or injury;

    (iii) a woman worker is in the period of pregnancy, childbirth or breast-feeding;

    (iv) other situations as regulated by legal or administrative regulations.

30. The trade union has the right to give its opinions when the termination of a labour contract is improper. If an employing unit has violated the law, other legal regulations or the contract, the union has the right to demand it to be reconsidered; when a worker applies for arbitration or takes legal proceedings, the union should give support and help according to the law.

31. The employing unit shall be notified in written form, 30 days in advance, if a worker wants to terminate a labour contract.

32. Workers can notify the employing unit any time to terminate a labour contract when:

    (i)   in the trial period;

    (ii) forced to work by the employing unit by violent threats or illegally confining personal freedoms;

    (iii) the employing unit fails to pay the compensation or provide the working conditions as regulated in the labour contract.

33. The workers of an enterprise can make a collective contract with the enterprise concerning labour compensation, working hours, rest and break periods, safety and hygiene, insurance and welfare, etc. The draft of the collective contract shall be adopted by the Workers' Congress or carried by the whole staff through discussion. Collective contracts are signed between the union representatives (on behalf of the workers) and the enterprise; where the union is absent, it can be signed between representatives elected by the workers and the enterprise.

34. Once the collective contract is signed, it shall be sent to the Labour Administration Department; if no objection is forthcoming within 15 days after receiving copy of the collective contract, the contract shall become effective thereafter.

35. The collective contract is signed according to the law is legally binding on both the enterprise and the workers of the enterprise. Standards of labour conditions, compensation and so on, in contracts between individual worker and the enterprise cannot be lower than in the regulations noted in the collective contract.

Chapter 4: Working Hours and Breaks/Holidays

36. The State shall institute a system of eight working hours maximum working time daily, with limit of 44 hours weekly on average.

37. For those working at piece-rate, the employing unit shall establish the work-quota and piece/work rate standard according to the regulation of Item 36 of this law.

38. Employing units shall guarantee that workers have at least one day off per week.

39. Enterprises that cannot adopt the regulations of Items 36 or 38 due to their production characteristics may adopt other work and rest arrangements with the permission of the Labour Administrative Departments.

40. Employing units should arrange holidays for workers for:

    (i)   New Year
    (ii)   Spring Festival
    (iii) International Labour Day
    (iv) National Day
    (v)   Other festivals and holidays regulated by law.

41. Employing units may extend working hours, usually not exceeding one hour per day, due to demands of production and business needs after consulting the unions and the workers; when working time extension is needed for particular reasons, working time can be extended for three hours per day, not exceeding 36 hours per month, when the physical health of the worker can be guaranteed.

42. Under one of the following conditions, working time can be extended unrestrained by the regulations of Item 41:

    (i)   when workers' life, health and safety are threatened, needing to be urgently dealt with, due to natural disasters, accidents or other causes;
    (ii) when accidents in production equipment, traffic and transportation and public facilities happen which need to be urgently repaired;
    (iii) in other situations as regulated by law.

43. Employing units cannot extend working times of workers against the regulation of this law.

44. Under one of the following conditions, the employing unit shall pay the workers wage compensation above the wage standard of normal working times:

    (i)   no less than 150 per cent of the wages when extension of working time is arranged;
    (ii) no less than 200 per cent of the wage when work is arranged on days off and cannot be made up afterwards;
    (iii) no less than 300 per cent of the wages when work is arranged on official holidays.

45. The State shall institute a annual paid holidays system.
    Workers who have worked for one year or more shall enjoy annual paid holidays, details of which shall be regulated by the State Council.

Chapter 5: Wages

46. Wage distribution shall follow the principles of 'distribution according to work' and according to the principle of 'same work, same wages'.
    Wage levels shall be raised incrementally in line with economic development. The State shall also regulate the general level of wages.

47. Employing units shall autonomously decide their own wage distribution and wage-level, according to the law, production level, management characteristics and the economic efficiency of the unit.

48. The State shall institute a system of minimum and guaranteed wages.
    Standards of minimum wages shall be regulated by the provincial, autonomous regional and municipal governments and reported to the State Council for the record.
    The wage paid to the workers by the employing unit shall not be lower than the local minimum wage standard.

49. The following factors should be taken into account when establishing and adjusting the minimum wage-standards:

    (i)   the average living expenses of the worker and average number of dependents;

(ii)   average national wage level;
(iii) productivity rate;
(iv)   level of employment;
(v)   differences in economic development levels between regions.

50. Wages shall be paid directly and monthly in monetary form to the worker and not be embezzled, or delayed without justifiable cause.

51. Employing units shall pay the worker wages according to the law for legal holidays, weddings and funerals and social activities taken part in according to the law.

[The next three chapters on safety, protection of women and young workers and training form a related grouping, dealing with the social dimension of work]

Chapter 6: Labour Safety and Hygiene

52. The employing units must establish and perfect their labour safety and hygiene systems, strictly abide by the State labour safety and hygiene regulations and criteria, carry out education for the above on behalf of the workers, in order to prevent accidents in the production process and to reduce occupational hazards.

53. The labour safety and hygiene facilities must meet the criteria set out by the State regulations.
The labour and safety and hygiene facilities of newly-built, amended and expanded industrial projects must be designed, put into operation and used simultaneously with the main industrial projects in hand.

54. The employing units must provide workers with labour safety and hygiene conditions which meet the State regulations and the necessary labour-protection wear and carry out health examinations regularly for employees involved in hazardous work.

55. Workers involved in specific work must be suitably trained and acquire specific work qualifications.

56. Workers must strictly abide by the safety operation regulations in the production process.
Workers have the right to refuse to work as directed by managers of the employing units which violate the regulations or incur risks; they have the right to criticize, report and accuse concerning acts which harm life, safety or physical health.

57. The State shall establish statistical reporting and attempt to deal with accidents involving casualties and occupational diseases. The Labour and Administrative and related departments at and above county-level and employing units shall compile statistics, report and deal with the above involved in all forms of work, according to the law.

Chapter 7: Special Protection for Women and Under-age Workers

58. The State shall institute special protection for women and under-age workers.
    Under-age workers refers to workers over 16 but below 18 years old.
59. It is forbidden to assign women workers work in mines, Class Four physical labour as regulated by the State and other prohibited jobs.
60. Women workers shall not be assigned work at high levels, low temperature or in cold water or be involved in Class Three physical labour as regulated by the State during their menstrual periods.
61. Women workers shall not be assigned Class Three physical labour as regulated by the State or other unsuitable work for pregnancy during their period of pregnancy. Women workers who have been pregnant for over seven months shall not be scheduled to work overtime or on night shifts.
62. Women workers shall enjoy no less than a 90 days' birth absence after giving birth.
63. Women workers should not be assigned Class Three physical labour as regulated by the State or other unsuitable work in the breast-feeding period or work overtime or on night shift, while breast-feeding babies below one year old.
64. Under-age workers shall not be assigned work in mines or hazardous or poisonous conditions or Class Four physical labour as regulate by the State or other unsuitable work.
65. Employing units shall arrange regular physical examinations for under-age workers.

Chapter 8: Vocational Training

66. The State shall adopt all measures to develop vocational training, explore and utilize skills of workers, enhance their qualities and raise their capabilities of employment and work.
67. The People's Government at all levels shall include the development of vocational training in their plans of social and economic development, encourage and support enterprises, institutions, social organizations and individuals with appropriate conditions to develop all forms of vocational training.
68. The employing unit shall establish a vocational training system and use vocational training funds according to regulations of the State to carry out vocational training for its workers with appropriate planning based on their practical needs.
    Workers engaged in skilled work categories must undergo training in advance.
69. The State shall define vocational categories and establish vocational skill standards and institute systems of vocational qualification

certificates for vocations thus regulated. Assessment and appraisal institutions ratified by the government shall take charge of the vocational skill assessment and appraisal of workers.

[The following chapter on social insurance does not go beyond codifying general considerations in this important area]

Chapter 9: Social Insurance and Welfare

70. The State shall develop the social insurance, establish social insurance systems and funds so that workers can obtain help and compensation when they are old, ill, injured at work, unemployed or giving birth.
71. The level of social insurance shall be compatible with the level of social and economic development and the resources of society.
72. The social insurance fund shall decide its source of income fund according to the insurance categories and as planned as a whole by society. Employing units and their workers must take part in the social insurance scheme and pay the insurance premiums according to the law.
73. Workers shall enjoy social insurance according to the law when they are:

    (i)   retired;
    (ii) ill or injured;
    (iii) disabled at work or leaving contracted occupational disease;
    (iv) unemployed;
    (v)   giving birth.

    When worker has died, his or her family member(s) can enjoy a family member stipend according to the law.
    The qualifications and criteria of social insurance that workers enjoy shall be established by law and legal regulations.
    The social insurance that workers enjoy must be paid on time and in the full amount.
74. The social insurance fund managing institutions shall manage and operate the social insurance fund according to the regulations of the law and be responsible for the value, guarantee and appreciation of the social insurance fund.
    The social insurance authorities monitoring institutions shall scrutinize the income and expenses, management and operations of the social insurance fund according to the legal regulations.
    The establishments and functions of the social insurance managing institutions and social insurance monitoring institutions shall be regulated by law.
    No organization or individual shall divert any part of the social insurance fund.

75. The State shall encourage the employing units to establish additional insurance for their workers according to their specific conditions.
    The State shall advocate that workers have individual savings-type insurance.
76. The State shall promote social welfare projects, and set up public welfare facilities for the rest and recuperation of workers.
    Employing units shall create conditions to improve collective welfare and enhance the welfare of their workers.

[The next three chapters on dispute-regulation, monitoring and inspection and legal considerations are particularly interesting for specialists in industrial relations]

Chapter 10: Labour Disputes

77. Labour disputes between employing units and employees shall be resolved through conciliation, arbitration and litigation according to the law, or through consultation.
    Principles of conciliation are applicable to the procedures of arbitration and litigation.
78. Labour disputes shall be resolved on the principles of legitimacy, justice and promptness and the legal interests and rights of both parties should be maintained according to the law.
79. When disputes happen, the litigants can appeal to the Labour Disputes Conciliation Committee of their unit for conciliation. When conciliation fails and one party demands arbitration, it can appeal to the Labour Disputes Arbitration Committee for arbitration. It can also directly appeal to the Labour Disputes Arbitration Committee for arbitration. When dissatisfied with this arbitration, it can litigate in the People's Court.
80. Labour Disputes Conciliation Committees shall be established in the employing units, and comprise employee representatives, employer representatives and trade union representatives, with the chairperson role assigned to the trade union representative.
    Agreement reached through conciliation shall be complied with by the parties.
81. The Labour Disputes Arbitration Committee shall comprise representatives of the labour administration and representatives of the trade unions and employing unit of the same level. The chairperson role of the committee is assigned to the representative of the Labour Administration Department.
82. The party appealing for arbitration should apply in written form to the Labour Arbitration Committee within 60 days of the dispute. The arbitration should generally be made within 60 days after receiving the application. The agreed arbitration judgement must be complied with by the parties.
83. When dissatisfied with such arbitration, the parties may go to the People's Court within 15 days of receiving the arbitration verdict.

When one party neither files suit nor complies with the verdict, the other party can appeal to the People's Court for enforcement.

84. For disputes involving the signing of collective contracts which cannot be resolved through consultation by the parties, the Labour Administration Department of the local People's Government can help with organizing and coordinating the parties involved for a resolution. For disputes complying with the collective contract which cannot be resolved through consultation by the parties, the Labour Disputes Arbitration Committee can be applied to for arbitration; when dissatisfied with the arbitration, litigation to the People's Court can be proposed within 15 days of receiving the arbitration verdict.

Chapter 11: Monitoring and Inspection

85. Labour Administration Departments of the People's Governments of and above county level are to supervise and inspect the employing units abide by labour law and regulations according to the law and are obliged to stop and demand correction of violations.

86. The monitoring and inspecting personnel of the Labour Administration Departments at and above county level have the right to enter the employing units when carrying out their duties to examine how they are abiding by the labour law and labour regulations, look into the necessary archives and inspect work sites.
The monitoring and inspecting personnel when carrying out their duties must show their identity cards, judge impartially and abide by the related regulations.

87. The related departments of the People's Government at and above county levels are to monitor that the employing units abide by labour laws and regulations within each defined set of duties.

88. Trade unions at all levels are to maintain the interests and rights of workers according to the law and monitor that the employing units abide by labour disciplines and regulations.
All organizations and individuals have the right to report and pursue any violations of labour laws and regulations.

Chapter 12: Legal Responsibilities

89. Labour rules and regulations formulated by the employing units which violate the laws and regulations can be warned and correction demanded by the Labour Administration Department; those workers harmed shall be compensated.

90. Employing units which extend working hours of the workers against the legal regulations can be warned, ordered to conform and fined by the Labour Administration Department.

91. Employing units that violate the legal interests and rights of workers in one of the following ways can be made to pay the workers wage remuneration, financial compensation, and can also be made to pay damages by the Labour Administration Department:

    (i)   embezzle, or delay the labour's wages without justifiable cause;
    (ii) refuse to pay extra wage compensation for extended working hours;
    (iii) pay workers at a level below the local minimum wage standard;
    (iv) fail to give financial compensation to workers according to legal regulations when the labour contract is terminated.

92. When employing units do not have labour safety facilities or labour hygiene conditions conforming to the State regulations or fail to provide the workers with necessary labour protection, utensils and facilities, they shall be obliged to conform and shall also be fined by the Labour Administration Department. Those causing serious consequences for workers can be sent to the People's Government at and above county level, which can decide to demand a production stoppage to rectify the situation. Those failing to adopt measures to deal with hidden accidents which lead to heavy accidents, causing life and property costs to the workers, shall be charged with criminal offences according to the regulation of Item 187 of the Criminal Law.

93. When employing units force employees to carry out hazardous work against the regulations, or causing heavy casualties, those responsible shall be accused of criminal offences.

94. Employing units that recruit or employ juveniles below 16 years shall be made to comply with the law by the Labour Administration Department and fined. If the offence is serious, their business licence can be revoked by the Industrial and Business Administration Bureaux.

95. Employing units that violate the regulations of the law for the protection of women and children workers and infringe their legal rights and interests shall be made to comply with the law and fined by the Labour Administration Department. Those causing harm to women and under-age workers shall be responsible for paying damages and compensation.

96. When employing units commit one of the following, their responsible personnel will be penalized by the public security institutions in the form of detention of less than 15 days, a fine or a warning if the responsible personnel are accused of criminal acts:

    (i) to force workers to work by violence, threats or illegally confining personal freedoms;
    (ii) to humiliate, punish physically, beat, search and detain them illegally.

97. Damages caused to workers due to invalid contracts by the employing units shall be compensated.

98. Employing units that terminate labour contracts or deliberately delay the signing of labour contracts conforming by the Labour

Administration Department regulations shall pay damages to the workers involved.

99. Employing units that recruit or employ workers whose labour contracts have not been terminated where this causes financial loss to the former employing units shall be responsible for all related damages according to the law.

100. Employing units that fail to pay social insurance premiums without justifiable causes shall be made to pay within a certain period of time and when overdue may also be charged supplementary fees.

101. Employing units that inhibit unjustifiably the Labour and related Administration Departments and their personnel to carry out their rights of monitoring and inspection, or victimize those who report irregularities shall be fined by the Labour or related Administration Departments; when committing a crime, the responsible personnel shall be charged with criminal offences.

102. Workers who terminate labour contracts against the regulations in this law or violate the security regulations in the labour contract and cause financial loss to the employing unit shall be responsible for damages according to the law.

103. Personnel of labour or related administrations who abuse their power, neglect their duties, practise favouritism and irregularities shall be charged with criminal offences or be given administrative penalties when not.

104. Personnel of the State and those managing Social Insurance Fund who divert social insurance funds and commit related crimes shall be charged with criminal offences.

105. Violations of the workers' legal rights and interests that are to be penalized according to other legal and administrative regulations shall be penalized accordingly.

Chapter 13: Appendix

106. The People's Government of provinces, autonomous regions and direct municipalities are to establish measures of implementation according to each specific condition and report to the State Council for the record.

107. This law shall be put into effect on January 1, 1995.

[To sum up, the 1994 Labour Law *formally* sets out a number of workers' basic rights, notwithstanding choice of job, rest and holidays, social insurance and so on. What is left out may be as important as what is included, such as the omission of the right to strike (removed in the 1982 amendments to the Constitution). Critics have pointed to China's failure to ratify several important International Labour Organization (ILO) conventions. These include numbers 87 and 98, explicitly guaranteeing respectively the right to collective bargaining and the right to freedom of association. To date, 16 ILO conventions have been ratified by successive Chinese governments since 1920, but only *three* in recent times (number 100 on equal remuneration in 1951, number 144 on tripartite consultation in 1976 and number 159 on vocational rehabilitation and employment of disabled persons in 1983). Such conventions are, however, not legally binding and depend on whether national governments adhere to recognized labour standards. Supplementary regulations detailing fines for breaches of the various parts of the 1994 Labour Law and further ones being drafted are noted in summary in official sources. See, for example, *Beijing Review*, 16 January 1995, p. 6.]

Notes

Chapter 1   Setting the Scene

1. The role of economic planning in the Chinese case, never as extensive as in the Soviet model, progressively diminished as the market-mechanisms were introduced over the 1980s (for details see Hsu, 1991). On the foundations of planning in the PRC, see Riskin (1987: Chapter 4).
2. For an elaborated discussion of theories of motivation in organizations, see Cascio (1986); Miner (1993). Knowledge of Western economic theory was (and probably still is) more extensive than that of academic work in organizational behaviour, at least in the mid-1980s (see Ji and Murray, 1992).
3. The debate on loss-making enterprises is set out at length in Nolan (1994b). See also Fan (1994): 'it is not clear whether it is desirable to restrict credit to loss-making enterprises as losses may or may not reflect operational efficiencies.' (1994, p.151). The relaxation of credit to cash-strapped state enterprises in early summer 1994 was announced by Vice-Premier Zhu Rongji, because of fears of labour unrest (see *Financial Times*, 24 May 1994, p.4).
4. The infra-structural services provided by the typical *danwei* in the industrial sector are listed in Leung (1988, pp. 57ff):

crèches	hospitals
kindergartens	clinics
schools: primary	canteens
middle	shops
higher	etc.
technical	

Specific detail is provided in Chapter 7, on benefits provided by enterprises.
5. The enthusiasm for TVEs is reflected in a number of studies, see for example Nee (1992); Weitzman and Xu (1992); Bolton (1993).
6. The *incremental* nature of the Chinese reforms have been a major contributory cause of China's superior performance *vis-à-vis* the former Soviet Union (see Fan and Nolan, 1994). On the costs of environmental pollution see Smil (1993).

Chapter 2   The Iron Rice Bowl: The Early Days

1. The Soviet interest in Taylor dates back to Lenin who coined the phrase 'Socialism plus Taylorism equals Communism' (see Beissinger, 1988). Trotsky was also impressed with this view (see Merkle, 1980, pp.115–21). 'Correct division of labour' was also the slogan of Ordzhonikidze, Special Commissar of Heavy Industry (cited in Dobb, 1966, p.468). 'Stakhanovite' inventive schemes – called by some 'Taylorism in Russian clothes' – became very common in the 1930s (see Warner, 1983).
2. Many Chinese senior managers and academics interviewed in various studies carried out by the present writer over the years had been sent to

study in the USSR, or taught by Soviet experts in the 1950s: their only foreign-language skill, in most instances, was in Russian (see Warner, 1992). Younger Chinese managers, some trained abroad, spoke English with varying degrees of fluency. Those in foreign-funded firms were most likely to be proficient in foreign languages.

3. This section has been specifically added to balance the emphasis on the Soviet influence which tends to dominate Western writing on industrialization in China in the 1950s. I am indebted to colleagues at the Heilongjiang Academy of Social Sciences for details on the above.

4. The Chinese lack of trained managers at the time of the Liberation led to their reliance on politically trained cadres. Schurmann (1966, p.279) believes they felt 'all decision making powers must be concentrated in the hands of the Party, regardless of the economic consequences'. For a later analysis of 'red cadres and specialists', see Laaksonen (1988); Bu (1994).

5. For example, the enterprise profit-retention scheme (launched in May 1959) allowed 5 per cent of the wage-bill to be retained for *ad hoc* bonuses and welfare benefits. In the early 1950s, however, it had been between 4 and 12 per cent (see Takahara, 1992, pp.49–50). After the Liberation, a Director's Fund had been established in each North-Eastern SOE to provide welfare facilities (see Lee, 1987, pp.37–8).

6. Soviet technical experts were sent to China up to 1960. There were over 10 000 such personnel at that time, mostly assisting with technical projects, but some with management training (see Warner, 1992, p.4). After the Sino-Soviet split, they departed precipitately, sometimes even taking their blueprints with them. They helped to set up many large industrial plants, for example in the iron and steel industry. Several (now antiquated) rolling-mills were donated under the ongoing economic and technical aid agreement, including one visited by the present writer (see Chapter 6, on Angang).

Chapter 3   Labour–Management Relations

1. Sources on the early history of the Chinese trade union movement are described at length in Chan (1981) whose historiography of the Chinese labour movement lists both Chinese and foreign language sources. Other authorities, such as Chesnaux (1969), Chen (1985) and Lee (1986) have useful bibliographies.

2. Membership figures of labour organizations in Communist societies always had to be treated sceptically. Such numbers were often largely used for propaganda purposes and were designed to show all-embracing popular support for and higher levels of mobilization in grass-roots bodies (see Pravda and Ruble, 1987).

3. Such collective agreements are not to be seen as evidence of 'collective bargaining' in the Western sense. The former are largely 'top–down' model accords formulated in the Ministry of Labour and Personnel at the time. A draft labour law, submitted to the State Council in March 1994, legally recognized the existence of 'collective contracts', according to a Xinhua News Agency summary (SWB, 5 March 1994).

4. The 'representative' role of Chinese workplace unions (however limited) is to act as a *grievance-channel* and to avoid workers expressing their

discontent by *informal* means, such as by 'go-slows', sabotage, and other forms of worker-resistance, well-documented by industrial psychologists (see Hollway, 1991, for example). On the role of Soviet trade unions in this capacity (see Borizov et al., 1994, p.17):

> Trade unions also had an obligation to defend the considerable legal rights of workers in the face of management violation in such areas as health and safety, disciplinary violations, dismissal, illegal overtime working and underpayment of wages and bonuses.

5. The trade union leadership in the period before the Tiananmen events of spring/summer 1989 was clearly aware of potential grass-roots discontent. They had extensive detailed questionnaire-surveys on attitudes to both union and Party available to them (see Rosen, 1989).
6. The Workers' Autonomous Federation and similar groups pose a problem for the analyst in that it is hard to ascertain their relative importance in the wave of discontent. Whilst they may have had an influence in the city-centre disturbances in 1989 out of all proportion to the adherents involved (see Walder and Gong, 1993) there is sparse evidence available regarding their impact on industrial behaviour. Later, independent groups such as the League for the Protection of the Rights of Working People have tried to officially register themselves but faced intimidation (see *China Labour Bulletin*, No. 2, April 1994, p.12).
7. 'Solidarity-style' activities in Eastern Europe were monitored very closely by the Chinese authorities at the time and subsequently. The CCP watched the forces leading to the collapse of Soviet Communism with concern but non-interference. Lessons drawn from the debacle informed the struggle both for and against reform in China (see Garver, 1993).
8. Corporatism is not necessarily pluralism either. It may however evolve as a *pragmatic* half-way house in the Chinese case (see Chan, 1993) but may be conceptually inappropriate in that interest representation is imperfect at best (see Leung, 1993). It is hard to conceive of the ACFTU becoming an *overly-active* force in this context.

Chapter 4   Economic Reforms and their Implications for Labour

1. Comparisons between the PRC and the USSR are not always unproblematic. The contrast between the 'European' and the 'Asian' paths to the political economy of the move from Stalinism are set out by Chang and Nolan (1994). Whether the term 'European' is the most apposite one here is, however, moot.
2. For a more detailed account of Anshan Iron and Steel, see Chapter 6. The effect of the latest reforms on their employment policies are set out in Chapter 7.
3. Since the early to mid-1980s, many Chinese SOEs have tried to limit the size of their workforce by reducing (or in some cases stopping entirely) recruitment of apprentices and so on (see Warner, 1986). Nonetheless, vocational training was encouraged as an essential part of the Dengist reforms (see CEDEFOP, 1987; Warner, 1992).

4. The attempts to introduce a 'market' for labour proved to be controversial and have remained so (see further references in sections 5.1 and 8.4). Wall (1993, p.13) characterizes these as *incomplete* markets, and as constituting the economics of 'the second-best'. More generally on markets, see Boisot and Child (1988, 1994).

5. Unemployment in urban areas has 'officially' been at a low level, a couple of per cent in the mid-1980s and not much more since then (see Minami, 1994, pp.204–5). The 'real' figures must be seen as considerably higher, given the flow of peasants into the cities in search of 'the good life', but often finding themselves unprotected by labour or social legislation. In many rural areas from which these migrants originate, living-conditions are often poor, with perhaps as many as 80 million peasants living on the poverty-line, a figure conceded in official reports (see Link, 1994). Interior provinces taken together have an average income over 75 per cent lower than coastal ones. A map of rural poverty is set out in Leeming (1992, p.158, figure 8.1).

6. Trained graduates are often able to increase their monetary rewards considerably, but the unavailability of subsidized housing if they moved outside SOEs has sometimes shown the new job in a joint venture to be a 'mixed blessing', given the high price of accommodation in major cities. Foreign-funded firms often preferred to hire those with existing housing (see Björkman and Schapp, 1994).

7. In the recent past, the Northern (or North-Eastern) industrial elite had, for several decades, the premium rewards; in recent years, however, Southern (or South-Eastern) workers have experienced very much higher material rewards. In some respects, this represents a geographical phenomenon of 'rust-belt' versus 'sun-rise' industries found elsewhere (see Leeming, 1992, pp.112–33). Productivity growth per worker in Liaoning Province has hardly risen since the early 1980s, it should be noted (see 1992, p.124).

8. Labour contracts are not in fact a new phenomenon as such, but had hardly ever applied to the Chinese industrial elite. Chinese trade unions had, since the 1920s, pledged to achieve security of employment. Ji (1992, p.172) states that the labour contract system was first tried out in the Special Economic Zones (in Shenzen and Zhuhai), later extended to enterprises in Guangdong, Liaoning and Shandong provinces and eventually to the whole country in 1986. Estimates of the numbers on labour contracts vary a good deal depending on the date and the source (Korzec, 1992). In the state-owned industrial sector the percentage has grown if only because all 'newcomers' to the workforce have had to have contracts since the mid-1980s (see Chapter 6 for further details). 'Temporary Regulations on the use of Labour Contracts in State-run Enterprises' were set out by the State Council in early July 1986 and were operational by the beginning of October of that year (see *Zhongguo Laodong Renshi Bao* – Chinese Labour Personnel Journal, 10 September 1986).

9. If convergence with 'Little Dragon' labour practices is growing (see also the discussion in Chapter 9), those concerned with workers' rights may not feel too sanguine about the prospects, given the range of abuses recorded by bodies like the Hong Kong based Asia Monitor Resource Centre, for example, which is financed by concerned trade unions there (on concern about human rights in the PRC generally, see Goldman, 1994).

10. An earlier equally large ACFTU survey in 1987 had also reported a substantial minority holding negative views on the contracts issue. Although the majority view supported labour contracts, it mainly represented permanent workers. Among those already on contracts, attitudes were more critical. In late 1986, a CP Youth League opinion poll in eight major cities reported even stronger negative views (see Ji, 1992, p.173). Contract workers no longer felt 'masters of the country'. On the unexpected consequences of the labour reforms, see Han and Morishima (1992).

11. A study of Organizational Commitment (OC) in nine Chinese enterprises (Yu et al., 1993) found the rather unexpected result that workers in state-owned enterprises experienced a greater sense of social injustice than their counterparts in non-state firms (in spite of the 'iron rice-bowl'). The Chinese researchers who carried out the investigation hold that 'the lower OC in state-owned firms does not stem mainly from employees' perception of poorer material treatments they receive, but rather from the failure to meet their psychological needs in those non-economic dimensions' (1993, p.193).

12. Trade union representation in foreign-funded firms may vary. Some have both unions and Congresses, others have neither (see Warner, 1989). A more recent Xinhua News Agency report in late 1993 highlighted the emphasis on unionization in such enterprises under the heading 'Foreign firms "obliged" to accept unionization as disputes increase'. It asserted that:

> Most foreign-funded enterprises have normal employer–employee relations. But labour disputes are growing in number because some employers ignore the legitimate rights and interests of their employees, said the official. These employers, he said, often fail to implement the contracts they have signed with their employees. The working conditions they provide are harsh and there have been cases involving employers violating personal freedoms of the work extra hours without proper payment. (SWB, 1 November 1993)

13. In this context, the following report is of interest:

> China has enlisted the Big Mac in its campaign to Smash the Iron Ricebowl. The *Workers' Daily* newspaper ... praised McDonald's for its flexible employment policies, and said state-run enterprises should learn from them. The Iron Ricebowl system guarantees Chinese state workers jobs and benefits for life. The *Workers' Daily* noted that many McDonald's employees worked flexible hours and on a casual basis. McDonald's has challenged our traditional worker systems and given us ideas and enlightenment ... (*China News Digest*, July 1992, p.1).

Chapter 5   Labour Reforms at City Level: Background

1. Comparisons with the two other enterprises studied – namely the Township enterprise (at Huanxin) and the privately owned firm (the Stone Group Corporation in Beijing – controversial because of its financial support for reform activities in Spring 1989) will be only referred to in passing here.

The Township enterprise had 2500 employees and the private firm 3150; both were relatively small *vis-à-vis* the main sample. Both enterprises were highly profitable and above the average level of returns in the sample (Interviews, August 1994).

2. See Appendix 1, for further details on the Revised Trade Union Law of 3 April 1992. The complete text is set out there, for reference purposes. For coverage of labour legislation, see Zheng (1987); Josephs, 1990; Xia (1991). The majority of laws (according to Leung, 1993) only protect employees of SOEs. A draft revised labour law, over ten years in the making, was submitted to the State Council in March 1994 and published in July of that year (see Appendix 2). A regulation to cut work-hours from 48 to 40 hours a *week* was passed at the time. A restriction of overtime to 48 hours a *month* has proved controversial, at least in the eyes of foreign-funded firms. Many workers in TVEs and foreign-funded firms have often little or minimal protection in terms of working conditions and safety, and often experience forced overtime, let alone those confined in prison labour-camps (*lao gai*) said to number over ten million, in over 1000 camps (see Link, 1994).

3. The unemployment benefit levels noted here are only guideline figures and should be compared with those mentioned in Chapters 7 and 8.

4. For references on training in general see Chapter 4, note 3.

5. Several different versions of the contribution levels for social (including labour) insurance, as reported to the present writer, are given in the text (see Chapter 7, section 7.3). Most references to the new scheme mention 2 per cent of the average monthly wage of the previous year as the individual worker's contribution.

6. The Dalian Economic Development Zone's regulations specified the following:

> *Wage Level of Enterprise Workers and Staff.* The wage level of enterprise staff and workers should not be lower than 120 per cent of the average wages of the state-owned enterprises with similar conditions in the same trades in the locality. Retirement and old-age pension should be 20 per cent of the actual wages. The waiting-for-work insurance money for staff and workers should be one per cent of their actual wages.
>
> *Housing Subsidy of Workers and Staff.* The housing subsidy of staff and workers should be 25 per cent of the actual wages.
>
> *Insurance Welfare Expenses.* During the employment period, the insurance welfare treatment (medical treatment subsidy, single-child subsidy, heating subsidy, transport subsidy, female work subsidy, etc) should be given according to relevant regulations as stipulated by the Chinese Government and applied to state-owned enterprise staff and workers, and the necessary expense should be listed in the enterprise costs according to actual conditions.
>
> *Life Subsidy for Ending Labour Contract.* If the labour contracts expire or are renounced because of other legal conditions, the enterprises should give staff and workers a life-subsidy according to their employment term in the enterprises: one month's actual wage for every past year not exceeding twelve months. If a staff member or worker is ill or injured, but this is not work-related, after the medical treatment period stipulated by the Chinese Government for labour contract workers expires, a life-

subsidy should be given to those who cannot take up their former jobs; in addition, medical treatment subsidy for three to six months should be given.

Work Time and Holidays for Workers and Staff. According to stipulations by the Chinese Government, the work-time of staff and workers should not exceed six days a week, and should not exceed eight hours per day. In principle, staff and workers should not work overtime. Under particular conditions, if overtime work is needed, then consent of the staff and workers is required, and overtime work pay should be computed at a rate of 150 per cent of the usual time-pay. Overtime work pay on legal holidays should be computed at a rate of 200 per cent of the usual time-pay.

Holidays stipulated by the State.
(1) Legal holidays: Spring Festival, 3 days; National Day, 2 days; May 1 International Labour Day and New Year's Day, 1 day each. There are altogether 7 days.
(2) Home leave:
     Visiting one's spouse: 30 days per year.
     Unmarried staff and workers visiting parents: 20 days per year or 45 days every 2 years.
(3) Wedding leave: 3 days (for late marriage: 10 days).
(4) Maternity leave: 90 days (for late childbirth: 134 days), 7 days for the husband to take care of his wife and child; 15 days added for difficult labour.
(5) Funeral leave: 3 days for members of one's immediate family.
     (Dalian Economic Development Zone brochure, 1993, pp.9–10)

7.   For further details, see Chapter 7. An assessment of how far the reforms were implemented is given for each of the ten enterprises investigated.
8.   A list of the pilot-enterprises runs as follows:

Shenyang Alloys Factory	Shenyang North Mansions
Shenyang Auto-Engine Factory	Shenyang Paints Factory
Shenyang Brewing Factory	Shenyang Real-Estate Company
Shenyang Electrical Machinery Factory	Shenyang Smelting Works
Shenyang Machine-Tools Factory No. 3	Shenyang Spring Factory
Shenyang Mansions	Shenyang Transformer Factory

9.   The 1986 State Regulations employ the term *citui* (to dismiss) rather than *kaichu* (to fire) as in previous documents (see Korzec, 1992, p.41).
10. Workers breaking labour discipline were previously suspended and placed 'under supervision', with their wages stopped for a period of up to two years.

Chapter 6   Selected Case-Studies at Enterprise Level

1.   Shougang is a classic example of a Chinese overseas-investing state corporation, unusual among SOEs, but a type now growing in potential importance. It has 18 overseas activities in 13 countries and regions,

including North America, Western Europe Union, Hong Kong, Middle East, South-East Asia and the former Soviet Union. More predictably, the privately-owned Stone Group Corporation had also expanded overseas to Australia, Hong Kong, Japan and USA, but on a more limited scale.

2. A new Dalian Port was under construction at Dayao Bay, six kilometres from the Economic Development Zone – eventually 20 berths will be built. This represents one of the four major transit-port projects in the PRC.

3. Dalian Locomotive and Rolling-Stock Works had a relatively high number of high-tech machines, such as computer numerically-controlled (CNC) machine-tools and associated equipment like advanced milling machines, computer-controlled testing equipment and so on. Such equipment was not however anywhere near state of the art technology as found in a comparable Western or Japanese plant (cf. Warner, 1989).

4. Dalian Shipyard does not appear to have confronted overmanning too stringently. Apart from the employment statistics, there was, however, no strong visual evidence of excess personnel when moving around the diverse areas of the Shipyard. Compared to its Japanese or Korean counterparts however, it clearly had an excess of manpower.

5. Harbin Pharmaceuticals was one of the 'flagship' reform enterprises in the city. It had the most 'modern' equipment and layout of the ten enterprises investigated, which was not surprising, as it was the most recently founded plant of all.

6. Harbin Power Equipment provided a sharp contrast with Pharmaceuticals. The plant was also founded in the late 1950s, but had not had the new capital investment visible in the latter case.

7. *Angang* was a 'company town' writ large, covering 154 square kilometres, in fact much of the urban area of Anshan. It physically dominated the city and provided most of its economic and social infrastructure.

8. *Jin Bei* Auto was the first 'share-holding' corporation in the PRC. Since its piloting, over 3700 SOEs, it was claimed, had tried the share-holding scheme, with 69 major ones listing their stocks on the Shanghai and Shenzen stock exchanges with many on the Hong Kong stock market (see *China Daily* 12 August 1993, p.1). Many shares have however begun to 'lose their shine' in terms of their performance falling faster than the Hang Seng index, probably because of initial over-valuation but also because of 'novel accounting practices' whereby welfare provisions are placed 'below the line', and not as an expense 'above the line' as in Western businesses (see *Financial Times*, 6 May 1994, p.26).

9. Data on Shenyang Smelting Works for the early 1980s are set out by Tidrick and Chen (1987, Chapter 2). In the 1980s, it employed somewhat fewer workers. It performed below the average of the World Bank sample and the national average at that time (1987, p.15).

10. See Chapter 5, note 8.

Chapter 7   The 'Three Systems' Reforms

1. *Shougang*'s (and *Angang*'s) exception to the rule *vis-à-vis* labour contracts should be noted. The Township enterprise had complete coverage of employees for labour contracts, and the private firm (Stone

Group Corporation) had one-year rolling contracts (see Interviews, August 1993).

2. DPA's payment-system was too complex and variegated to go into a standard labour contract.

3. DLRS's relations with their Ministry probably gave them a different status on labour contracts.

4. Workers operating their own business off the site (or even on it, in some cases) was a growing phenomenon in China. The tighter disciplinary clauses (such as on absenteeism) noted in this chapter were in part designed to confront such problems. Earlier State Regulations (of 10 April 1982) codified the penalties for 'violating labour discipline', based on the original 1957 rules (see Korzec, 1992, p.40).

5. Harbin Pharmaceuticals faced an expanding market for its products. It was already the largest production base for semi-finished antibiotics in Heilongjiang Province.

6. The interviews with managers here took place in the presence of senior trade union officials, unlike instances in other firms. In the latter cases, only the personnel concerned with the specific function in question, such as production, were present.

7. No reasons were given by the Personnel Department for this limited extent of labour contracts. Comparisons with Shougang are apposite. By international standards, both were relatively overmanned. As employees in the iron and steel industry were traditionally among the key members of the Chinese industrial (and political) elite, grass-roots opposition to changing their employment status might explain their exemption to date *vis-à-vis* the 'comprehensive' labour contract status (see Brislin, 1994 on intra-elite conflict and the economic reforms).

8. *Jin Bei* Auto was the only firm in the sample where we encountered a contemporary overt Japanese influence in terms of either technology or management, other than the private Stone Group Corporation. Previous investigations by the present writer had however covered some firms with similar training cooperation (see Warner, 1989).

9. Compare these levels with unemployment benefits (see Chapter 5, section 5.3). The payment once six months had elapsed was relatively low in terms of the average industrial worker's wage in the firm or in the city. The incentive to complete the retraining programme successfully was therefore strong.

10. Seventy-five per cent of basic wage was the figure cited for the newly unemployed in the interviews with Beijing Municipal Labour Bureau (see Chapter 5, section 5.3). Nationally, urban workers may receive less than this, between 50 per cent and 70 per cent. As the current minimum wage was 200 yuan a month on average, many laid off may get as little as 50 yuan for this period, leaving them below the urban poverty-level.

11. This example appears to be the model for wage reform laid down from above (for previous top–down examples see Takahara, 1992). It is clear that as 'a labour-market has hardly existed, government wage policy lies at the heart of the question' (1992, p.2). See also the discussion in Chapter 9.

12. There was apparent general conformity (as reported in interviews) with the national law on social insurance, in the SOE sector at least. It is likely that the 'safety-net' for these firms' workers has been implemented, but no

details were readily available of how comprehensively and speedily benefit-payments were made.

13.   The average income in the Township enterprise, it was claimed, was around 4800 yuan per annum and in the private Stone Group Corporation 'above average' and higher than the middle of the range, but less than the top, 'in comparable joint ventures' (Interviews, August 1993). Compare this level with the national annual wage across Chinese industry of approximately 2700 yuan with bonuses added of just over 500 yuan a year (see Table 7.2) (SSB, 1993).

14.   The Dalian figures may be somewhat exaggerated, however. A survey of foreign-funded firms in Beijing and Shanghai estimated average pay of around 6500 yuan and for Guangdong just over 10 000 yuan a year (see Björkman and Schaap, 1994).

Chapter 8   Discussion

1.   This figure on losses in SOEs was generally quoted. The appropriate level of government subsidies and credit to 'bail-out' such firms may be seen mainly as a subsidy to employment in those cities. In order to contain the drain on resources, wage-levels were frozen in all such enterprises nationally in September 1993. Some managers in loss-making SOEs were recently only able to pay 60 to 70 per cent of wages and salaries (see Link, 1994, p.32). An ACFTU study found that wage arrears in ten cities in Heilongjiang Province totalled 2.66 billion yuan in 1993. Seven in ten firms had paid their wages three to six months late. The official Chinese government explanation was the introduction of the new tax-system (see *Beijing Review*, 13 June 1994, pp.20–1) had turned profits into temporary losses for many firms. Just under half of all state-owned firms were described by the State Statistical Bureau in the first quarter of 1994 as 'being in the red' (see Chapter 1).

2.   The cadre contracts were the responsibility of a separate Ministry, namely that of Personnel (see following note 3).

3.   The MoLP had been split into two separate Ministries of Labour (*laodong bu*) and Personnel (*renshi bu*) just prior to the new wave of 'all-in' reforms.

4.   The adaptation was largely to the requirements of the emerging local 'labour market'. Severe shortages of 'key personnel' lay behind this necessity, although there was a 'labour surplus' generally, both internally and externally (see Minami, 1994, pp.204ff).

5.   Gao's (1994) explanation is rather odd in that it implies a 'class' gain from the increase in 'individual' job-choice. The author seems to be falling over backwards to justify the 'labour-service market' in theoretical terms, as well as ideological legitimacy. (For an earlier discussion of this last point, see Chapter 4 on the first steps in debate in the mid-1980s.)

6.   The official inflation figure was 25.9 per cent by the end of 1993, and 27.4 per cent in September 1994 (see *Financial Times Survey: China*, 7 November 1994, p.iii). The 'real' rate of urban inflation was probably much higher. The authorities' concern for sensitive handling of the current situation, especially where related to rationalization of industry and employment was reflected in an editorial in the *People's Daily* (*Renmin*

Ribao, 23 May 1994, p.1) admitting conflicts were inevitable between centre and localities, enterprises and employees, and so on.

7. Sichuan Province was planning to sell-off the best of 33 SOEs in mid-1994 'to make the best use of State-owned assets' in Chengdu, Chongqing and other cities and towns. These were principally in machine-building, electronics, metallurgical, chemical, building materials, food processing, pharmaceutical, textile and light industries. Most of these are already profit-making enterprises. Foreign investors will be able to buy firms outright, or invest in a joint venture as shareholder. In some cases, the workers' employment is to be protected; in others, they will be re-employed by the local government (*Beijing Review*, 30 May 1994, p.28).

Chapter 9 Human Resource Management 'With Chinese Characteristics'?

1. For example, ICI's joint venture in China used the term 'Human Resources Development Manager' for the person responsible for this area of personnel management. See also Björkman and Schaap (1994) and Child (1994) on personnel and HRM practices in joint ventures.
2. In the Japanese case, the work of Westney (1987) is instructive. This study covers 'knowledge-transfer' in the late nineteenth century regarding the implanting of new institutions such as the Post Office, Police, and so on.
3. See Whitehill (1991) on Japanese corporate values. A useful comparison is drawn between Chinese and Japanese macro- and micro-level experience by Minami (1994). Personnel and HR management in Japanese firms is discussed in Ballon (1992) and Okazaki-Ward (1993). On overseas Chinese enterprises and managerial behaviour, see Redding (1990).
4. It is still necessary for top personnel to be Party members in most instances. The Party Organization Department holds the file (*dang'an*) on the person concerned. A person cannot transfer to another enterprise without the *dang'an* being released by the former employing organization (see Björkman and Schapp, 1994).

Chapter 10 Conclusions: Summing-Up

1. See Child (1994) for an application of an organizational theory framework to the Chinese management context. See also Shenkar and von Glinow (1994): some theories like population ecology are not appropriate, but others such as those relating to the structure and process of Chinese enterprises generally are so.
2 For a further discussion, see Warner (1993) on this point. This particular contribution has aroused a fair degree of controversy, as it has tended to criticize HRM specialists in the field.
3. Estimates of future economic growth-rates tend to suggest a somewhat lower level, at best. See World Bank (1993) for example. Optimists still believe a level close to the 9 per cent annual growth of the last decade is feasible; pessimists estimate it closer to 6 per cent. Wall (1993) lists a number of worries relating to predictions of Chinese growth-rates:

Some of it is illusory. It doesn't exist. It is a fallacy of national income accounting ... some outputs are measured by their inputs ... (some) simply consist of the monetization of activities previously outside the market' (1993, p.13).

4.   As Saich has rather robustly characterized it:

The pursuit of economic riches without genuine marketization and democratization and where power remains hierarchically structured with information dependent on position is resulting in corruption being institutionalized. A system of state, society, Party and bureaucratic reciprocities is the operational norm. Public enterprises controlled by the State can become in practice fiefdoms plundered by those who run them, with a market system in which goods and services are less important than power and prestige. The combination of Party appointment to controlling positions and a dual economy is creating a hybrid economic formation that one might refer to as 'nomenclature capitalism'. The real good of value in this form of market is information that can be traded for money or, more often for further power. This path of projected development may not be very appealing but it is potentially a very real one. (Saich, 1993, pp.1159–60)

5.   The estimates by the Ministry of Labour and ACFTU include strikes, slow-downs, demonstrations and so on in the 10 000 or more cases of industrial action. Over 250 000 disputes have been officially noted since 1988, with only one-fifth officially recorded by labour bureaux. Another estimate raises this total to over one million such cases for 1987–92. Labour disputes are said to be frequent among foreign-funded ventures (see *China Labour Bulletin*, March 1994, p.9; June 1994, p.5). The *Bulletin* is produced by Han Dongfang, a co-founder of the Beijing Workers' Autonomous Federation, imprisoned for 22 months in 1989. He was released after contracting tuberculosis in jail and sent to the US. Han produces the publication, in Hong Kong, of which over 1000 copies are smuggled into mainland cities, although many more thousands are said to be faxed and photocopied (see the *Observer*, 29 May 1994, p.8).

6.   Cited in *China Labour Bulletin*, December 1994, p. 7.

References

ACFTU (1988) *The Eleventh National Congress of Chinese Trade Unions* (Beijing: All China Federation of Trade Unions).

Andors, S. (1977) *China's Industrial Revolution* (London: Martin Robertson).

Aoki, M. (1988) *Information, Incentives and Bargaining in the Japanese Economy* (Cambridge: Cambridge University Press).

Associated Press News Agency, various, see text.

Ballon, R.J. (1992) *Foreign Competition in Japan: Human Resource Strategies* (London: Routledge).

Banks, J. (1974) *Trade Unionism* (London and New York: Collier/Macmillan).

Barnowe, J.T. (1990) 'Paradox Resolution in Chinese Attempts to Reform Organizational Cultures', in (eds) J. Child and M. Lockett, *Reform Policy of the Chinese Enterprise*, Vol.1 (Part A) of *Advances in Chinese Industrial Studies* (Greenwich, Conn., and London: JAI Press) pp.329–48.

Beasley, W.G. (1963) *A Modern History of Japan* (London: Routledge).

Beijing Review, various – see text.

Beissinger, M.R. (1988) *Scientific Management, Socialist Discipline and Soviet Power*, (Cambridge, Mass.: Harvard University Press).

Björkman, I. and Schapp, A. (1994) 'Human Resource Management Practices in Sino-Western Joint Ventures', *Working Paper*, Swedish School of Economics, Helsinki.

Boisot, M.H. and Child, J. (1988) 'The Iron Law of Fiefs: Bureaucratic Failure and the Problems of Governance in the Chinese Economic Reforms', *Administrative Science Quarterly*, Vol.33, No.3, pp.507–27.

Boisot, M.H. and Child, J. (1994) 'China's Emerging Economic Order: Modernization through "Weak" Markets and Quasi-Capitalism?', Paper given to conference on 'Management Issues for China in the 1990s', St John's College, Cambridge, March 23–25.

Bolton, P. (1993) 'Privatization and the Separation of Ownership and Control', Paper to CEA – Chinese Economics Association (UK), Fifth Annual Conference, at London School of Economics, 14–15 December.

Bond, M.H. (1986) (ed.) *The Psychology of the Chinese People* (Hong Kong: Oxford University Press).

Bond, M. and Hwang, K.K. (1986) 'The Social Psychology of the Chinese People', in (ed.) M. Bond, *The Psychology of the Chinese People* (Hong Kong: Oxford University Press) pp.213–66.

Borisov, V., Clarke, S. and Fairbrother, P. (1994) 'Does Trade Unionism have a Future in Russia?' *Industrial Relations Journal*, Vol.25, No.1, pp.15–25.

Brandt, C. (1958) *Stalin's Failure in China, 1924–1927* (New York: W.W. Norton).

Brislin, S. (1994) 'The Changing Centre – Provinces Paradigm and the Policy-Making Process in Post-Mao China', Paper to INSEAD Conference on 'The Future of China', Fontainebleau (France), 4–5 February.

Brown, E.C. (1966) *Soviet Trade Unions and Labor Relations* (Cambridge, Mass: Harvard University Press).

Brown, D.H. and Branine, M. (1994) 'Adoptive Personnel Management: Making Sense of Managing the Human Resources in China's Foreign Trade Corporations', Paper to conference on 'Management Issues for China in the 1990s', St John's College, Cambridge, 23–25 March.

Brugger, W. (1976) *Democracy and Organization in the Chinese Enterprise, 1948–1953* (Cambridge: Cambridge University Press).

Bu, N. (1994) 'Red Cadres and Specialists as Modern Managers: An Empirical Assessment of Managerial Competencies in China', *International Journal of Human Resource Management*, Vol.5, No.2, May, pp.357–85.

Byrd, W. and Tidrick, G. (1987) 'Factor Allocation and Enterprise Incentives', in (eds) G. Tidrick and J. Chen, *China's Industrial Reforms* (Oxford: Oxford University Press) pp.60–102.

Cascio, W.F. (1986) *Managing Human Resources: Productivity, Quality of Work Life, Profits* (New York: McGraw-Hill).

CEDEFOP (1987) *Vocational Training in the PRC* (CEDEFOP, Berlin 1987).

Chan, A. (1993) 'Revolution or Corporatism? Workers and Unions in Post-Mao China', *Australian Journal of Chinese Affairs*, No.29, pp.31–61.

Chan, M.K. (1981) *Historiography of the Chinese Labour Movement* (Stanford, Calif: Stanford University Press).

Chang, H.J. and Nolan, P. (1994) 'Europe *versus* Asia: Contrasting Paths to the Reform of Centrally Planned Systems of Political Economy', Paper to conference on 'Management Issues for China in the 1990s', St John's College, Cambridge, 23–25 March 1994.

Chen, P.K. (1985) *The Labour Movement in China* (Hong Kong: Swindon Books).

Cheng, T. and Selder, M. (1994) 'The origins and social consequences of China's *Hukou* system', *China Quarterly*, No.139 (September), pp. 644–68.

Chesneaux, J. (1969) *The Chinese Labor Movement, 1919–1927* (Stanford: Stanford University Press).

Chiang, C. (1990) 'The Role of Trade Unions in Mainland China', *Issues and Studies*, Vol.26, No.2, pp.94–100.

Child, J. (1990) 'The Structure of Earnings in Chinese Enterprises and some Correlates of their Variation', in (eds) J. Child and M. Lockett, *Reform Policy and the Chinese Enterprise*, Vol.1 (Part A) of *Advances in Chinese Industrial Studies* (Greenwich, Conn. and London: JAI Press) pp.227–46.

Child, J. (1994) *Chinese Management during the Age of Reform* (Cambridge: Cambridge University Press).

Child, J., Loveridge, R. and Warner, M. (1973) 'Towards an Organizational Study of Trade Unions', *Sociology*, Vol.7, No.2, pp.71–91.

Child, J. and Xu, X. (1989) 'The Communist Party's Role in Enterprise Leadership at the High-Water of China's Economic Reform', *Working Paper*, Beijing: Economic Management Institute.

China Daily, various, see text.

China Labour Bulletin – see text.

Chinese News Digest – see text.

Chinese Trade Unions, various, see text.

Choucri, N., North, R.C. and Susuma, Y. (1992) *The Challenge of Japan before World War II and After: A Study of Growth and National Expansion* (London: Routledge).

Daily Telegraph, various, see text.

Davis, D. (1993) 'Job Mobility in Post-Mao Cities: Increases on the Margin', *China Quarterly*, No.132 (December) pp.1062–85.

Dittmer, L. (1994) *China under Reform* (Boulder, Colo., and Oxford: Westview Press).

Dobb, M. (1966) *Soviet Development since 1917* (London: Routledge).

Dong, F. (1987) 'On the Labour System and Whether Labour is a Commodity', *Guangming Ribao*, 4 October, p.4.

Duus, P. (1989) 'Introduction', in (eds) P. Duus, R.H. Myers and M. Peattie, *The Japanese Informal Empire in China, 1895–1937* (Princeton, NJ, Princeton University Press) pp.ix–xi.

Duus, P., Myers, R.H., and Peattie, M.R. (1989) (eds) *The Japanese Informal Empire in China, 1985–1937* (Princeton, NJ: Princeton University Press).

Easterby-Smith, M., Malina, D., and Lu, Y. (1994) 'How Culture Sensitive is HRM? A Comparative Analysis of Practice in Chinese and UK Companies', *Working Paper*, Management School, University of Lancaster, England.

Echoes from Tiananmen (Hong Kong), various, see text.

Economic Daily, see text.

Economist, The, various, see text.

Edelstein, J.D. and Warner, M. (1979) *Comparative Union Democracy: Organization and Opposition in British and American Trade Unions* (New Brunswick, NJ: Transaction Books).

Fairbank, J.K. (1987) *The Great Chinese Revolution: 1800–1985* (New York: Harper and Row).

Fan, Q. (1994) 'State-owned Enterprises in China: Incentives and Environment' in (eds) Q. Fan and P. Nolan, *China's Economic Reforms: The Costs and Benefits of Incrementalism* (London: Macmillan) pp.137–58.

Fathers, M. and Higgins, A. (1989) *Tiananmen: The Rape of Peking* (London: *The Independent* and Doubleday).

Financial Times, various, see text.

Feuerwerker, A. (1958) *China's Early Industrialization* (Cambridge, Mass: Harvard University Press).

Gao, S. (1994) 'Market Economy and the Labor Force Market', *Beijing Review*, 3 January, pp.14–16.

Garver, J.W. (1993) 'The Chinese Communist Party and the Collapse of Communism', *China Quarterly*, No.133 (March) pp.1–26.

Goffmann, E. (1959) *The Presentation of Self in Everyday Life* (Garden City, NY: Doubleday).

Goffman, E. (1961) *Asylums* (Harmondsworth, Mddx.: Penguin Books).

Goldman, M. (1989) 'Vengeance in China', *New York Review of Books*, Vol.36, 5 November, pp.10–13.

Goldman, M. (1994) *Sowing the Seeds of Democracy in China: Political Reform in the Deng Xiaoping Era* (Harvard: Harvard University Press).

Gong, Y. (1989) 'Chinese Trade Unions' Function of Democratic Participation and Social Supervision', *Chinese Trade Unions*, Vol.2, No.1, pp.2–5.

Gongren Ribao (Workers' Daily), various, see text.

Granick, D. (1987) 'The Industrial Environment in China and the CMEA Countries' in (eds) G. Tidrick and Y. Chen, *China's Industrial Reforms* (Oxford: Oxford University Press), pp.103–31.

Granick, D. (1990) *Chinese State Enterprises: A Regional Property Rights Analysis* (Chicago and London: University of Chicago Press).

Granick, D. (1991) 'Multiple Labour Markets in the Industrial State Enterprise', *China Quarterly*, No.126 (June), pp.269–89.

Guest, D. (1992) 'Right Enough to be Dangerously Wrong: An Analysis of the "In Pursuit of Excellence" Phenomenon', in (eds) G. Salaman et al., *Human Resource Strategies* (London: Routledge) pp.5–19.

Guillermaz, J. (1972) *A History of the Chinese Communist Party* (New York: Random House).

Han, J. and Morishima, M. (1992) 'Labour System Reform in China and its Unexpected Consequences, *Economic and Industrial Democracy*, Vol.13, No.3, pp.233–61.

Henley, J.S. and Nyaw, M.K. (1986) 'Introducing Market Forces into Managerial Decisionmaking in Chinese Enterprises', *Journal of Management Studies*, Vol.23, No.6, pp.635–56.

Hussein, A. (1993) 'Reform of the Chinese Social Security System', Working Paper, Development Economics Research Programme, London School of Economics, October.

Henley, J.S. and Nyaw, MK (1990) 'The system of management and performance of joint ventures in China : Some evidence from the Shenzen special economic zone', in (ed.) N. Campbell and J.S. Henley, *Joint Ventures and Industrial Change in China*, Vol.1 (Part B) of *Advances' in Chinese Industrial Studies* (Greenwich, Conn. and London : JAT Press), pp.277–96.

Hofstede, G. (1980) *Culture's Consequences: International Differences in Work-Related Values* (Beverley Hills, Calif., and London: Sage).

Hofstede, G. (1991) *Culture and Organizations: Software of the Mind* (London and New York: McGraw-Hill).

Hollway, W. (1991) *Work Psychology and Organizational Behaviour: Managing the Individual at Work* (Newbury Park, Calif. and London: Sage).

Howe, C. (1971) *Wage Patterns and Wage Policies in Modern China, 1919–1972* (Cambridge: Cambridge University Press).

Howe, C. (1992) 'Foreword', in M. Korzec, *Labour and the Failure of Reform in China* (London: Macmillan) pp.vii–x.

Howell, J. (1992) 'The Myth of Autonomy: The Foreign Enterprise in China', in (eds) C. Smith and P. Thompson, *Labour in Transition: The Labour Process in Eastern Europe and China* (London: Routledge) pp.205–26.

Hsu, R.C. (1991) *Economic Theories in China, 1979–1988* (Cambridge: Cambridge University Press).

IDE: International Research Group (1981) *Industrial Democracy in Europe* (Oxford: Oxford University Press).

IDE: International Research Group (1993) *Industrial Democracy in Europe Revisited* (Oxford: Oxford University Press).

Independent, The, various, see text.

Independent on Sunday, The.

Jacka, T. (1992) 'The Public-Private Dichotomy and the Gender Division of Labour', in (ed.) A. Watson, *Economic Reform and Social Change in China*, (London: Routledge) pp.117–43.

Ji, L. (1992) 'Management by Objectives and China's Reform of the Employment System', in (ed.) W.C. Wedley, *Changes in the Iron Rice Bowl: The*

Reformation of Chinese Management, Vol.3 of *Advances in Chinese Industrial Studies* (Greenwich, Conn., and London: JAI Press) pp.169–81.

Ji, L. and Murray, V. (1992) 'Obstacles to the Development of Organizational Behaviour', in (ed.) W.C. Wedley, *Changes in the Iron Rice Bowl: The Reformation of Chinese Management*, Vol.3 of *Advances in Chinese Industrial Studies* (Greenwich, Conn. and London: JAI Press) pp.155–68.

Jiang, Y. (1980) 'The Theory of an Enterprise-Based Economy', *Social Sciences in China*, Vol.1, No.1, pp.48–70.

Jiang, Y. and Zhou, S. (1992) Critique of Economic Reform, *Economic Daily*, 10 November, p.2.

Josephs, H.K. (1990) *Chinese Labour Law* (London: Butterworths).

Kaple, D.A. (1994) Dream of a Red Factory: *The Legacy of Stalinism in China* (New York: Oxford University Press).

Korzec, M. (1992) *Labour and the Failure of Reform in China* (London: Macmillan).

Laaksonen, O. (1988) *Management in China During and After Mao* (Berlin: de Gruyter).

Lansbury, R.D., Ng, S.K. and McKern, R.B. (1984) 'Management at Enterprise Level in China', *Industrial Relations Journal*, Vol.15, No.1, pp.56–64.

Lee, L.T. (1986) *Trade Unions in China: 1949 to the Present* (Singapore: Singapore University Press).

Lee, P.N.S. (1987) *Industrial Management and Economic Reform in China, 1949–1984* (Oxford: Oxford University Press).

Legge, K. (1989) 'Human Resource Management: A Critical Analysis' in (ed.) J, Storey, *New Perspectives on Human Resource Management* (London: Routledge) pp.19–40.

Leeming, F. (1992) *The Changing Geography of China* (Oxford: Blackwell).

Leung, W.Y. (1988) *Smashing the Iron Rice Pot: Workers and Unions in China's Market Socialism* (Hong Kong: Asia Labour Monitor Centre).

Leung, W.Y. (1993) 'Stalinist Unions Under Market Socialism', *Working Paper*, Dept of Political Science, University of Hong Kong.

Li, H. (1989) 'The Democratic Management of Enterprises and Workers' Awareness of Democracy', *Chinese Economic Studies*, No.2 (Summer) pp.69–80.

Link, P. (1994) 'The Old Man's New China', *New York Review of Books*, Vol.41, 9 June, pp.31–6.

Littler, C.R. and Lockett, M. (1983) 'The Significance of Trade Unions in China', *Industrial Relations Journal*, Vol.14, No.4, pp.31–42.

Littler, C.R. and Palmer, G. (1987) 'Communist and Capitalist Trade Unionism: Comparisons and Contrasts' in (eds) A. Pravda and B.A. Ruble, *Trade Unions in Communist States* (London: Allen & Unwin) pp.253–72.

Liu, J., Wang, W., He, P. and Liu, J. (1988) (eds) *Qiye Gongzi Gaige Shiyong Shouce* (A Practical Handbook of Enterprise Wage Reform) (Beijing: China Urban Economy and Society Press).

Liu, T. (1989) 'Chinese Workers and Employees Participate in Democratic Management of Enterprises', *Chinese Trade Unions*, Vol.2, No.1, pp.5–10.

Lockett, M. (1980) 'Bridging the Division of Labour? The Case of China',. *Economic* and *Industrial Democracy*, Vol.1, No.4, pp.447–86.

Lockett, M. (1988) 'Culture and the Problem of Chinese Management', *Organization Studies*, Vol.9, No.3, pp.475–96.

Lu, P. (1991) (ed.) *The Moment of Truth: Workers' Participation in China's 1989 Democracy Movement and the Emergence of Independent Unions* (Hong Kong: Asia Monitor Resource Centre).

Ma, C. (1955) *History of the Labour Movement in China* (Taipei: China Cultural Service).

Mahoney, T.A. and Deckop, J.R. (1986) 'Evolution of the Concept and Practice in Personnel Administration and HRM', *Journal of Management*, Vol.12, No.2, pp.223–41.

Meaney, C.S. (1988) *Stability and the Industrial Elite in China and the Soviet Union* (Berkeley, Calif: University of California Press).

Merkle, J. (1980) *Management and Ideology: The Legacy of the Scientific Management Movement* (Berkeley, Calif.: University of California Press).

Minami, R. (1994) *The Economic Development of China: A Comparison with the Japanese Experience* (London: Macmillan).

Miner, J.B. (1993) *Role Motivation Theories* (London: Routledge).

Nakagone, K. (1989) 'Manchukuo and Economic Development', in (eds) P. Duus et al., *The Japanese Informal Empire in China, 1895–1937* (Princeton, NJ: Princeton University Press) pp.133–58.

Nevis, E.C. (1983) 'Using an American Perspective in Understudying Another Culture: Towards Hierarchy of Needs for the People's Republic of China', *Journal of Applied Behavioural Science*, Vol.19, No.3, pp.249–64.

Nish, I. (1985) *The Origins of the Russo-Japanese War* (London: Longman).

Nolan, P. (1994a) 'Introduction: The Chinese Puzzle', in (eds) Q. Fan and P. Nolan, *China's Economic Reforms: The Costs and Benefits of Incrementalism* (London: Macmillan) pp.1–20.

Nolan, P. (1994b) 'Large Firms and Industrial Reform in Former Planned Economies: The Case of China', *Cambridge Journal of Economics* (in press).

Observer, (The) – see text.

Okazaki-Ward, L. (1993) *Management Education and Training in Japan* (London: Graham and Trotman/Kluwer Academic).

People's Daily, various, see text.

Nee, V. (1992) 'Organizational Dynamics of Market-Transition : Hybrid Forms, Property Rights and Mixed Economy in China', *Administrative Science Quarterly* 37: 1–27.

Perry, E.J. (1993) *Shanghai on Strike: The Politics of Chinese Labour* (Stanford, Calif.: Stanford University Press).

Perry, E.J. (1994) 'Shanghai's Strike Wave of 1957', *China Quarterly*, No.137 (June), pp.1–27.

Poole, M. (1986) *Industrial Relations: Origins and Patterns of National Identity* (London: Routledge).

Poole, T. (1993) 'Workers Fear Loss of Rice Bowl for Life', *The Independent*, 20 May, p.14.

Poole, T. (1994) 'Market Forces Unscramble the Chinese Egg', *The Independent*, 19 March, p.15.

Portes, R. (1993) 'From Planning to Markets – Eastern Europe and Comparisons with China', Paper to CEA – Chinese Economics Association (UK). Fifth Annual Conference at London School of Economics, 14–15 December.

Pravda, A. and Ruble, B.A. (1987) (eds) *Trade Unions in Communist States* (London: Allen & Unwin).

Pye, L. (1991) 'The Individual and the State: An Overview Interpretation', *China Quarterly*, No.117 (September) pp.443–66.

Redding, G. (1990) *The Spirit of Chinese Capitalism* (Berlin and New York: de Gruyter).

Reuters News Agency, various, see text.

Richman, B. (1969) *Industrial Society in Communist China* (New York: Random House).

Riskin, C. (1987) *China's Political Economy: The Quest for Development since 1949* (Oxford: Oxford University Press).

Rosen, S. (1989) (ed.) Special Issue: 'The All-China Federation of Trade Unions' Survey of China's Workers and Staff', *Chinese Economic Studies* (Summer).

Saich, T. (1993) 'The Fourteenth Party Congress: A Programme for Authoritarian Rule', *China Quarterly*, No.132 (December), pp.1136–60.

Sano, Y. (1977) 'Seniority-based Wages in Japan: A Survey', *Japanese Economic Studies*, Vol.5, No.1, pp.48–65.

Schurmann, F. (1966) *Ideology and Organization in Communist China* (Berkeley, Calif: University of California Press).

Shenkar, O. and Ronen, S. (1993) 'The Cultural Context of Negotiations: The Implications of Chinese Interpersonal Norms', in (eds) L. Kelley and O. Shenkar, *International Business in China* (London: Routledge) pp.191–207.

Shenkar, O. and Ronen, S. (1987) 'Culture, Ideology or Economy: A Comparative Exploration of Work Goal Importance Among Managers in Chinese Societies', *Academy of Management Journal*, Vol.30, No.3, pp.564–7.

Shenkar, O. and von Glinow, M.A. (1994) 'Paradoxes of Organizational Theory and Research: Using the Case of China to Illustrate National Contingency', *Management Science* (in press).

Schram, S.R, (1963) *The Political Thought of Mao Tse-Tung* (New York: Praeger).

Sklair, L. (1991) *Sociology of the Global Systems* (New York/London: Harvester Wheatsheaf).

Smil, V. (1993) *China's Environmental Crisis* (New York: M. E. Sharpe).

South China Morning Post, various, see text.

SSB (State Statistical Bureau) *Statistical Outline of China* (*Zhongguo Tongji Zhaiyao*) (Beijing: China Statistical Press) various years.

Stockman, N. (1994) 'Gender Inequality and Social Structure in Urban China', *Sociology*, Vol.28, No.3, pp.759–78..

Storey, J. (1989) (ed.) *New Perspectives on Human Resource Management* (London: Routledge).

SWB, *BBC Summary of Short-Wave Broadcasts* (London: British Broadcasting Corporation) various, see text.

Swearingen, R. (1978) *The Soviet Union and Post-War Japan* (Stanford Calif.: Stanford University Press).

Takahara, A. (1992) *The Politics of Wage Policy in Post-Revolutionary China* (London: Macmillan).

Thomas, S. (1993) 'Chinese Enterprise Reforms in the Post-Tiananmen Era: The View from Liaoning Province', in (eds) L. Kelley and O. Shenkar, *International Business in China* (London: Routledge) pp.45–62.

Thompson, P. (1992) 'Disorganized Socialism: State and Enterprise in Modern China', in (eds) C. Smith and P. Thompson, *Labour in Transition: The Labour Process in Eastern Europe and China* (London: Routledge) pp.227–59.

Thompson, P. (1992/3) 'Afloat in a Better Sea', *China Now* (Winter), No.143, pp.26–8.

Tidrick, G. and Chen, J. (1987) (eds) *China's Industrial Reform* (Oxford: Oxford University Press).

Times Higher Educational Supplement, various, see text.

Trade Union Law (1992), see Appendix 1.

Tung, R.L. (1991) 'Motivation in Chinese Industrial Enterprises' in (eds) R.M. Steers and L.W. Porter, *Motivation and Work Behavior* (New York: McGraw-Hill) pp.342–51.

Vogel, E. (1991) *The Four Little Dragons* (Cambridge, Mass: Harvard University Press).

Walder, A. (1986) *Communist Neo-Traditionalism: Work and Authority in Chinese Industry* (Berkeley, Calif: University of California Press).

Walder, A. (1989) 'Factory and Manager in an Era of Reform', *Chinese Quarterly*, No.118 (June) pp.242–64.

Walder, A. and Gong, X. (1993) 'Workers in the Tiananmen Protests: The Politics of the Beijing Workers' Autonomous Federation', *Australian Journal of Chinese Affairs*, No.29 (January) pp.1–29.

Waldron, A. (1992) *The Great Wall of China: From History to Myth* (Cambridge: Cambridge University Press).

Wales, N. (1945) *The Chinese Labour Movement* (New York: Day).

Wall, D. (1993) 'All that Glitters is not Gold: Worries about the Quality of China's Rapid Economic Development', *CEA–Chinese Economic Association (UK) Newsletter*, Vol.5, No.2, June, pp.10–14.

Wang, Z.M. (1989) 'Participation and Skill Utilization in Organizational Decision Making in Chinese Enterprises', in (eds) B.J. Fallon, H.P. Pfister, J. Brebner, *Advances in Industrial Organizational Psychology* (Amsterdam: Elsevier) pp.19–26.

Wang, Z.M. (1992) 'Managerial Psychological Strategies for Chinese–Foreign Joint-Ventures', *Journal of Managerial Psychology*, Vol.7, No.3, pp.10–16.

Wang, Z.M. (1994) 'Decision Making and Multi-Phase Socio-Technical Adaptation in Chinese Industrial Organizations', Paper, for International Symposium on Decision Making under Different Economic and Political Conditions, Royal Dutch Academy and Kurt Lewin Institute, Amsterdam, 1–3 June.

Wang, Z.M. and Heller, F.A. (1993) 'Patterns of Power Distribution in Managerial Decision Making in Chinese and British Industrial Organizations', *International Journal of Human Resource Management*, Vol.4, No.1, pp.113–28.

Warner, M. (1983) *Organizations and Experiments* (Chichester and New York: Wiley).

Warner, M. (1986) 'Managing Human Resources in China', *Organization Studies*, Vol.7, No.4, pp.353–66.

Warner, M. (1987a) (ed.) *Management Reforms in China* (London: Pinter).

Warner, M. (1987b) 'Industrial Relations in the Chinese Factory', *Journal of Industrial Relations*, Vol.23, No.2, pp.217–32.

Warner, M. (1989) 'Microelectronics and Manpower in China', *New Technology, Work and Employment*, Vol.4, No.1, pp.18–26.

Warner, M. (1991) 'Labour management relations in the PRC: the role of trade unions', *International Journal of Human Resource Management*, 2(2), 205–20.

Warner, M. (1992) *How Chinese Managers Learn: Management and Industrial Training in the PRC* (London: Macmillan).

Warner, M. (1993) 'Human Resource Management "with Chinese Characteristics"?', *International Journal of Human Resource Management*, Vol.4, No.1, pp.45–65.

Warner, M. (1994) 'Japanese Culture, Western Management: Taylorism and Human Resources in Japan', *Organization Studies*, Vol.15, No.4, pp.509–34.

Wedley, W.C. (1992) (ed.) *Changes in the Iron Rice Bowl: The Reformation of Chinese Management, Vol.3 of Advances in Chinese Industrial Studies*, (Greenwich, Conn. and London: JAI Press).

Weitzman, M.L. and Xu, C. (1992) 'Vague Defined Cooperatives and Cooperative Culture: A Reconciliation of a Paradoxical Phenomenon in Transitional Economies', *Working Paper*, Economics Department, Harvard University, Cambridge, Mass..

Westney, E. (1987) *Imitation and Innovation: The Transfer of Western Organizational Patterns to Meiji Japan* (Cambridge, Mass.: Harvard University Press).

White, G. (1987) 'Labour Market Reform in Chinese Industry', in (ed.) M. Warner, *Management Reforms in China* (London: Pinter) pp.113–26.

Whitehill, A.M. (1991) *Japanese Management: Tradition and Transition* (London: Routledge).

Whiteley, R. (1990) 'Eastern Asian Enterprises Structures and the Comparative Analysis of Forms of Business Organization', *Organization Studies*, Vol.11, No.1, pp.47–74.

Wilson, J.L. (1987) 'The People's Republic of China', in (eds) A. Pravda and B.A. Ruble, *Trade Unions in Communist States* (London: Allen & Unwin) pp.219–52.

Wood, A. (1994) 'China's Economic System: A Brief Description with some Suggestions for Further Reform', in (eds) Q. Fan and P. Nolan, *China's Economic Reforms: The Costs and Benefits of Incrementalism* (London: Macmillan) pp.21–45.

World Bank, (1990) *World Development Report* (Washington DC: World Bank).

World Bank (1993) *World Development Report* (Washington, DC: World Bank).

Young, S. (1992) 'Wealth but Not Security: Attitudes to Business in the 1980s', in (ed.) A. Watson, *Economic Reform and Social Change in China* (London: Routledge) pp.63–87.

Xia, J.Z. (1991) (ed.) *Issues of China Labour Legislation* (*Zhongghuo Laodong Lifa Wenti*) (Beijing: China Labour Publisher).

Xinhua News Agency, various, see text.

Yahuda, M.B. (1994) 'North China and Russia', in (eds) D.S.G. Goodman and G. Segal, *China Deconstructs: Politics, Trade and Regionalism* (London: Routledge), pp. 251 - 70.

Yu, K.C., Wang, D.C. and He, W. (1993) 'A Study of the Organizational Commitment of Chinese Employees' in (ed.) W.C. Wedley, *Changes in the Iron Rice Bowl: The Reformation of Chinese Management*, Vol.3 of *Advances in Chinese Industrial Studies* (Greenwich, Conn. and London: JAI Press) pp.181–96.

Zhang, G.X. (1988) 'Changes in the Chinese Trade Union Management in the Light of the Current Reforms', MA Thesis, Institute of Social Studies, The Hague (Netherlands).

Zheng, H.R. (1987) 'An Introduction to the Labour Law of the People's Republic if China', *Harvard International Law Journal*, Vol.28, No.2, pp.385–431.

Zhungguo Laodong Renshi Bao (Chinese Labour Personnel Journal)–see text.

Index